Green Cultural Studies

Green Cultural Studies

Nature in Film, Novel, and Theory

Jhan Hochman

University of Idaho Press
Moscow, Idaho
1998

Copyright © 1998 The University of Idaho Press
Published by the University of Idaho Press
Moscow, Idaho 83844-1107
Printed in the United States of America
All rights reserved

02 01 00 99 98 5 4 3 2 1

Library of Congress Cataloging-in-Publication Data

Hochman, Jhan, 1952–
    Green Cultural Studies: Nature in Film, Novel, and Theory /Jhan
Hochman.
        p.   cm.
    Filmography: p.
    Includes bibliographical references and index.
    ISBN 0-89301-209-2 (alk. paper)
    1. Nature in motion pictures.   I. Title
PN1995.9.N38H63   1998   97-45524
791.43'66—dc21   CIP

Contents

Introduction

PART I
THERIOMORPHS AND ANTHROPOMORPHS

1. A Theriomorphic Bestiary   21
   The Silence of the Lambs
2. Human Parasites in Animal Hosts   43
   Women in Love

PART II
THE FOREST AND THE TREES

3. The Forest Primarily Evil   71
   Deliverance
4. A Peculiar Arborary   93
   Beloved

PART III
FOR LAND'S (NOT PROPERTY'S) SAKE

5. The Deed and Its Undoing   111
   The Conservationist
6. Owning Up to Belonging   131
   Daughters of the Dust

PART IV
NATURE, IN THEORY

7. An Environmental Impact Report   159
   Of Grammatology
8. Beyond a Creeping Metonymy   171
   Simians, Cyborgs, and Women

Epilogue   187
Notes   189
Bibliography/Filmography I   221
Bibliography II   231

INTRODUCTION

The human ob-literation of nature marks a twofold "literation." First, culture scrawls itself on nature's flesh. Animals are tagged, branded, genetically rewritten, fatally punctuated by bullets and arrows, and fatally scored by blades and traps. Animal skin is made into vellum and parchment. Trees, standing or pulped, are carved and written upon—their cellulose flesh processed into celluloid. Land is inscribed by rows, strips, grids, *bound*aries; rock is inscribed by explosion, cutting, painting, graffiti. Rivers are redrawn by dams, levees, and locks; and skies once thought to exhibit divine messages are *cursed* by airplanes leaving new messages in thin air, tainted (*tincta* means inked stroke) by exhaust from cars *cursing* the land below.

Not only forced to serve as surface, nature is also commanded to write. Ink, comprised largely of tissue from slaughtered plants and animals, gets its name from the Greek *enkaustikós,* meaning to burn in (whence *encaustic* also derives) and like most writing matériel, is used as a *stain* or *blot* on nature's corpus (the Latin *fuco* means not only to dye and to paint but also to falsify). Mined metals and petroleum products—*raw* materials for which (eco)catastrophic wars are fought and people and nature less sensationally sacrificed on an ongoing basis—are turned into consumer goods, specifically, recording instruments such as computers, cameras, audio, and printing equipment.[1] In terms of nature, representation is a caustic enterprise.

Even as nature is destroyed and served up as the material on which and with which culture uses to write itself, nature is also conceptually cooked in a cultural cauldron, an often toxic brew releasing scenic to horrific phantasms of represented nature. And this amalgam of cultural concepts about nature created out of nature's flesh breeds further cultural concoctions and protean chimeras. Someone has already said that representation is unavoidably mis-representation, and taking, mis-taking.[2]

Culture's double utilization of flesh as raw material for purposes of physical and representational construction necessitates what Andrew Ross has already called "green cultural criticism,"[3] or what I prefer, green cultural studies (gcs), in order to link it with the many-headed politico-ethical family of cultural studies. Absent a green component, cultural studies' prevailing concerns are with (popular) texts/practices primarily impacting upon ethnicity/race, gender, sexuality, economic class, and age (particularly youth subcultures). A struggling newcomer to this nexus of concerns is nature (plants, animals, and elements).[4] The task of green cultural studies is the examination of proliferating cultural representations of nature—i. e., lexical, pictorial, and actual manipulations of plants, animals, and elements—for their potential to affect audiences affecting nature-out-there or what I often call *worldnature*.

Before advancing any further, I should attempt to carefully define use of the terms *nature*, *worldnature*, *Nature*, and *culture*. Throughout this book I critique, sometimes with admitted difficulty, the word *nature* when used by others in its senses of Power or Force, Laws, demiurge or deity, System or Intention, Essence, in short, that nature construed as transcendentally metaphysical or immanently essential. I would prefer this nature be understood as *Nature* in order to first make obvious, and then largely eliminate, nature's association with the highly suspect realms of the otherworldly and transcendental.

On the other hand, I prefer to use *nature* in a more worldly fashion in order to collectivize individual plants, nonhuman animals, and elements. And to avoid otherworldly or transcendental associations with nature, I often substitute *worldnature* for *nature*. Furthermore, I infrequently, and only with ample clarification, include human animals and their activities within the terms, *nature/worldnature*. The reason is not to once again reclassify humans as apart and superior to animals or to the rest of nature, but to make it politically difficult for humans to claim that by simply being part of nature they know what to do about and with it.

The reader should be warned that my differentiation between nature/worldnature and Nature is not airtight. For example, how classify apparently sensible, universal, N/natural patterns? Is number nature or Nature? Are life and death nature or Nature? Equally leaky and related to this problem is the division between nature and culture. Does *species* correspond to something of nature, or is it a powerful cultural construction? Are fractals of nature or culture? Is the indicated absence of something nature or culture?

And then, the question behind all those: Why differentiate nature/worldnature, Nature, and culture? A short answer is: So culture does not easily confuse itself with nature or Nature, or claim to know Nature as a rationale for replacing worldnature with itself and its constructions. The longer answer, I hope, flows through the capillaries of this book.[5]

As I understand and practice it, gcs positions itself as a comprehensive critique of both cultural *praxis* (action backed by theory) and *practice* (action less theoretical than traditional or habitual), by taking little for granted; knowledge, culture, and civilization all become subject to its critique. Not only a wide range of basic cultural formations, but myriad forms of representation attract the attention of gcs, from billboards to literature, menus to paintings, gardens to guidelines for National Park rangers. While ecocriticism is established in a few university English and environmental studies departments, most humanities divisions, to my knowledge, have no established green approaches to their subjects. This is, perhaps, understandable since many are still preoccupied with opening or closing themselves to issues of race, class, gender, and sexuality. Green approaches, while tolerated in the work of this or that individual, remain outside the concerns of most humanities divisions (the word *humanities* might have something to do with this).

Green cultural theorists are prevailed upon not only to become intimate with the cultural history of nature,[6] but must also be knowledgeable about the workings and history of the particular media depicting it. While the ultimate goal of green cultural studies should be to decrease the cultural manipulation and decimation of plants, animals,[7] and elements its exploration and critique of different cultural formations give it an additional value. Paying especial attention to depictions of nature in film, novel, and theory as I do throughout this book can cast new light, not only on texts, but on makers, movements, and mediums. For example, by examining *Women in Love*, the traditional view of Lawrence's passion for nature becomes problematic (his infatuation is more for Nature). By looking at naturalism, as I have done outside this book, I find it to be against nature because it constructs *nature* as a debilitating internal and external Force, as a determinative Nature. And, in examining the film *Deliverance*, we see how film renders viewers separate and superior to film-nature even as it brings them into proximity. Nature becomes, then, prop(erty) and commodity not unconnected to the idea and practice of worldnature as prop for film and property for the larger culture.

As textual study, this book foregrounds what is often configured as mere background: the contribution of represented animals, plants, and land to theme, narrative structure, and character. As cultural studies, it weighs particular representations of nature against grand cultural narratives about nature. At times, individual chapters like those on *Deliverance* and *Daughters of the Dust* supply material only implied by the text. One reader of the manuscript called such exploring "discursive." While I feel these few side-excursions supply valuable material missing from the films, I have clearly marked the paths in the event the reader does not want to venture down them.

The first three two-chapter parts of *Green Cultural Studies* consist of one chapter on a film and another on a novel. Part I, Theriomorphs and Anthropomorphs, employs a chapter on *The Silence of the Lambs* and a chapter on *Women in Love* for countertendencies: nature projected into, and nature injected with culture, respectively. Part II, The Forest and the Trees, juxtaposes a chapter on *Deliverance* and a chapter on *Beloved* for an opposing politics of number—fear and denigration of the mass (*Deliverance's* forest), and veneration of the individual (*Beloved's* trees)—by correlating these to intersecting articulations of race, class, and gender. Part III, For Land's (Not Property's) Sake, contrasts Nadine Gordimer's treatment of possessed South African land in *The Conservationist* to Julie Dash's depiction of people owned by, or belonging to, their seductive Sea Island homeland in *Daughters of the Dust*. Finally, Section IV, Nature, In Theory, critiques sites of indiscriminate blurring of nature and culture in seminal works by theorists Jacques Derrida and Donna J. Haraway.

What becomes apparent through these pages is how textual criticism, when politicized, magnifies rather than enervates the importance of textual study. Forcing texts to talk in the interrogational light of historical change might seem like textual torture to some. But I view such critical work as a crucial method of bringing the text out from the often stuffy departments of literature and cinema studies, into the open—even if polluted—air of the public sphere. There, the text can interact with events larger than authorial biography and literary/cinema history, and can address concerns larger than motif, theme, structure, and oeuvre. Such a text *en plein air* can interweave with more than the period the text is supposed to reflect, refract, or help create. This methodology produces not only the precious and pleasurable text, but the political text whose reading and analysis, whose reception, prepares one for bombardment by more quotidian representations and practices.

Still, texts need "airing" less than readers and viewers, whose receptive practice spark new or continued awareness and involvement. No longer is it enough that threat and controversy is relegated to this or that occasional book or film. Reading and viewing must become world-relevant; it must become dangerous, so that any text, even corporate and state propaganda, stands to backfire in the face of its producers. Recalling the potential danger of literate slaves, is it too fantastic to imagine the potential and beautiful treachery of textually- and visually-literate wage-slaves and students? These creatures become dangerous by trying to understand—through the political analysis of *any* text—the culture which prods and channels them into company, marketplace, state, church, school, family, and into buying, believing, and obeying. Why the need for a new breed of dangerous wage slaves and students? So that we can become less a danger to ourselves, to other people, and to the plants, animals, and elements of the fifth world. [8]

The History of Green within Cultural Studies

Cultural studies began in green. Stuart Hall, a central figure in British cultural studies, paid tribute to the field's *urtexts*, not only the works of the Italian Marxist, Antonio Gramsci, but the German cultural critics of the Frankfurt School whose work was translated into English in the 1970s.[9] In 1944, Frankfurt School philosophers, Max Horkheimer and Theodor Adorno had already theorized alienation from and (Baconian) "blind domination" of nature as the central problem with Enlightenment.[10] Adorno and Horkheimer thought that if Enlightenment could be turned against itself in order to open up its dead and deadly ends, or if culture's grounding in nature could be recalled, people might come to understand the truth of culture: "By virtue of this remembrance of nature in the subject [i.e., the individual] in whose fulfillment the unacknowledged truth of all culture lies hidden, enlightenment is universally opposed to domination."[11] Hyperbole notwithstanding, Horkheimer's and Adorno's assertion is crucial for cultural studies in three ways. First, culture can be inferred to grow out of, without being determined by, nature. Culture is therefore neither self-generating nor wholly self-perpetuating but is embedded in and dependent upon nature. Second, remembrance of nature propels one toward grounding and critiquing culture, and especially pertinent for cultural studies, toward theorizing ways out of culturally-generated and thus—one hopes—avoidable dominations. Third and most important, in Horkheimer and Adorno's work the seeds of a poststructuralist blurring of nature and culture are sown. These philosophers critique a condition of reification, or naturalization, that situation where culture replaces nature as the realm of the given, the unchangeable. On the other hand, they fault the way nature has become alienated from human experience as an unusual, unnatural realm to humans. In Horkheimer and Adorno, nature does not risk vilification as threatening, violent, or deadly, nor is nature imperiled by the poststructuralist strategy of putting the word *nature* within quotation marks, which leads some to see nature as a mere cultural idea rather than the plants, animals, and elements comprising worldnature.

Consistent with the Frankfurt School's cultural critique, Jennifer Daryl Slack and Laurie Anne Whitt see cultural studies as a two-pronged front: "The project of cultural studies is grounded on a moral and political critique of late capitalism, and more generally of oppressive cultural and social formations."[12] Following Slack and Whitt, I argue first that there is nothing so routinely subjugated and destroyed by late capitalism (but also the marxist/communist drive to industrialize as a necessary step for proletarian liberation) as the multiplicity of corpora and phenomena grouped together by the term *nature*, i.e., plants, animals, and elements (worldnature). Second and most crucial for green cultural studies are the capitalist/communist/technical[13] dominations of worldnature that are informed by a textual nature prone to represent nature unimaginatively and flatly, as a two-dimensional backdrop to the human drama. Material and representational domination is reciprocal and double. Each stands to aggravate or potentiate the other, reifying nature as a realm fit primarily for multiple manipulations and annihilations.

Three more recent patriarchs of cultural studies proper, British historians Raymond Williams, Richard Hoggart, and E. P. Thompson, make the case for a genuine working-class culture and history opposed to royal or bourgeois histories, but also against working-class culture's displacement by mass or popular culture.[14] In general terms, these historians, as informed by marxism, conceive of workers as the locus of instrumentalism and deculturation, not only by Althusseurian repressive (e.g., police and military) and ideological (e.g., schools and churches) state apparatuses, but additionally, by the spread of popular or mass culture.[15] Workers and working-class culture became the first sprouts of nascent culture study with roots in Marx. While Marx saw nature as matter, raw material, and "tool house,"[16] nature was for him the foundation of culture and of labor, a necessary factor for their theorization. Despite the deadness of Marxian nature, it remains, even while backgrounded, the foundation of cultural work and study.[17]

A notion of an oppressed working class became the basis by which others who were and are subjugated in the workplace were embraced by cultural studies including youth, people of color, and women. Race, gender, and age thus became wedded to class, and domination became multipronged: a relatively small group commodifying and justifying its manipulation of a much larger group defined by their race, gender, age, and class. These larger groups were burdened with the overclass' use of adjectives like *brute-ishness*, *brute-ality*, *coarseness*, *wildness*, *innocence*, *ignorance* and verbs like *massing*, *spreading*, and *swarming*, terms also applied to nature. Such words indicate a need for surveillance, control, and, *checking*, in the double sense of both inspecting and stopping the spread of.

Putting aside cultural studies disagreements about the degree to which individuals are entirely and inescapably dominated by interpellation, or accept, consent to, or struggle within a framework of hegemony, cultural studies fundamentally posits political and social power directed at a vast group of raced, classed, gendered, sexualized, and aged people by a small, traditionally unmarked group, increasingly recognized as wealthy, Western, white, heterosexual, adult males. Yet what cultural studies seems not to recognize is the overclass' characterization of subalterns in terms also used to anathematize nature. It could even be argued that poverty, femaleness, youth, or rich melanin content become problems primarily through traditional linkage to reified negative nature: living close to nature as a kind of poverty, nature as a punishing mother goddess or innocent child, youth as wild, or nature as the past or immaturity of culture. Hannah Arendt spoke of the relationship between dark skin and nature in the context of early white racist psychology:

> What made [Africans] different from other human beings was not at all the color of their skin but the fact that they behaved like a part of nature, that they treated nature as their undisputed master, that they had not created a human world, a human reality, and that therefore nature had remained, in all its majesty, the only overwhelming reality— compared to which they appeared to be phantoms, unreal and ghost-like. They were, as it were, "natural" human beings who lacked the specifically human character, the specifically human reality, so that

> when European men massacred them they somehow were not aware
> that they had committed murder.[18]

Because worldnature is routinely and reductively construed as unconscious raw material, any entity associated with nature stands to lose its
rights to ethical culture and gains admittance into culture only or primarily
as a material, aesthetic, recreational, or suffering object. People of color,
women, the lower classes, and youth,[19] all reduced to labor, gain admittance into culture predominately as means to another's profit or leisure, or
as suffering objects that must be saved for the overclass' redemption, a ritual compensation for destroying what it professes to want to save.

These connections make nature's inclusion in cultural studies—as green
cultural studies—reciprocally important. Since people and nature are made
abject in similar terms and by similar practices, attention to the actual and
representational way nature is treated provides insights into overarching
theories and strategies of power as they impact on people; conversely, green
cultural studies has the potential to reconfigure nature still essentialized as
mere matter, a continuum from dead to not fully alive, and reconfigure it as
essential, a living fifth world. In this way, nature gains potential for increased
theoretical and geographical space in, and despite, cultural practice.

Problems Facing the Greening of Cultural Studies

Nature, however, is up against fierce antagonism, not only from conserva-
tives, but from leftist suspicion of environmentalism's whiteness and its
alleged callousness toward people, and further, from within cultural studies
itself. Entry of nature into cultural studies is hampered by the discipline's
guardedness against any mention of *nature*. Fredric Jameson, however, is
not squeamish about using the n-word: "Postmodernism is what you have
when the modernization process is complete and nature is gone for
good."[20] Implied here is not only late capitalism/postmodernity's decimation of worldnature, but also the disappearance in some postmodernisms
(namely, cultural studies) of nature as a conceptual and linguistic referent.
Herein is a coincidence: Often when the subaltern becomes a trenchant
problem for those on top, the urge to heal real division is attempted by
waving away so-called divisive categories such as race, class, and gender as
mere constructions having no basis in reality. African Americans are asked
to repress concerns with race or ethnicity because of "the basic fact that all

human beings—though far from being alike—are similar at least insofar as they are human."[21] Indeed. But meanwhile, "the basic fact[s]" of the socio-culturescape give every indication that racism and sexism are chronic. And now that nature and its advocates have become a problem for culture in general, perhaps some leftist theorists want to settle this conflict similarly. In other words, by suddenly conjuring a utopian oneness of nature and culture—a nature subsumable under culture or a culture naturalizing itself as Nature or nature—culture gives itself powers previously attributed to Nature. Might this "Hey, we are you, you are us" be an expiation of cultural guilt through facile erasure of difference?

Perhaps these eraserheads, these well-intentioned reconcilers of the split between nature and culture, are saying what most of us who feel has-sled by environmental critiques want to hear: Yes, it is possible to shunt or repress culture's increasing decimation of worldnature by denying the superiority of culture over nature. But even if the idea of cultural superior-ity becomes discounted, the practices based on an ideology of superiority are built into nearly every interstice and fiber of cultural practice. This cou-pling of enlightened words and ideas with devastating practice produces nothing but hypocrisy, intended or not. A guilty white who proclaims that blacks and whites are essentially the same should not expect a forgiving pat on the shoulder by an understandably indignant black skeptic; nor should reconcilers proclaiming human solidarity with nature expect that minimiz-ing the distance of difference between nature and culture is a solution to the nature-culture problem. Far better it would be for critics to admit and theorize the intensity of culture's manufactured distance from and gridifi-cation of worldnature before too easily latching onto facile and convenient epiphanies that humans are nature, know Nature, or that nature is (like) us. Otherwise, it is likely that similar cultural obscenities will be reproduced in subtler, more incorrigible forms. To cast this argument as an aphorism: Waving away a conflict is not waving good-bye to it.

Within the larger political backlash among moderates against "environ-mental extremists" and a leftist castigation of environmentalism on the basis of its whiteness and its supposed privileging of nonhuman victims,[22] nature faces more specific representational/rhetorical hazards in cultural studies. First, in cultural studies the terms *natural*, *naturalness*, and *natu-ralized* tend to be synonyms for *reified* and *essentialized*, terminology which, contrary to the marketplace-use of *nature* and *natural* to confer positive values on products, associates *nature* with the inescapable cage of natural determinism. Graeme Turner writes: "Cultural studies defines itself in part . . . through its ability to explode the category of 'the natural'—revealing the history behind those social relations we see as the products of a neutral evolutionary process. It is understandably worried at the prospect of becoming a 'natural' discipline itself."[23] By disparaging *natural* and replacing *nature* or *natural* with the more humanly alterable *history* or *cultural construction*, cultural studies risks vilifying worldnature as an external straitjacket or internal tether, the kind of nature opposed to a culture over-optimistically referred to as nurture.

The cultural-studies baggage of an outwardly and inwardly determining negative Nature might, in part, issue from Zola's naturalism. There are Zola's deterministic surroundings: "it will only be necessary to work upon . . . the surroundings if we wish to find the best social condition. In this way we shall construct a practical sociology and our work will be a help to political and economical sciences."[24] While Zola's surroundings are primarily urban, the twentieth-century American naturalists Steinbeck and Norris relocate Zola's surroundings to nature. Examples are Steinbeck's Oklahoma dust bowl at the opening of *The Grapes of Wrath* and Norris's Death Valley at the closing of *McTeague*. Reading nature as determining enemy in these two novels becomes rather easy despite Steinbeck's depiction of the dust bowl as a culturally-caused calamity,[25] and McTeague's and Marcus's aridity of values as more a product of culture than of nature.[26] But Zola also describes the determining innards of flesh:

> I chose to portray individuals existing under the sovereign dominion of their nerves and their blood, devoid of free will and drawn into every act of their lives by inescapable promptings of their flesh. Thérèse and Laurent [characters in *Thérèse Raquin*] are human beasts, nothing more. In these beasts I set out to trace, step by step, the hidden workings of the passions, the urges of instinct, and the derangements of the brain which follow on from a nervous crisis.[27]

With both outer and inner determinants, the individual is reduced to both a laboratory animal and an abject beast. And while culture and nature are both capable of being the disease, only culture is posited as the cure: Surroundings must be corrected to mitigate internal nature's constant supply of abjection.

Before Zola, nature was Hobbes's "natural state of war" where without a political commonwealth "the life of man [is] solitary, poor, nasty, brutish and short."[28] A related sentiment is shared by the green cultural critic, Andrew Ross, who feels that environmentalism, like Nature, is a politics of restriction: "Green politics has this unfortunate reputation of being the politics that says 'No,' or at least 'No more'; there's this very strong strain of asceticism that runs through the house style of environmental writing. Culture critics don't find narratives of restraint to be very sexy."[29] Ross could also, but thankfully does not, make similar remarks about identity politics or multiculturalism—that they too are an unsexy, ascetic politics of restraint that say "No more" to pleasurable indulgence in manipulation, discrimination, gatekeeping, scapegoating, and generalized self-aggrandizement, thereby breeding a culture of frustrated racists, sexists, and homophobes. Ross, instead of asceticism, favors a democratization of cultural affluence, a post-scarcity politics that might seem to square with exclusively-human social politics but not, unfortunately, with an ever-exterminated worldnature.

Nature also faces a second hazard as it attempts to green up cultural studies: The poststructuralist-deconstructionist blurring of the nature/culture boundary, an unfortunate blurring that impacts on worldnature. By an overreading of poststructuralist thought, worldnature itself, not just nature as concept or de-referentialized signifier or sign, becomes culturally constructed. In physics, there is what Timothy Ferris calls the "Copenhagen interpretation" which he translates as, "no observer means no phenomena," a cousin of the poststructural "no culture means no nature" or "no sign means no referent." Physicist Murray Gell-Mann calls the Copenhagen interpretation "stupid."[30] Gell-Mann's comment also applies to the Copenhagen's poststructural cousin for this reason: a worldnature conceived as culturally constructed is a looking glass nature, nature as sensorially abstract, cognitively or sign-ificantly concrete.

Asserting an ontological worldnature is not to claim an epistemological Nature as the realm of truth or knowable referent(s) recognized through the heroism of human thought. Cannot one aver nature's existence without claiming a particular framework to which that existence must conform? While existence and essence may not be separable at thought's vanishing point, distinguishing them is hardly avoidable. It is, of course, paramount to cultivate suspicion of claims of common sense, common knowledge, and of truth, but it seems puerile centrism or regressive religiosity (seeing ourselves as gods) to render all existence dependent on human senses, language, and culture.

Even in the Fichtean apogee of German Idealism—denial of the thing-in-itself and affirmation of a pure, transcendental ego which produces the world—there is no consciousness, language, or culture without the pure, transcendental ego planting within human egos (loosely, culture) and the non-ego (nature, reality). In Fichte, culture does not construct (here, a synonym for *produce*) nature and reality so much as does pure, transcendental ego through the vehicles of human egos. While still making nature dependent upon the higher and anthropomorphic power of pure, transcendental ego, not even Fichte had the hubris to claim that human consciousness, language, or culture alone produced the world (nature).[31]

Perhaps the confusion about the cultural construction of nature is the word *construction*: to construct a house, an artifact, means to cause to exist, as well as to fashion. However, the cultural construction of nature can only, without admitting nonsense, admit to meaning the latter. That culture fashions and manipulates worldnature, and has invented the word *nature* with its multiple meanings, hardly needs arguing.

One could, perhaps, optimistically argue that worldnature has not yet been swallowed by culture, or that the trend of nature's destruction by intellectual and industrial culture is reversing since nature is now dubbed—supposedly to indicate a new awareness of nature—environment. This term, however, runs another risk related to chronic, excessive anthropocentrism. *Environment* is not inclusive of all plants, animals, and elements; as of this writing, environment has increasingly come to mean a nature tangibly important only to human health or livelihood. We thereby cease to pay as much attention when distant nature is destroyed by manipulation, development, consumerism, and dumping as long as our environment or neighborhood stays intact. This merely anthropocentric brand of environmentalism would be fine if nature were not precluded as important in itself, and for itself, outside human considerations.

More shrapnel against nature issues from an unrestrained exploding of the nature/culture boundary: The idea that technology is nature, is an aid to *reinventing* nature. Here, I have Donna Haraway in mind, a formidable critic of the biological sciences but problematic advocate of nature:

> In the belly of the local/global monster in which I am gestating, often called the postmodern world, global technology appears to *denature* everything, to make everything a malleable matter of strategic decisions and mobile production and reproduction processes.

Technological decontextualization is ordinary experience for hundreds of millions if not billions of human beings, as well as other organisms. I suggest that this is not a *denaturing* so much as a *particular production* of nature.[32]

Unlike the previous instance of boundary blurring, where concrete nature was vulnerable to absorption by culture, Haraway's suggestion that technology is a "particular production of nature" is a subset of the argument that everything, including culture and technology, is nature.

The contention that everything is nature is surely difficult to dispute. But what might result from such a statement? Haraway's suggestion seems already to have been coopted by developers, scientists, and technophiles who argue that they and their products are part of nature. Already, one car commercial's slow pan-shot of a dashboard in closeup reveals the dashboard's gradual metamorphosis into a rocky landscape. Other commercials portray cars as revered hunting animals, superior to wolves who can only admire and envy the vehicle's speed and traction. Haraway's assertion that technology is nature also seems a veiled attempt to call upon nature to justify technology, to naturalize technology as intrinsic to humanity, as good. The naturalization argument is, as has already been claimed by cultural studies itself, problematic. By such reasoning, circumcision and clitoridectomy can also be called natural, not a genital mutilation "denaturing" the human body, but a "particular production" of nature, producing merely altered or fixed bodies (terms already used to refer to the mutilated bodies of pets).[33] Let me venture some amateur psychology for why technoculture gets naturalized, even promoted, by the environmentally-minded: Technology's out-of-sight and out-of-mind processes of extraction, production, distribution, consumption, and disposal make damage to nature seem nonexistent or minimal. Even dropping bombs on unseen targets better connects cause to effect.

Allowing that technology is a particular production of nature is probably one thing Haraway means by *The Reinvention of Nature,* subtitle to her *Simians, Cyborgs, and Women* (*Nature* is not within quotation marks even though Haraway presumably means the concept of nature or the cultural construction of nature, not worldnature itself). Haraway should have been more careful with the phrase, *reinvention of nature.* Imagine the indignation if heterosexuals, men, and whites called for, respectively, the reinvention of gays and lesbians, women, and people of color. Would it not be more accurate to call for the reinvention of culture, or even the less catchy and dramatic, reinvention of cultural concepts of nature? One such possible reinvention is of culture as a technological weapon of mass destruction unleashed on nature.

Toward a Greener Cultural Studies

So that nature does not disappear into culture, and culture does not authorize and naturalize itself as nature or Nature, closer scrutiny is necessary when blurring the boundary between nature and culture, and when wielding the word, *nature*, with too broad a stroke. Scrutiny *is* employed by Alexander Wilson in his far-ranging (Dollywood to outer space) and potentially far-reaching *The Culture of Nature*. While Wilson argues against border reification, he does so without sanctioning cultural acts as part of nature—as natural—and without viewing nature as a mere construction or extension of culture. Even when describing Disney's staged nature films, Wilson is—unlike theorists milking the drama of the counter-intuitive—careful with casting nature as mere appendage of culture: "Nature is *in part* a human construction after all."[34] And though Wilson is obsessed with seeing the separation of nature and culture as *the* cause of the degradation of nature and the impoverishment of culture, his plans to physically break down the distance between culture and nature call for an expansion of wilderness and undomesticated nature and a limit to urban, suburban, or exurban culture. Wilson only runs into problems, relative to a larger scheme of things, with his overly-optimistic notion of "ecological restoration":

> Some landscape work is able to galvanize both communities and professions. A promising example is ecological restoration, an emerging discipline—and movement—dedicated to restoring the Earth to health. Restoration is the literal reconstruction of natural and historic landscapes. It can mean fixing degraded river banks, replanting urban forests, creating bogs and marshes or taking streams out of culverts.[35]

The notion that humans can restore nature to health might remind the reader of ideologies of ethnic purity, health, and cleanliness applied to the so-called improvement of human populations whose non-indigenous or "exotic" individuals or minorities must be relocated, "improved," or massacred for a greater "good." The restoration model entails manipulation and objectification, even if for the presumed good of the subject *and* object (admittedly, this is a step above instrumentalism exclusively for the subject). Nature restoration is based on an egregious and positivist presumption that humans know what restored nature looks and acts like, know what is healthy for plants, animals, and habitat or the bioregion or ecosystem. The drive toward restoration can also indicate an impatience with natural time; on their own, plantlands, grasslands, forests, and wetlands might flourish if people radically lessened their impact on them. It is not that restoration should never be performed, only that the practice is highly problematic. Instead of trying to restore nature, a better strategy might be for the too-scientific and too-instrumental ego to back off in order that plants, animals, and land can restore themselves and benefit from observation and protection rather than manipulation. Backing off might be reproached as an example of separating ourselves from nature or praised because it allows nature to take its course. Call backing off what you will, my point is that fixating on the merging of nature and culture as *the* solution, and their separation as *the* problem, is an attempt to overcome binarism that stumbles back into it by privileging unity over difference. A kind of postmodernism—notwithstanding Jameson's characterization of postmodernity as a state where "nature is gone for good"— might be an antidote: Fusing and separating might be seen as alternating strategies both of which, ethico-political exigencies depending, can be engaged.

One could argue that Gilles Deleuze and Félix Guattari—though far more concerned with breaking down, rather than reasserting, the culture/ nature, animal/human boundary—offer a more promising scenario than either Haraway or Wilson. Deleuze and Guattari's view is one dialectically careful not to abandon the advantages accruing to borders and boundaries, to separations in terms of molar individuals and subjects on planes of organization. Their view of becoming-in-the-world, in contrast to a fixed being-in-the-world, merges structuralism (boundaries, limits, identities) and poststructuralism (transgressions, joyous confusions, protean fluctuations) into a shape-shifting multiplex postmodernism. After pages of lexical spawning, of darting and diving in fluid non-separation—where "molecular multiplicities" are "haeccities" "deterritorializing," "involuting," becoming "bodies without organs" on a "plane of consistency," in short, where the human can, at least, "become-animal"—Deleuze and Guattari slow down to counsel sobriety: "But once again, so much caution is needed to prevent the plane of consistency from becoming a pure plane of abolition or death, to prevent the involution from turning into a regression to the undifferentiated. Is it not necessary to retain a minimum of strata, a minimum of forms and functions, a minimal subject from which to extract materials, affects, and assemblages?"[36] And when or where are these minimal strata and subjects to be retained, even if temporarily? In the realm of politics:

> It is, of course, indispensable for women to conduct a molar politics, with a view to winning back their own organism, their own history, their own subjectivity: "we as women . . ." makes its appearance as a subject of enunciation. But it is dangerous to confine oneself to such a subject, which does not function without drying up a spring or stopping a flow . . . . It is thus necessary to conceive of a molecular women's politics that slips into molar confrontations, and passes under or through them.[37]

Deleuze and Guattari's sense of movement is their strength. First, they advocate "becoming-other" along a "plane of consistency" (an improvement over imitation or identification), and second, they move from the plane of consistency, that plane of *temporary and strategic* becomings where no impervious boundaries exist between nature and culture or animal and human, to a "plane of organization," that realm of subjects and individuals, of *temporary and strategic* fixities.

If green cultural studies is to be an effective politico-cultural tool in the service of nature and culture, it will need to study not only how to become nature, by attempting to merge with the real or imagined subjectivity of a plant, animal, or mineral and of air, water, earth, and fire; it will also need to pull back and grant these beings and entities unromanticized difference, an autonomy apart from humans, a kind of privacy and regard heretofore granted almost exclusively to humans. Nature and culture cannot be willed together by glibly naturalizing culture, or by culture simplistically proclaiming itself part of nature, or by stupidly making worldnature into an appendage of culture and worldnature into a culturally-constructed product. Any substantial, reciprocal, merging of nature and culture will take generations of internal cultural struggle. Green cultural studies and human culture would do well to ensure that plants and animals are granted separateness, independence, and liberation (an apartness distinct from excusing and advocating separation because of superiority) before mucking about too much with forced fusions and coalescences. Otherwise it is nature who/that will suffer most by this shotgun marriage with culture(s) made monstrous by thousands of years of naturalized atrocities against plants, animals, and elements.

I
Theriomorphs and Anthropomorphs

Where, in chapter one, human characters are burdened with the attributes of animals and, in chapter two, animal characters are burdened with the attributes of people.

1

A THERIOMORPHIC BESTIARY
The Silence of the Lambs

Everything is more than it seems in *The Silence of the Lambs* (1991): a prisoner impersonates his guard, a man gets inside the skin of a woman, beetles become self-moving chess pieces. But in this chapter's meander from one kind of animal to another, the metamorphoses are all concerned with people becoming animals, i.e., theriomorphosis. While the usual concern in such cases is the effect on people so animalized, theriomorphosis also effects animals, from those forced to lend positive or enviable attributes (totems), to those saddled with heavy and unwieldly human loads (scapegoats, tabooed animals). Frequently the animal is contrived as both totem and taboo.

Birds

With Hannibal Lecter's (Anthony Hopkins) admonishment to Clarice Starling (Jody Foster), "You fly back to school now little starling," Clarice becomes associated with a bird. In British slang, a *bird* is a girl or young woman, akin to the American *chick.* At least Hannibal, with his near-British accent and penchant for anagrams and riddles, would have made the connection between bird name and gender. Clarice's birdness connects her to Jame Gumb's (Ted Levine) women victims, also associable with birds. When Clarice goes to search the home of Jame's first victim, Fredrica Bimmel, several duck replicas "walk" in the front yard, a thriving bird hotel stands on a pole out back, and a little wooden, wind-blown Indian paddles his canoe in full feathered headdress. Fredrica's father raises and kills pigeons, or to be exact, squabs.[1] Feathered skins or fur pelts (it is difficult to discern) hang from the side of an outbuilding, a parallel between the father's slaughter and skinning of pigeons or small animals and the killing and skinning of Fredrica. *Pigeon* is slang for both a person easily duped and an attractive female. Perhaps Fredrica was duped by Jame just as Catherine Martin, another of Gumb's victims, was duped by Jame feigning a sprained arm (as birds sometimes feign a sprained wing?). Inside Fredrica's room, birds can be heard to fly and tweet outside, and two wall photos inside a four-picture wall frame show a smiling Fredrica with her father as he seems to offer her a still-alive squab. On the frame in the middle of the four photos is a drawing of birds on a tree limb. When Clarice enters Fredrica's sewing room, the camera fixes on Mr. Bimmel's pigeon coops and a bird bath outside the room's central window.

Catherine Martin's last name, like Clarice's, is a kind of bird (swallow to be more precise). She is singing while driving home at night when we first see her and is glimpsed by the treacherous bird watcher Jame through his night binoculars. She has a cat with the birdlike name of Cheeper (a reference to an "indoor" cat being a bird watcher?) who watches her intently as she drives up to her apartment. When Catherine is in Gumb's basement well, she tries to snare the poodle, Precious, with a *chicken* bone after *whistling* to get his attention.

But why would these women be connected to birds? Birds, especially doves and pigeons, like lambs, goats, and cattle, can be traced in Western tradition, at almost any point within the last several thousand years, back to forebears that "served" or were served as (sacrificial) victims. The word *victim* comes from the Latin *victima*, meaning sacrificial animal.

Leviticus 1:14 instructs the religious killer on the proper bird to sacrifice: "And if the burnt sacrifice for his offering to the Lord *be* of fowls, then he shall bring his offering of turtledoves, or of young pigeons." Jame, however, expects quite a bit more from his fowl sacrifice than protection or absolution. He aims to clip these women's wings (recall the diamond-shaped pieces of skin removed from Bimmel's upper back, where wings might be positioned) and don them so as to be reborn as a woman from the ashes of an irritating maleness, or as a (feminine) angel from a pyre of (masculine) devilishness (*bim*, as in Bimmel, means woman, and is the same prefix used in *bimbo*).

Associations of the Egyptian Benu bird (the Greek phoenix) come to mind. Here is Herodotus on the subject:

> Its plumage is partly red and partly gold, while in shape and size it is
> very much like an eagle. They (the Heliopolitians) tell a story about

this bird which I personally find incredible: the Phoenix is said to come from Arabia carrying the parent bird encased in myrrh; it proceeds to the temple of the sun and there buries the body. In order to do this, they say it first forms a ball as big as it can carry, then hollowing out the ball, it inserts its (dead) parent subsequently covering over the aperture with fresh myrrh. The ball is then exactly the same weight as it was at first. The Phoenix bears this ball to Egypt, all encased as I have said, and deposits it in the temple of the sun. Such is their myth about this bird.[2]

The bird's work both ensures the sun's daily rebirth and reenacts the sun's original burial and rising. So does the work of the sacred scarab: the beetle was said to roll Re, the sun god, into the eastern sky. This belief is presumed to have arisen because the scarab had been observed depositing its eggs into a warm ball of earth and burying the ball. The young beetles were later seen to emerge from the dark earth, like the phoenix from the temple, and the sun from the underworld.[3]

Jame, phoenix- and scarab-like, buries *pupae* (Latin for girl or doll) into the warm throats of his women victims to symbolize and ritually ensure his rebirth as beautiful. When Jame videotapes himself, he wears a richly-colored cape comparable to the Phoenix's red and gold flame-like plumage and the headdress/scalp of a bird/woman on his head, somewhat like the Egyptian sun gods Re and Horus depicted with the head of a falcon or hawk. In ridding himself of the weight of his genitals by tucking them behind his thighs and raising his caped arms into the air, Jame prepares to ascend like a bird, or an angel, into the warm light of femininity.

True to the popular version of the phoenix myth, Jame cannot get where he wants to live. Like the phoenix, Jame dies so that Catherine, the martin, who rises from a kind of burial and flies to relative freedom, can be reborn, no doubt newly vigilant about strange men in need.[4] And Clarice (meaning clear and bright), the starling, is reborn as an FBI special agent, and a person finally bereft of "that awful screaming" of the lambs. When the tables are turned and Jame becomes the sacrificial bird, the dove with a crucifix and *love* tattooed on his hand, his death not only spares the lives of "roomy" women, but enables the sunlight to flood the basement as a result of the climactic shootout. Venus, goddess of love, is a herald of the sun in the predawn sky; thus phoenix, sun, and Venus are associated.[5] Jame represents the Christ/dove (he has a small tattoo on his right side depicting a stab wound complete with drops of blood) and the phoenix and bird-headed sun god (while videotaping he wears make-up and a scalp of long golden hair) and thus dies in the dark so the sun may rise again.

In the references cited above, birds are coveted and sacrificed because of their feminized, angelic flight and beauty. Most birds fly and are considered beautiful or at least fascinating because of flight. Features like these, however, prevent attention to others. Birds reductively and essentially defined by flight become little more than feathers and wings that could confer flight on humans acquiring those parts[6]—in Jame's case, by butcherous means. But birds summed up by flight, feathers, and wings are as inadequate a description as are women defined by torsos. Jame's zealousness about the body-equals-being equation should be a valuable, if not ominous, sign of strained synecdoche to any fledgling auspex.

Flight and a certain beauty are exaggerated in importance because of their difference from human qualities, though, of course, humans fly mechanically and possess their own beauty. Preoccupation with birdness in *The Silence of the Lambs* still means what it has meant for thousands of years, a fascination with, and envy of, what is different, merging effortlessly with practices of imitation and domination. But Jame is foiled by believing in essentials and essential differences: In the process of murdering "birds" to become a "bird," Jame is killed by a "bird" not meeting the most distinctive bird characteristic, flight, or in his case, escape. Clarice is that bird of unexpected feather, a won't-be-victim partially because of her clear vigilance against patronization (recall Clarice's anger at Crawford's treatment of her in the funeral home). Like the ornithologist who erroneously believes birds incapable of a mass attack on humans in Hitchcock's *The Birds,* Jame's unchecked faith in the demarcations of humanly-constructed symbolic/taxonomic systems becomes his downfall.

If Jame was aware of the fallacy he embraced, he could have easily killed and skinned Clarice, a disturbing moral that constitutes knowledge as an efficient enabler of gynocide/Avescide. But the indissoluble reverse of this moral, where critique, specifically Clarice's enmity towards patriarchy and her deviation from traditional cultural constructions, usurps the master-slave relationship is also—especially in terms of birds—problematic. For this reason: a critique of culturally-constructed "birdness" and an attack (understood as one) on homocrats will not be taken up by our "feathered friends" anytime soon (on this count birds appear silent to humans). Even if it were possible, a critique by birds would have to be acknowledged and the offending behavior renounced *by people* for change to occur. This is the major difference between the project to end animal oppression and the project to end human oppression: With human to human relationships, victims are finally responsible for ending victimization; with humans and animals, it must be the victimizers.

Jame's faith in control by taxonomic/symbolic methods of cultural construction lead him toward reductive *definition-by-difference.* As counterweight, *definition-by-similarity* might serve. In Western zoological taxonomy, definition-by-similarity is already in place: birds and humans both belong to the subphylum, *Vertebrata.* The resonance of definition-by-similarity, however, pales in comparison with the strength of definition-by-difference because culture inculcates the differences between birds and humans, not their similarity. If birds are ever thought to be as similar to humans as they are different, creatures whose front appendages (*arms*) are conjectured to have become wings, who are bipedal, whose beaks are a combination of nose and mouth, whose bodily symmetry is also bilateral, whose intraspecies "songs" change dialect with location, and build nests or homes, birds start to seem less exotic. If similarity to *Homo "sapiens"* is stressed as much as difference, we might start to wonder how birds cannot possibly notice or care what is happening to them when hunted, caged, tortured, and sacrificed for food and pleasure. Jame defined his women as objects radically different from human flesh so he could cut them up. Perhaps women's already-culturally-inculcated birdness aided him.

While definition-by-difference fosters order, unity, and a certain enlightenment notion of individuality—even the individuality of a large group called birds—defining-by-difference also works to constitute and reinforce *us* and *them* and provides a ready-made infrastructure upon which a hierarchical shell can be placed. Though it is possible to inscribe difference without hierarchy and to maintain hierarchy without overt domination, the three form a too-familiar trio.

Hierarchy is most often thought to serve the one who ranks, but Jame's strategy of defining by difference hierarchizes in reverse fashion, *them* over himself or, at least, women's bodily appearance over men's.[7] This is a form of totemism. But, of course, Jame's desire for a woman's appearance equally damns those defined as superior. Jame must possess or become that which is greater. In order to kill what he desires and admires, "covets" as Lecter put it, he must convert his victim into a nonhuman object (recall Jame telling Catherine down in the pit, *"It* puts the lotion on *its* skin," where *it* replaces *Catherine*). It might be said that, for Jame, a woman (because she is reduced to a superior outer layer of the body) is not killed, but an emptiness (woman as vessel) is eradicated to gain access to and keep alive what is superior (outer form). Partitioned into form and emptiness, or form and material, he simultaneously deifies and objectifies his women victims. This makes the women paradigmatic sacrificial victims, and links them to their analogues, lambs and birds, and especially to pigeons and doves, and more recently, chickens. While wings and feathers may have made birds a fitting sacrifice for gods, bird brains and bird lives did not (in the case of pet birds, vocalization or beauty is sought, while flight and quality of life are denied). Brains and lives which, as the expression "brain death" indicates, almost define each other when referring to humans, and form *the* human-claimed domain of supremacy on which no other creature may trespass without intense surveillance.

In an us/them duality, wings, feathers, and meat are the superior parts of the bird because they can be imitated, possessed, and worn or eaten, turning their excellence into ours. Whether reductive definitions-by-difference lead to a hierarchy of us over them or them over us, definition is dangerous for the defined. In Jame's case this means women must die so that he may "live."

Cats

Although Jame aspires toward the flight and beauty of birds, the film depicts him as a cat, a killer of birds. Like Cheeper, Catherine Martin's cat with the birdish name, Jame watches through his catlike, night-vision binoculars as Catherine comes home. When Jame vans Catherine away unconscious, Cheeper watches from a window. Catherine's kidnapping tears her away from my initial desire to metonymically associate her with the cat; instead she becomes a bird in the jaws of a cat (Jame).

As Clarice later searches Fredrica Bimmel's house, she encounters the Bimmel's cat. The cat also appears upstairs in Fredrica's room in a photo of Fredrica and a friend, and seems to inspire Clarice with the idea to search Fredrica's sewing room, where in the closet, she finds the epiphany-producing dress with the sewed-on diamond shapes that reveals Jame's plan to make a "woman-suit." A small white china cat in front of the music box appears to invite Starling to search it and find Polaroids of Fredrica. Clarice, while looking for clues to Jame's whereabouts, seems to follow all these cats. Perhaps a viewer's first impulse would be to connect the cat to Fredrica, but more fruitful results are obtained when the cat is seen as a sort of specter of Jame in Fredrica's room, like Fredrica's bedroom wallpaper with a motif of moths or butterflies, and the sewing room that contains the dress with the diamond shapes matching the areas of skin Jame cut from Fredrica. But Jame's most obvious connection to cats is his stalking of Starling in the dark,[8] and the curious position he dies in—like a dead cat on its back with its front legs held up in rigor mortis. The sunlight that surges into the room when Jame dies can also be said to further associate him with the sun, especially the Egyptian sun god Horus, sometimes depicted as either a lion, or—like Jame wearing his woman-scalp while posing like a bird/woman in front of his videocam—a falcon-headed man.

Can relating Jame to house cats be a strained allusion to both the killing of "birds," and doing so without eating them, as many fed house cats do? Even if this is pushing it, Jame's catlike identity comes from associating his killing with a domesticated or wild cat's supposedly vicious and remorseless killing behavior,[9] a hackneyed representation of any carnivore's killing—except a human's, of course. Cats, even the domestic ones who torture their prey only to leave it, cannot accurately be called vicious, a word derived from *vice,* which is more intimately connected to maliciousness and depravity, terms more apropos of a cultural construction of humans than of cats. The so-called vicious house cat that "plays" with its prey, or kills and leaves it, is a cat domestically constituted, here, fed; and the wild cat's "viciousness" (why not effectiveness, efficiency, even benevolence?) allows a quicker and perhaps less painful death. Most importantly, virtually all killing by cats is motivated by eating: even fed cats kill what they *would* eat. Jame's killing is based on desires unrelated to eating—he kills what he (unlike Hannibal Lecter) would probably never eat: His own species. Jame's killing, as anomalous as it is, and as much as it is fobbed off on cats or "animals" (herbivores too?), is deeply grounded in *human* practice: it is humans who kill, not just for food, but for the unpalatable trophies of fur, feathers, and skin.

Dogs

Though the novel is richer in its use of dogs than the film, dogs do play a small role as dogs, which I will only briefly comment on, and, this time, without any politicized discussion. Catherine is the character who benefits from dogs. A snapshot of her as a baby lying with her head on a dog's abdomen is shown on TV to assist her mother, Senator Ruth Martin's plea for Catherine's release. Near the movie's end, it is perhaps her possession of Precious, Jame's dog, that saves her from being killed. The proximity of dogs to Catherine protects her because dogs are preeminent watch-animals and enemies of cats (Jame).

The part of the film I want to examine, and this time less seriously, is Jame's death, the sunlight exploding through the window, and Catherine escaping the well with Jame's dog, Precious. Continuing with the idea that Jame shares similarities with the phoenix, ancient Egypt can be employed to tie up events surrounding Jame's death.

The rise of the Dog Star, Sirius (also Canis), from the underworld proximate to the sun in July, coincided with the flooding of the Nile that irrigated the fields and precipitated sprouting vegetation. Sirius was thus linked to the sun and rebirth.[10] Comparing these events with those surrounding Jame's death results in the following rather far-fetched and playful reading: Jame (as Benu bird or phoenix) dies, enabling the sun to burst through the window (the phoenix dies and lives to insure the sunrise); Precious rises from the pit (the underworld) along with the sunlight (like Sirius), and so does Catherine (like a plant from irrigated ground)—recall she is soaked from being punitively hosed by Jame—in vegetative rebirth. The novel must be called in to support the not-so-apparent *plantness* of all Jame's victims: "He [Jame] took off his clothes and put on the robe—he always finished a *harvest* [of skin] naked and bloody as a new-born."[11] Catherine walks unsteadily out of Jame's house holding on to Precious even when the cop tries to take the dog away. Precious, the dog *star*, saves Catherine's skin.

Beetles

Characters Pilcher (from *pilchard*, a small fish) and Roden (back formation from *rodent*), the Smithsonian entomologists who examine the pupa found in Fredrica Bimmel's throat, play chess with what looks like a combination of dead beetles and one or two live ones when Starling first greets them. Clarice wonders if a certain move counts, and Roden replies, "Course it counts, how do you play?"

Though the beetles are objectified as chess pieces, they appear anomalous on the grid of the chessboard (perhaps it is just the beetles' bad acting).

Though the various sizes of beetles do conveniently fit within the squares, the beetled chessboard provides an excellent device depicting a nature-culture clash. The squares, though without walls, can easily be imagined as a series of boxes or cages, or a kind of grid, the latter an exemplary product of an instrumental reason transforming relatively autonomous entities into non-autonomous objects for measurement and of knowledge. It is no coincidence that straight, interlocking or crisscrossing horizontals and verticals also allude to cultural entrapment: the bars found throughout the film constrict in order to convert into objects of knowledge and surveillance. It could be maintained that scientifically gridding or measuring beetles makes easy the beetles' transference from tools of measurement to tools of entertainment. Objectification in one field flows easily into others.

Roden's reply to Starling's question points to a certain generalization of experience, a kind of solipsism on Roden's part that befits a stereotype of nerdy scientists out of touch with anything outside their field of study. Roden's "How do you play?" intimates plenty of other people playing chess with beetles, thereby eradicating oddness from their anomalous game. Playing chess with beetles seems normal to Roden even though it requires knowledge of beetles to employ them as chess pieces: different species or varieties must serve as pawns, knights, and castles. Roden's generalization of his own experience, though absurdly humorous, makes sense if we see its advantage: a number of people engaging in the same activity is validating. If one does not see others doing the same thing, imaginary others who do can be conjured. But validation by imaginary others is unnecessary in science and entertainment where objectification (of humans as well as animals) is standard, not to mention lucrative.

Moths

"The significance of the moth," Hannibal tells Clarice, "is change, caterpillar into chrysalis, or pupa, and from thence into beauty. Our Billy [Jame, a.k.a., Buffalo Bill] wants to change too." Transformation of pupa (less beautiful) into moth (more beautiful) is the analogue of Buffalo Bill's/Jame Gumb's view of change from man (unbeautiful) to woman (beautiful). Along with an association between women and birds, a link between moths and birds has everything to do with heavenly beauty. Jame's raising of his caped arms—as if they were wings—before his basement videocam links him to the bird he would become and the moths he raises. But the moth's significance goes further, since this is the death's head moth, *Acherontia styx,* named for Hades' two rivers, the Acheron and the Styx, which are further connected to the rivers in which Jame dumps his victims.[12] It should be mentioned that the poster advertising the movie depicts Dali's famous painting—a skull composed of naked women—on the moth's thorax.

It is not just death's head moths that are associated with destruction, but moths in general. Moths are well-known for their damage to cloth. Throughout both Old and New Testament, moths are synonymous with destruction. For example, "For the moth shall eat them [the wicked] up like a garment" (Isaiah 51:8), and "Sell that ye have, and give alms; provide yourselves bags which wax not old, a treasure in the heavens that faileth not, where no thief approacheth, neither moth corrupteth" (Luke 12:33). Further, it is not inconceivable that the idea for the classic horror film *Mothra* (1962) came from an association between moths and destruction.

There are two types of death's head moth, *Acherontia styx* (the moth in the movie) and *Acherontia atropos.*[13] Atropos, not seen in the movie, is one of the three ancient Greek Moerae or Fates having intimate links to thread or the fabric of human life. Clotho is the spinning fate (birth), Lachesis, the assigner of human fate (life), and Atropos, the fate breaking the thread (death). These Fates are all goddesses and often depicted with spindles. Clarice, upon entering Jame's home, realizes Jame is Buffalo Bill when she sees a moth land on an array of spindles (perhaps a linkage to spinning or sewing as traditional women's work and to women's direct ability to reproduce the thread or fabric of human life). Atropos, in particular, is variously pictured either with cutting instruments, a sundial, or a pair of scales. Jame is tied to Atropos as the cutter of his victims' life thread, and like Atropos, Jame has cutting instruments: the camera pans his basement workshop and reveals a table of knives. Not only does Jame cut numerous life threads, but akin to the destruction of fabric by the well-known clothes moth, *Tinea pellionella,* Jame destroys the integrity of the skin of his victims. No scale is seen in Jame's lair, but the sunlight rushing into the basement when Clarice shoots him might stand in for a sundial. The moths familiar to many of us—although they are nocturnal—often fly into light, and if that light is fire, into death. Wearing his see-in-the-dark binoculars, Jame also seems nocturnal, and though he dies in the light, his attraction to it is doubtful.

Jame's perception of pupa-to-moth as change from ugly-to-beautiful is as reductive as scripture's moth of destruction. Jame's reduction differs only in that change is given positive value. Jame is even credited by the entomologist, Roden, with loving the pupa when Roden examines it under a microscope: "Somebody grew this guy, fed him honey and nightshade, kept him warm. Somebody loved him." The purported love Jame has for his moths is understood by Roden because it is akin to the love, often attributed to scientists, for the things or creatures studied. More often it is *not* a love of or interest in moths as living things since scientists often kill the creatures they study for the knowledge they gain from either an animal's suffering, death, or corpse. This is especially true of entomologists who entrap, kill, and torture specimens (only important insofar as they are members of a species, from which the word *specimen* derives) to *understand* them. What most entomologists do love is perhaps what Jame loves, the constructed or imagined value of insects, their transformative, destructive, mutative, and indomitable qualities as a group, not as individual animals.[14]

Because knowledge of individuals is so difficult, time-consuming, and useless to the goal of instrumental knowledge or the domination of a group (in the film's case, of species), the individual becomes a degraded instance of species the way Plato construed chairs as lesser instantiations [of the one, Form of the Chair:] ". . . a consummate craftsman or guardian in any sphere will need the ability not *merely* to fix his regard on the many [specimens], but to *advance* to the recognition of the one [species] and the organization of all other *detail* [specimens] in the light of that recognition?"[15] Gerard Manley Hopkins, as exemplary Christian, extremes Plato's notion of Forms into one Form—Christ, in the poem, "The Windhover." Here the "brute beauty" of a bird is dwarfed by the beauty of Christ (the chevalier), to whom birds owe their beauty: "Brute beauty and valour and act, oh, air, pride, plume, here/Buckle! AND the fire that breaks from thee then, a billion/Times told lovelier, more dangerous, O my chevalier!"[16] When concerned people speak of the preservation of biodiversity, or species, individual animals often don't matter as much (or at all) as the cultural construction or abstraction. "Biodiversity" or "species," abstractions akin to Plato's Forms and Hopkins' Christ, are construed superior to concrete individuals. But the abstraction of species, though it comes from the same word in Latin meaning seeing or appearance, has only been cognitively apprehended, never sensorially perceived. Only individuals have. *Species*, while a compelling theory of patterns in nature, is a human invention of science worshipped because humanity adores, first and foremost, itself, its image, and its inventions. Roden demonstrates his love of moths by trapping, killing, and mounting them on pins (recall the camera pan over pinned moths or butterflies up to Roden looking through the microscope) in order to show the beauty of taxonomy—the order humans were clever enough to discover or fabricate. Jame loves moths by buying and raising them, inserting pupae into the throats of human corpses, and pulling off their chrysalises because he likes the idea of change.

Wolves (and Owls)

Dr. Fredrick Chilton, smarmy overseer (and overhearer) of the Baltimore State Hospital of the Criminally Insane, deems his prisoner, Hannibal, "the Cannibal," Lecter, a "monster." The Latin *monere,* from which the word *monster* is derived, means to warn, foretell, or predict, activities attributed both to diviners and animals whose flight patterns or disemboweled organs some diviners are skilled at reading (the practice of haruspicy). Socrates disdains conflation of those who possess the merely human skill of reading signs ("mantia," my formation from *mantic*) with those possessed of the gift of divine madness (mania). The conflation is evident in Hannibal who resides in a home for the (criminally) insane and is depicted as virtually prescient (he, as befits his surname, reads Clarice's life when he first meets her and when he knows that Clarice approaches without seeing her when last they meet at the courthouse). The confusion between mantia and mania is understandable, despite Socrates' crucial distinction. Ancient gods often became or were depicted as some form of animal. Sign-animals are supposed to have been messengers of the gods, and it is contested ground whether divination, "the greatest of arts," is a human skill or a divine gift.[17] In Hannibal, not only is there a conjunction of mania and mantia, but of diviner and sign. In order to read his animals (the birds/women and the cat/Jame), the logic might go, Hannibal becomes a monster like the riddling sphinx (recall his anagrammatic riddles, Louis Friend [iron sulfide] and Hester Mofet [the rest of me]). Hannibal, as sphinx, is part woman and part bird which enables him to read Clarice (recall that Hannibal longs for a tree and is offered a tern-inhabited island from inside his cage), and part lion enabling him to understand Jame-as-cat. But Hannibal becomes not only an animal-as-sign but a sort of divining auspex and haruspex (leaving, as well as divining, signs) when he hangs the disemboweled Lieutenant Boyle as a terrible birdlike warning from the prison cage.

The Random House Dictionary defines the modern word *monster* as "a legendary animal combining features of animal and human form or having the forms of various animals in combination, as a centaur, a griffin, or sphinx." Both in its ancient roots and the modern definition, fear is operative: animals as feared portents and the fear of animals as monsters or monstrosities mutually reinforcing one another. The inventory of future events of living persons always contains the great and feared event—death. The future then becomes easily equated with fear. Fear of future death reinforces present or past fear of terrifying animals capable of killing people. An associative chain results: future equals animals-as-signs equals death equals animals-capable-of-killing-humans. Hannibal is the embodiment of all these correspondences: mantia equals mania equals bestiality.

Hannibal-as-animal is evident from the outset. After Chilton defines Hannibal as a monster, he continues, "Pure psychopath. It's so rare to capture one alive. From a research point of view Lecter is our most prized asset." The caged and cagey Hannibal is the incorporation of captive zoo animal and research animal. Chilton continues: "We've tried to study him of course, but he's much too sophisticated for the standard tests. Oh my, does he *eat* us." Chilton, after a few more remarks, tells Clarice, "And oh are you ever his taste . . . so to speak." Chilton then shows Clarice the picture of a nurse whose tongue Hannibal ate and whose face he ravaged. Hannibal is cast as both cannibal and man-eating animal. Camera work emphasizes recurring bars between viewer and characters, while the soundtrack carries a rumbling bass reminiscent of low growling which evolves into a high-pitched howling-wind sound. Along with the red light under which Chilton shows Clarice the nurse's picture, the labyrinthine path to and dungeon-like quality of the lower prison, we enter the cave of not just any animal but the hellish sanctum of an evil animal.

As Clarice walks down the hall to Hannibal's cell the first prisoner growls a long "Hiiiiiii" and Miggs hisses like a snake, "I can *smell* your cunt" (my emphasis) and rushes the bars like a stereotypical zoo monkey. Hannibal, in contrast, stands back vigilant and deathly calm. Top-lighting transforms his face into a skull, a visual metonym of his murders. Almost as much as Miggs, Hannibal has a certain "animalian" ability to discern the scent of Clarice's perfume and skin lotion, and later the blood from Clarice's cut leg. When Clarice passes the psychological questionnaire to Hannibal, he challenges her with, "Do you think you can *dissect* me with this blunt little tool," (my emphasis) thereby associating Clarice with cruel (and flaccid) male science. Clarice dupes Hannibal with her offer of vacations at Plum Island replete with terns' nests, which Hannibal later learns is Anthrax Island, home of an animal disease research center. But Hannibal's last and most obvious tie to animals is the werewolfian restraining mask (or muzzle) he wears when taunting Senator Martin at the airport.

Hannibal clearly belongs to a predatorial species. A wolf seems most likely because of the muzzle, but also because Hannibal is a cannibal, a person sometimes associated with wolves (and other predators like leopards). But cannibals are also like vampires, both of whom share the consumption of human tissue (flesh and blood). Vampires are closely associated with wolves and werewolves (meaning man-wolf).[18] The vampire/cannibal connection is explicit in the courthouse elevator: When Clarice rides up to visit Hannibal, the accompanying cop asks her, "[Is] he [Hannibal] some kind of vampire?" An associational path can now be traversed: cannibal becoming vampire becoming wolf.

This chain can first be explicated by the weaker cannibal-wolf correlation, and then the much stronger and more involved vampire-wolf relationship, which includes the owl. At least since the Old Testament, references to the wolf as a symbol of evil abound. In Zephaniah 3:3, the evil judges of the city Nineveh are called wolves, and in Jeremiah 5:6, "a wolf of the evening" is said to "spoil them [those who don't follow God]... every one that goeth out thence shall be torn in pieces: because their transgressions are many, and their backslidings are increased." In Matthew 7:15 wolves are referred to as "ravening." The "medieval mind," says Barry Lopez in *Of Wolves and Men*:

> More than any other mind in history, was obsessed with images of wolves. A belief in werewolves was widespread and strong. Pagan festivals in which wild men, mythic relatives of wolves, played the central roles were popular. Peasants were in revolt against their feudal lords, and the hated nobles were represented by wolves in the proletarian literature. Medieval peasants called famine "the wolf." Avaricious landlords were "wolves." Anything that threatened a peasant's precarious existence was "the wolf."[19]

Though I find no evidence wolves eat each other (they apparently do kill one another on occasion), it is said wolves killed humans and ate unburied corpses. They also threatened domestic animals, which likely resulted in the New Testament hatred of wolves as both killers of lambs and the wolfish enemies of Christianity that threatened the lambs of God, especially Christ (see Acts 20:29 and Matthew 7:15).

Though a quantity of evidence directly linking wolves to cannibals has not been easy to find (linkages to other carnivores such as leopards are easier), confirmation does show up in Plato's *Republic*. "The story goes," says Socrates, "that he who tastes of the one bit of human entrails minced up with those of other victims is inevitably transformed into a wolf."[20] As eaters of flesh, sometimes including human flesh and especially organs, it isn't difficult to see how wolves and other carnivores became metaphors for cannibals, particularly Hannibal, who ate a census-taker's liver and a nurse's tongue.

Hannibal, however, is much easier to connect to wolves through the conduit of vampirism rather than cannibalism. Besides the security cop's remark, Hannibal is like a vampire because he smells the dried blood on Clarice's leg after she cuts herself on the storage garage door. Like Dracula's power over Renfield in Bram Stoker's *Dracula*, Hannibal has the ability to manipulate people, as he does when he convinces the Renfield-like-Miggs to kill himself. Crawford also warns Clarice before she meets Hannibal, "You don't want Lecter inside your head." As a crucifix was apotropaic against vampires, a TV gospel program torments Hannibal as punishment for "killing" Miggs. When Hannibal asks Clarice to get him a cell with a view, his request to see water is similar to certain eastern European beliefs (Dracula is Romanian) in the soul's hydrotropia:

> The relation of the dead person to water is remarked on elsewhere: in one part of Albania it is reported that, if a funeral procession comes by, any containers of water must be emptied; in Romania, that they must be covered up, since the soul, being hydrotropic, might otherwise fall into one and drown. Here the soul is shown to seek water but also to be endangered by it. . . . In Bulgaria, after a death, containers of water are either covered or emptied.[21]

Not only is water (the ocean) important to Hannibal, but also sex. He asks about the potential sexuality of Clarice's relationship with Jack Crawford and asks her if she ran away from the sheep and horse ranch because the rancher forced her into fellatio and sodomy. Vampires are known for their consuming sexual desires: "It is generally assumed that the 'wild signs' (*wilde Zeichen*) imply that the corpse was believed to have an erection. The vampire of folklore is a sexual creature, and his sexuality is obsessive—

indeed, in Yugoslavia, when he is not sucking blood, he is apt to wear out his widow with his attentions, so that she too pines away, much like his other victims."[22] Of course, the vampire's penis is not the only body part which comes back to life; like a revenant, Hannibal is thought dead in the courthouse, but comes back in the ambulance to kill again. And Hannibal, like Dracula,[23] is strong and cunning, strong enough to hang Officer Boyle's corpse near the top of the courthouse cage and Officer Pembry's atop the elevator car; cunning enough, also, to make his extraordinary escape.

Another indication of Hannibal's vampirism is a mounted and stuffed owl discovered by Clarice's flashlight when she begins her search of Hannibal's storage garage. Before the owl became a symbol of wisdom in Christian tradition it was a symbol of evil, an abomination not to be eaten (Leviticus 7:17, 18) and a symbol of death and of desert, a creature inhabiting the land after God destroyed it (Isaiah 34:11, 15). Like the wolves under Dracula's command,[24] the owl hunts at night or just before dawn. Dracula commands many of the creatures of the night to the point that he can become them: "he is brute, and more than brute; he is devil in callous, and the heart of him is not; he can, within limitations, appear at will when, and where, and in any of the forms that are to him; he can, within his range, direct the elements: the storm, the fog, the thunder; he can command all the meaner things: the rat, and the owl, and the bat—the moth, and the fox and the wolf."[25] The most conspicuous creature of these animals, in the context of this chapter, is the moth. Dracula can control any moth "within his range" but especially *Acherontia atropos*, the death's head moth that he sends to Renfield in the insane asylum.[26]

As nature, in the form of poisonous plants, and poisonous and powerful animals, has been pushed or relegated to the outskirts of threat, human monsters increasingly take their place. Film monsters have moved, more and more, from monsters like Godzilla, Mothra, and King Kong to a plethora of human and humanesque monsters like Frankenstein, Dracula, Freddie Kruger, and an array of revenants, witches, psychopaths (Hannibal and Jame), cyborgs, and androids. Despite the humanization of monsters, or better, the monsterization of humans, the marks of what are monstrous, evil, and terrifying about humans are still mostly associated with animals— past, present, future, or imaginary—that are perceived to be threatening to humans.

Monsters Jame and Hannibal, in fact, are merely more subtle hybrids of human and animal like the satyr, harpy, minotaur, and werewolf. Though many strange mixtures, especially that of animal and human can evoke fear, this is not the case with *monster* hybrids of human and animal like Spiderman, Batman, Swamp Thing, and Tinkerbell. In order for the animal/human hybrid to be non-threatening, at least one of two criteria must be met: (1) human appearance or characteristics take precedence over animal appearance or characteristics; or (2) the animal hybridized with the human is considered to be non-threatening or beneficial.[27]

What allows a liking or compassion for monsters Hannibal and Jame are *human traits*: Hannibal's keen and cultured mind and Jame's tortured one make them human. Their *animal traits* make them frightening: stalking and killing with supposed pleasure, eating human flesh, night-vision, and a heightened sense of smell. Jame's sartorial cannibalism, though a human practice, remains horrid because humans are his victims. The film is subtle about connecting Jame's cannibalism to the human practices of skinning and making clothing from fur, feathers, and animal skin: the viewer must connect Mr. Bimmel and Jame as pelt farmers, and murdered women to murdered animals.

A tendency to see the animalism of Hannibal's cannibalism is strong, though cannibalism is, through historical construction, much more a human activity than an animal one. Even a charge of human cannibalism should be confronted with skepticism.[28] Except for starvation, the foremost reason for cannibalism—absorbing the victim's identity or power—is not likely to motivate carnivorous animals as much as the probably more semiotically-oriented human animal.

The transference or displacement of unsavory human practices onto *nature* or *animals* (nouns that smother even more variety than *human*) is a masquerade of species. Animal masks hide the human faces that should more properly represent cultural construction, and disguise our ability to reconstruct or deconstruct those constructions. Portraying humans as monsters draws even more attention to human cultural construction than constructing humans as machines, which stresses a need to deconstruct and reconstruct human behavior and get people off the backs of animals. But describing animals with traits we would rather disavow does not simply serve a desire to see "humanness" above animals and just below gods. Degrading representations of animals further allow people to deem necessary, accept, or ignore the slavery and totalitarianism (complete absence of rights and representation, a legal and philosophical subjectivity) from which animals run and under which they squirm. While *The Silence of the*

Lambs might evoke sympathy for screaming lambs, sympathy for slaughter, caging, and ghettoization of screaming wolves (and predators in general) is precluded by representations that reinforce stereotype (even if non-intentional or subtle). Such recourse to animal representations masks the human face attached to monstrous practice.

Lambs

A charcoal drawing of Clarice, in the foreground, holding a lamb and three Calvaric crucifixes in the background, lies on Hannibal's table in the Shelby County Courthouse. After hearing of Clarice's failed attempt at rescuing spring lambs, Hannibal, the werewolf, has a Last (Passover) Supper before his escape. The meal consists of a version of the paschal lamb: "lamb chops, extra rare." Curiously, Lieutenant Boyle finds this familiar meat exotic. He says, "Wonder what he wants for breakfast, a damn thing from the zoo?" perhaps to exaggerate Hannibal's love of flesh. Just after killing Lieutenant Boyle Hannibal hangs him from the prison cage, crucifixion-style, bright lights illuminating the eviscerated and bloody corpse. "Hannibal" is then found dead on top the elevator but the real Hannibal, like Dracula and Christ, "comes back." Hannibal returns while inside an ambulance (where is the red *cross*?) that is going through a tunnel, a kind of trance connecting the realm of death and life. Hannibal sacrifices Boyle and Pembry to stage his own death and rebirth. This prototypical Mass, crucifixion, and resurrection reconfigures the flock of Christian *lambs—* who eat the Agnus Dei (Lamb of God)—into a pack of wolves/ vampires/cannibals. After all, lambs do not eat lambs. Wolves do. Christian reference to the Lamb's body (and the Shepherd—shepherds protect their lambs in order to kill or sell them to be killed) that is eaten by a Christian flock of innocent lambs, draws attention away from the repugnant human cannibalism of eating Christ, and strangely displaces it onto (vegetarian) lambs. Meanwhile, when Christ is in the guise of the Lamb who quietly accepts his own sacrifice, transubstantiated wine and wafer subtly serve as naturalization and reinforcement of human carnivorism. But it could be much worse. At least lamb is not eaten at Communion.

Mass must not have influenced Clarice because she is deeply disturbed about lambs being readied for slaughter. These lambs even scream, unlike the Old Testament Lamb who is silent: "He [the Messiah] was oppressed, and he was afflicted, yet he opened not his mouth: he is brought as a lamb to the slaughter, and as a sheep before her shearers is dumb, so he openeth not his mouth" (Isaiah 53:7). From the tradition of this quotation, we might be surprised that lambs scream (or pigs squeal or cows low) when killed. But it is not surprising that we are surprised. Since the slaughter-house (a.k.a. *abattoir*, shambles) is isolated terror and suffering need not be considered. Consideration or feeling stands to threaten the profits that managers and owners make from degraded workers who kill and butcher largely out of economic desperation,[29] and from consumers conditioned from infancy to eat meat. Clarice was not lucky enough to be distant from the slaughterhouse; the screaming was right out back. Like a fledgling ani-mal-rights guerrilla, she breaks in to free the lambs but fumbles the attempt. As a last resort she grabs one lamb and runs. That lamb, too, is eventually killed and Clarice is *jailed* and exiled in a Lutheran home for orphans, a fitting place for a not-fully-interpellated Christian or *Homo carnarius* (flesh lover).

Clarice grows up and accepts the killing of lambs (perhaps made easier by moving away from the shambles) but not the screaming that some asso-ciate with the mushy, childish, and effeminate side of her constitution. The screaming *inside her head* must be stopped. She attempts this through metaphor, substituting people—Christian lambs and women in need—for screaming lambs. If she rescues Catherine Martin, Clarice might also save herself. Near the film's conclusion, Catherine comes out of Jame's house holding Precious and one of the cops tries to relieve her of the dog. Catherine clutches the dog closer and walks away with the precious Precious. It is no mistake Precious looks like a lamb. Catherine's exit with Precious transforms into a more successful reenactment of Clarice's attempt to save the spring lamb years before. On the other hand, with Catherine being readied for slaughter and skinning she is the homologue of the spring lamb, which makes Jame the counterpart of Clarice's unsym-pathetic rancher/uncle and Frederica Bimmel's poulterer/father. Catherine becomes the lamb surrogate through metonymy, through contiguity to Precious-as-lamb. Catherine can therefore be seen as both young Clarice (resemblance) and lamb (metonymy). Rescue of Catherine presumably relieves the screaming of the lambs inside Clarice's head, the kind of silence referred to in the movie's title.

Material lambs, however, continue screaming in shambles everywhere. While Clarice tells Hannibal her story, we are given the opportunity to understand this. But our potential sympathy for lambs is displaced onto our sympathy for Clarice's disturbed nights, and onto the relief that she can sleep once again. Clarice, by witnessing victimization, becomes a victim, which mediates, lessens, or removes the primary victim, the lambs. Carol Adams has already isolated and named the phenomenon whereby human suffering or suffering is substituted for animal suffering. She calls any entity so displaced (here, animals) the "absent referent":

> Metaphorically, the absent referent can be anything whose original meaning is undercut as it is absorbed into a different hierarchy of meaning; in this case the original meaning of animals' fates is absorbed into a human-centered hierarchy. Specifically in regard to rape victims and battered women, the death experience of animals acts to illustrate the lived experience of women [especially to the phrase "I felt like a piece of meat" stated by women describing their own rape].[30]

Linguistically appropriating animal treatment without appreciating animal suffering also occurs in the often-heard sentence, "They treated me like an animal." An animal might serve here as absent referent but, taking Adams further, something more insidious than absence seems likely. Cruel treatment of animals becomes naturalized (the naturalized referent) as *the* way to treat animals. "They treated me like an animal" could be restated, "It is, or may be, fitting and natural to treat an animal in such fashion but not me, a human being." Naturalizing the different treatments of animals and humans gives them the force and veracity of God-given acts. One can be sure that when any person says she or he was treated like an animal, the treatment was cruel.

Does this film (and novel), besides absenting animals as suffering referents à la Adams, naturalize practices of slaughtering and butchering animals, or does it draw critical attention to them? It seems to criticize lamb-killing through Clarice's tale of victimized lambs; however, this is undercut by the word *silence* from the title of the film and novel. Critical attention to both absented and naturalized lamb cruelty in the world outside the film is replaced by attention to Clarice overcoming a disturbing mental/emotional experience. The cruelty of humans would have been better brought to the fore by the more disturbing, anti-Hollywood title, *The Screaming of the Lambs.*

But *screaming* has problems too. The verb usually applies to human vocalization. Humanizing the sound of lambs elicits sympathy comparable to that for suffering humans, but it also reinforces a suspect, even if under-standable and effective, practice of humanizing animals in order to demand decent treatment, or evoke empathy for them. Configuring an entity into human form as the only way to respect its existence indicates a problem of imagination as does the opposite tendency, in which animals, as animals, cannot be understood as capable of feeling pain or pleasure in ways similar to us (what I call the Cartesian syndrome).[31] Human autophilia is a plausi-ble reason why *The Bleating of the Lambs* was not chosen over *The Screaming of the Lambs,* and the mainstream phobia against disturbing endings is the probable reason both titles were passed up for *The Silence of the Lambs.*

2

HUMAN PARASITES IN ANIMAL HOSTS
Women in Love

Nothing is subtle about the appearance of animals in D. H. Lawrence's novel, *Women in Love*. While a variety of animals are peripheral to *The Silence of the Lambs*, fewer animals play prominent roles in *Women in Love*. The animals in *The Silence of the Lambs* are, with few exceptions, subtle theriomorphs implanted in human characters, or hosts. Animal characters selected from *Women in Love*, however, are separate and animated, portrayed as animals. While *The Silence of the Lambs*' human hosts are infested with theriomorphs, *Women in Love*'s animal hosts teem with anthropomorphs. Theriomorphs and anthropomorphs are human parasites because both are the result of human conception.[1] Parasites, specifically the anthropomorphs in *Women in Love*, are an admixture of benefit, harm, and commensalism to their hosts.

Before discussing the anthropomorphs in *Women in Love* (1920), I want to examine Lawrence's, "Reflections on the Death of a Porcupine" (1925) for the author's ideas about animals outside the context of fiction. "Reflections" prepares the ground for a discussion of *Women in Love* and complicates Lawrence's reputation as civilization's enemy and nature's enlightened lover or acolyte. In 1947, W. H. Auden summed up the prevalent view of Lawrence's relationship to nature: Lawrence "loves them [plants, animals] neither as numinous symbols nor as aesthetic objects but as neighbors."[2] Either Auden did not read Lawrence's "Reflections" or he did not notice its inconsistency with his observation. Perhaps after the following discussion, Auden's statement will look a bit hasty.

"Reflections on the Death of a Porcupine"

Lawrence's feelings about animals are more complex than those about plants, land, and universe. He loves the unanimaled, unpeopled world,

even the "ice-destructive" mountain heights of Gerald Crich (a main character in *Women in Love*), more than their "improvement," "development,"
or replacement by culture. Lawrence's animals, however, can be desirable
or undesirable. This makes his depiction of nature difficult to sum up easily. Auden offers the animal factor as a plausible explanation why
Lawrence's views on nature are still more complex than Auden's above
characterization. Perhaps the complexity arises from animals' interaction
with people:

> Lawrence possessed a great capacity for affection and charity, but he
> could only direct it towards non-human life or peasants whose lives
> were so uninvolved with his that, so far as he was concerned, they
> might just as well have been non-human. Whenever, in his writings,
> he forgets about men and women with proper names and describes
> the anonymous life of stones, waters, forests, animals, flowers, chance
> traveling companions or passers-by, his bad temper and his dogma-
> tism immediately vanish and he becomes the most enchanting com-
> panion imaginable, tender, intelligent, funny and, above all, happy.
> But the moment any living thing, even a dog, makes demands on him,
> the rage and preaching return.[3]

Lawrence's "Reflections on the Death of a Porcupine" both verifies and
refutes Auden's point. Near the opening of the essay, Lawrence, after
spending several hours removing embedded quills from the snout of a
squirming and yelping dog, loses his patience and shoos the dog away,
even though twenty or so quills still remain in his muzzle. The dog refuses
to go so Lawrence hits him with a stick: "I could not bear to have that dog
around any more. Going quietly to him, I suddenly gave him one hard hit
with the stick, crying: 'Go home!' He turned quickly, and the end of the
stick caught him on his sore nose. With a fierce yelp, he went off like a wolf,
downhill, like a flash, gone. And I stood in the field full of pangs of regret,
at having hit him, unintentionally, on his sore nose."[4] This corroborates
Auden's point that Lawrence does not want anyone, even if in trouble,
troubling him. But Lawrence does not stop with the material cause (the
dog) of his trouble, but goes to the efficient cause (the porcupine).

Even before the dog's quilling, Lawrence says he hates porcupines
because they gnaw on and sometimes kill trees, and because "Everyone
says, porcupines should be killed; the Indians, Mexicans, Americans all say
the same" (349). When Lawrence is out walking a few days before the dog

incident and sees a porcupine moving away from him, it is not surprising that he "stood near and watched, disliking the presence of the creature. It is a duty to kill the things" (349). But at this point Lawrence says, "the dislike of killing him was greater than the dislike of him" (349).

But after the dog is quilled, the case against porcupines becomes overwhelming; so-called evidence of porcupinian evil drives Lawrence to want to kill porcupines. He grabs his gun and, with the woman on whose ranch he lives, hunts down and kills the first porcupine he sees, excusing himself by saying that he was urged on by the woman. The insufficient excuse, however, is filled out with an extensive rationale:

> Wherever man establishes himself, upon the earth, he has to fight for his place, against the *lower* orders of life. Food, the basis of existence, has to be fought for even by the most idyllic of farmers. You plant, and you protect your growing crop with a gun. Food, food, how strangely it relates man with the animal and vegetable world! How important it is! And how fierce is the fight that goes on around it. (203, my emphasis)

Remarkable here is how rationalization bypasses act: the porcupine is never mentioned as a threat to either Lawrence or his horticultural pursuits. While it is true Lawrence holds the porcupine responsible for infringing on *his* life, at least partly because dogs are conceived of as human property (though the dog was not his), it can be safely said Lawrence hunted *a* porcupine primarily because he already hated it as an anonymous individual but with a species name (he doesn't know if the one he killed was the one who quilled the dog). Perhaps Auden should have written that Lawrence loves anonymous creatures, unless they belong to an ignominious (derives from Latin for badly-named) species. The porcupine makes the mistake of reinforcing, presumably by protecting itself from the dog, all of Lawrence's received, un-critiqued cultural baggage.[5] Because Lawrence expends little effort questioning stereotypes, his view of animals is hackneyed and eventually deadly to the animal(s) he debases.

From here it is but a small jump to endowing humans with the characteristics of already contemptible animals, which makes humans easier to hate, harass, or kill. Recall that in *Women in Love,* Gerald compares Loercke, Gudrun's artist-friend, to a bestiary of hate: vermin, rat, dry snake, insect, maggot, and flea.[6] Gerald eventually wants to rid himself of Loercke. Anthony Burgess picks up on the theriomorphism of humans by noticing in

Lawrence's *oeuvre* a general attribution of natural motivations and natural characteristics (especially animal) to Lawrence's human characters:

> Why, in my view, is *Women in Love* one of the ten great novels of the century? Chiefly because, through the dangerous guesswork of intro-spection, Lawrence has come to certain conclusions about human emotions and motivations that draw men and women closer to nature—the world of plants, animals, sun and moon—than the old fic-tional emphasis on man as a social animal would allow.[7]

This, however, presents unfortunate results for nature if it leads to the notion that, because humans are part of nature and are themselves animals, human action cannot be anti-natural, that since we are natural, our actions must also be. After all, how could an animal—considered motivated by nature—commit an unnatural act? Lawrence justified killing the porcupine with the argument that man is an animal who therefore cannot commit an unnatural act; in other words, his act was natural because most animals kill for food. But it is a strained synecdoche to assert that since animals can be and are killed for food, any particularized killing of an animal is justifiable. Or perhaps it is a maimed metonym: Since Lawrence killed the porcupine near to the woman's ranch (a place that raises animals, usually for food) the killing must have—through associative proximity—been for the purposes of obtaining food. But my tropic speculation is disingenuous. Lawrence knew that food had nothing to do with his killing: The porcupine neither threatened Lawrence's food nor his safety, nor did Lawrence eat the porcu-pine after he blew it away.

The food excuse remains insufficient, even to Lawrence, because he sub-sequently calls on tradition to bolster it. The argument is fully transfigured through a slightly embellished reiteration of the Elizabethan great chain of being (nature at bottom, God at the top, with humans between). The crite-rion giving rise to Lawrence's hierarchy is not derived simply from a food chain, but from degrees of being alive. The test of aliveness is *"Can thy neighbor finally overcome thee?"* If he can, then he belongs to a higher cycle of existence" (357). Lawrence gives two examples of this existential hierarchy: "Life is more vivid in the Mexican who drives the wagon, than in the two horses in the wagon. Life is more vivid in me, than in the Mexican who dri-ves the wagon for me" (357). Lawrence stresses that hierarchy only con-cerns time and space—existence—not the fourth dimension of being (heaven) on whose plane everything is incomparable, and so, neither higher nor lower. He also emphasizes that he speaks not about individuals, but about "species, race, or type." The trick for Lawrence is that in order to have more being, a species, race, or type must subordinate "the lower creatures or races, and assimilate them into a new incarnation" (361). "The aim of conquest," writes Lawrence, "is a perfect relation of conquerors with conquered, for a new blossoming" (361).

Two inferences can be made from Lawrence's philosophy of being. First, porcupines, horses, and Mexicans should take to heart that their domination or killing by more being-ful creatures preserves earthly order and will eventually end by blossoming in the promised land of a "new incarnation." Second, domination is always best done by a large group of similar, imperialistic individuals. It would do little good for one horse to overcome one Mexican, or one Mexican to subdue the Anglo Lawrence, unless horses and Mexicans, *en masse*, subdued the respective rungs above them. Thus, Lawrence's porcupine-killing (and his race/class hierarchy over Mexicans and horses) is consistent with his view of the natural order of existence.

It does not take a logician, however, to find problems with Lawrencian overcoming as a measure of aliveness, as the best way to accumulate being. Moreover, it is curious to see how killing a hated animal gives rise to such a universe of rationalization, displacing responsibility, from Lawrence onto Universal or Natural Law. Even the words *The Death*, in the essay's title, displace Lawrence's murder onto an act perpetrated by an abstract Universe or Nature; the title did not begin with the words, *My Killing*, or better, *I Killed*. Perhaps it is to Lawrence's credit that he felt the need to articulate a world-view to justify one act, however serious. At least it indicates discomfort with what he did.

Lawrence's elaborated appropriation of the great chain of being reinforces the great chain's rationale for human use, domination, and extermination of anything below humanity. The appropriation also bears comparison to the appropriative act in the readymades of artist Marcel Duchamp. But Duchamp's urinal, for example, keeps its identity as a urinal even after Duchamp turns it upside down to transform it into the "Fountain" he signs as an art object. Not so with Lawrence's appropriation of the great chain. The chain is apt to get lost behind the veneer of Lawrence's philosophy, might even be validated because it is Lawrence's conception (the author's exalted status lends authority to a racist/speciesist theory, even if it is piss-poor). Duchamp, at least, turned his urinal upside down and drew attention to one of the ways objects become sacrosanct (the artist's signature), and can be transformed. Lawrence takes his object (the great chain) and does little new except anchor it firmly in three-dimensional existence, not in "four-dimensional Being."

Remember back to Auden's observation that Lawrence "loved" plants and animals "neither as numinous symbols nor as aesthetic objects but as neighbors." Further recall that Lawrence killed the porcupine—killing as a way to possess—neither for food, existence, or being, but because it was a negative anthropomorphic symbol. I suspect he would not have wanted to kill that positive anthropomorphic symbol, the horse (including the one pulling the Mexican's cart), even if the horse had kicked a dog. Contra Auden, the Lawrencian porcupine *is* negatively aestheticized, a symbol of evil, an icon of ugliness, and in Lawrence's essay, "Aristocracy" (1925)—a kind of appendix to "Reflections"—cowardly and greedy:

> Deserts made the cactus thorny. But the cactus still is a rose of roses.
>
> Whereas a sort of cowardice made the porcupine spiny. There is a difference between the cowardice of inertia, which now governs the democratic masses, particularly the capitalist masses: and the conservative fighting spirit which saved the cactus in the middle of the desert.
>
> The democratic mass, capitalist and proletariat alike, are a vast, sluggish, ghastily greedy porcupine, lumbering with inertia. Even Bolshevism is the same porcupine: nothing but greed and inertia.
>
> The cactus had a rose to fight for. But what has democracy to fight for, against the living elements, except money, money, money!
>
> The world is stuck squalid inside an achieved form, and bristling with a myriad spines, to protect its hulking body as it feeds, feeds: gnawing the bark of the young tree of life, and killing it from the top downwards. Leaving its spines to fester and fester in the nose of the gay dog.[8]

It is a wonder Lawrence did not torture or mutilate the porcupine he murdered, a porcupine replete with human parasites that turn it into an enemy of "Life," reinforce the *widespread* perception of porcupinity, and deeply trouble Lawrence himself.

The metaphor trap is double. In the quotation above, not only are porcupines anthropomorphized as cowardly and greedy—descriptions more befitting humans than animals whose motives are usually less clear—but the masses are animalized into a porcupine. Conflating *entities*, not merely terms, becomes dangerous to porcupines and people. Lawrence, when he saw *the common man*, saw a cowardly, greedy porcupine. When he saw porcupines, he saw the lumbering masses. Theriomorphism and anthropomorphism have become reciprocal and potentiating. But the process goes further. For the masses to be degraded by calling them a porcupine, the porcupine must already be endowed with greed and cowardice, traits closely associated with humans. Conversely, in order for porcupines to be demeaned as substitutes for the masses, the masses must already be endowed with the so-called traits of a porcupine (hulking and lumbering). Metaphor comes to the verge of vertiginous identity.[9] Nonetheless, while the masses still benefit from their status as human, porcupines take on the double evil of human masses and animals.

Because "Reflections" was published five years after *Women in Love*, it might be argued Lawrence changed for the worse. Perhaps this is the case since no animals in the novel were murdered. Or perhaps the particular animals he chose simply benefited from more favorable anthropomorphs.

Mareman

While a centaur is male, a *mareman* is hermaphroditic. Though no mareman exists in "Coal-Dust,"—a chapter in *Women in Love*—Gerald Crich, rich, blond industrialist who is the upper male, human portion, rides, with a vengeance, the lower, female, animal portion—his "red Arab mare"— "almost as if she were part of his own physique" (126).[10] The scenario suggests several binaries in a master/slave relationship: male over female, West over East, North over South, human over animal, culture over nature. While these dominations are not dependent on the fusion involved in the mareman image, this fusion suggests the problems that must be overcome when a political agenda calls for flexible and multiple individual subjectivities to win out over a politics where individuals have a rigid, fixed identity. In this novel, Gerald aggressively attempts to deny or pacify the degraded mare portion of his multiplicity, in order to crush a complication of his identity into homogeneity. This mareman suggests a body at war with itself and has implications for a body at war with the world.

As sisters Gudrun and Ursula walk home from teaching school they must stop for a passing train. Gerald, heir to his father's colliery that this train serves, trots his red Arab mare up to the tracks. The colliery train approaches and slowly passes, making a horrible racket and scaring the nameless mare into a rearing, kicking frenzy. Gerald will have none of this squeamishness and forces the mare to stand close to the passing train, spurring her flanks over and over while she rears and bleeds. Ursula, appalled at Gerald's brazen mistreatment of the mare, screams, "Let her go, you fool, you *fool*——!" (125). Gudrun is so angry she blanks out momentarily; when she recovers, she is coldly distant. The train finally passes, and as she opens the gate to let the struggling horse cross, Gudrun screams at Gerald, "I should think you're proud" (127).

Three chapters later, in the presence of their friends Rupert and Hermione, Ursula calls Gerald on his abuse. After much argument the conversation ventures across the species boundary and wanders into gender. Rupert Birkin is the venturer: "And woman is the same as horses: two wills act in opposition inside her. With one will, she wants to subject herself utterly. With the other she wants to bolt, and pitch her rider to perdition" (159). The operative metaphors are: horses, mares, and domesticated animals equal women, and riders equal men. No one objects here to the metaphors[11] and the conversation culminates with:

> "It's a dangerous thing to domesticate even horses, let alone women," said Birkin. "The dominant principle has some rare antagonists."
>
> "Good thing too," said Ursula.
>
> "Quite," said Gerald, with a faint smile. "There's more fun." (159)

Gerald enjoys his supremacy, especially with a resistant object, and Ursula seems content with this role, as she voices no objection to generalized objectification.

Something is uncannily easy about this slippage from species to gender. Is it that both animals and women are, or were, considered primarily mindless bodies, (the body being mere matter and the mind the locus of suffering)? This concept is strange when physical pain is usually felt in the body. Or does it have to do with analogous positions of rider and horse and man and woman during a common position for intercourse? In two well-known (hetero)sexual positions, male over, or on top of, female, and male behind female, the male is, or appears to be, dominant, probably an association with fighting and riding. In the rear approach, the male is said to "mount" the female as a person mounts a horse. In either position, a centaur or mareman posture is created. And, of course, the verb *ride* is used to refer to the male's sexual position and motion. Women have even been called *fillies*. That the horse under Gerald is a mare drives home the correspondence.

So what is going on between Gerald and this mare? Is he having sex with her overexcited, rearing body while two sisters/voyeurs watch? Is he raping her by jabbing his spurs into her flanks until she bleeds, and forcing her to wear the bondage gear of bit and reins? Perhaps Gerald imagines "she wants it," since a creature believed to be a mere body supposedly needs a mind to control it and another body to satisfy it. In its most negative sense, Gerald's act is pornographic: perhaps feeling he is arousing the sisters, he forces the terrified mare to endure a violent (sexual) act. Even minus the sheer cruelty, Gerald is a "rapist."[12]

There is another possibility—one that dispenses with the horse's femaleness. The animal between Gerald's legs is his gigantic penis, and when the horse rears, its body becomes a sky-jabbing erection worthy of Priapus. Gerald, prancing with his (engorged) red horse, is an exhibitionist and "Gudrun liked to look at him" (124). It is curious that juxtaposing the more massive and powerful horse with the human body does not evoke Gerald's humility. What saves him is his position vis à vis the horse.

Later, the horse becomes a metaphor for male potency and power when Ursula, Gudrun, Gerald, and Loercke examine a picture of Loercke's statuette of a young, naked girl, "passing towards cruel womanhood," who sits sideways atop "a massive, magnificent stallion, rigid with pent-up power, its neck . . . arched and terrible, like a sickle, its flanks pressed back, rigid with power" (489). Here, positions of gender are reversed—female on top, male on bottom. But the girl, though human, seems diminished and shamed on the horse, unable to get a sexual charge from her mount (one possible explanation is that she sits with legs hanging to one side). Her puberty (and gender?) embarrasses her even though she sits on top of the mature, *rigid* stallion. The statuette seems designed to humiliate the girl, a view corroborated by the fact that Loercke coerced her to pose for him by beating her. Undiscussed is the horse's humiliation since it must tolerate a person sitting on top of it. (Ursula does object to the "stiff," "stupid," and "brutal" way the horse is depicted.) The girl looks humiliated by puberty, and not necessarily mortified from having been beaten. But despite the viewers' ignorance, the powerful "pent-up" (and probably penned-up) stallion is *broken*.

Besides being described as a mare, Gerald's mount is said to be an Arabian horse from Constantinople. The obvious connotation, today at least, is West (Gerald) over East (spurred mare) or North over South—

hegemonies based on bloodletting. Contemporaneous with the writing of *Women in Love,* the Allies agreed to partition Turkey in 1915 and then fought over Constantinople: "Europeans regarded Turkey as the sick man of Europe, the Ottoman state as doomed to extinction, and the Turkish people as barbarous and incompetent."[13] Whether Gerald, Gudrun, and Ursula were such Europeans is unmentioned, but Ursula, in conversation with the railroad-crossing gatekeeper, says that Gerald should have left his horse in Constantinople: "He'd better have left her to the Turks, I'm sure they would have had more decency towards her" (128), perhaps sarcastically implying that Gerald had to go a long way to beat the Turks at barbarism. But then, Gerald possibly thought he was taming a "barbarous" country by taming a "wild beast" that was doubly wild because she came from a "barbarous" country.

To Gudrun and Ursula, Gerald seems anathema to a turn-of-the-century England where the Royal Society for the Prevention of Cruelty to Animals (RSPCA) "epitomized respected philanthropy" and identified "animal protection with solid English virtue."[14] English kindness was juxtaposed to foreign barbarity to the point that an English dog breeder avoided breeding with an alien stock on the grounds that it "must be inferior *because* it is foreign."[15] Perhaps the idea of Turkish barbarity came partially from their treatment of animals, especially horses, where ". . . the horse, a member of the clan, is the epitome of the sacrificial animal. . . . "[16] Or perhaps the stereotype came from ancient texts like *The Histories* wherein Herodotus describes horse sacrifices. For example: "The only god they [The Massagetae from the Turkish side of the Caucasus] worship is the sun, to which they sacrifice horses: the idea behind this is to offer the swiftest animal to the swiftest of gods."[17] But while the British might have superciliously objected to relatively quick and violent killings, even now objections are seldom voiced to the slower deaths of horses enslaved by both Brits and Turks, or to the ownership and treatment of horses that would be an abomination were humans the chattel.[18] The Turkish treatment of animals is purportedly still an issue for Europe. On a recent news program about building a European Community, a panel member suggested that one reason Europe did not want to admit Turkey was "cultural difference," citing as an example Turkey's treatment and eating of certain animals tabooed in Europe.

Gerald's horse is described as red, a curious color for a horse. But knowing that Lawrence had the Bible "poured every day into [his] helpless consciousness,"[19] offers a possible explanation for the horse's redness:

And there went out another horse *that was* red: and *power* was given
to him that sat thereon to take peace from the earth, and that they
should kill one another: and there was given unto him a sword. (Rev.
6:4, original emphasis)

Horses lend size and power to the horseman's stature: "The horse, like a
colonized subject, makes a man [and woman] a master. Its association with
knighthood, chivalric orders, lordly privilege, and high degree reinforces
the image of mastery that a man on horseback represents."[20] The horseman
is fittingly destructive since he subjugates the horse for riding.

Gerald resembles the rider of the Biblical red horse because he is an
extraction-crazed mine owner, who takes coal from the earth and is
described in sword-like terms: "A sharpened look came on Gerald's face.
He bit himself down on the mare like a keen edge biting home" (125); "he
held on her unrelaxed, with an almost mechanical relentlessness, keen as a
sword pressing in to her" (126). Gerald is a sword using his spurs (little
swords) to make his mare (and nature) do his will. Lawrence tampers with
Revelation by placing Gerald, the nonbeliever and apocalyptic violator of
n/Nature (especially through mining), atop a gentle horse so that Gerald
must die instead of Revelation's heretical multitudes. Gerald is a hero of
epic proportion because, Lawrence writes, he confronts no mere mortal
adversary, but Nature:

The difference is, that whereas in Shakespeare or Sophocles the
greater, uncomprehended morality, or fate, is actively transgressed
and gives active punishment, in Hardy and Tolstoy the lesser, human
morality, the mechanical system is actively transgressed, and holds,
and punishes the protagonist, whilst the greater morality is only pas-
sively, negatively transgressed, it is represented merely as being present in background, in scenery, not taking any active part, having no
direct connexion with the protagonist. Oedipus, Hamlet, Macbeth set
themselves up against, or find themselves set up against, the unfathomed moral forces of nature, and out of this unfathomed force comes
their death.[21]

Gerald, the only main character who dies in this novel, is repeatedly shown
pitted against N/nature as epic mine owner and animal subjugator.
Gerald's corpse even reminds Birkin of a "dead stallion," perhaps alluding
to the mare Gerald tortured. Gerald's tragic fall is far, like Hamlet's, Lear's,

and Oedipus's, because Gerald tries to subdue lofty Nature. But the message is ambivalent: Either we should grapple with nature and *live* while alive (a life weakly lived is hardly the stuff of epic), or merely drift through in less-than-epic proportions. The dilemma is a human, especially male, solipsism—what happens to nature is absent from both options. While the larger patterns and events of nature might be indomitable, the inhabitants comprising earthly nature are not.

Gerald's cruelty is depicted both in the excessive force he uses to make his mare stand at the crossing and in his repeated puncturing of her flanks. No cruelty is seen in owning, riding, or working a horse, which are often thought to be good for both people *and* horses. At the wedding in the first chapter, "the bride's carriage, adorned with ribbons and cockades" pulls up to the church. *"Gaily* the grey horses curvetted to their destination. . . " (19, my emphasis). Perhaps Lawrence confuses the gaily decorated carriage with the horses' happiness. But maybe the horses *are* happy, since *he* created them. Lawrence does have much at stake in seeing beasts of burden as joyful. Horses, he affirms, give humans metonymic nobility:

> Horses, always horses! How the horse dominated the mind of the early races, especially of the Mediterranean! You were a lord if you had a horse. Far back in our dark soul the horse prances. He is a dominant symbol: he gives us lordship; he links us, the first palpable and throbbing link with the ruddy-glowing Almighty of potence. He is the beginning even of our god-head in the flesh. And as a symbol he roams the dark under-world meadows of the soul. He stamps and threshes in the dark fields of your soul and of mine. The sons of God who came down and begot the great Titans, they had "the members of horses" says Enoch. Within the last fifty years man has lost the horse. Now man is lost. Man is lost to life and power. While horses thrushed the streets of London, London lived.[22]

While London lived, "cruelty to horses accounted for 84 percent of the total convictions and 60 percent of the narrative reports [to the RSPCA from 1857–60]":

> If an animal was unwilling or unable to go as fast or as far as its driver wished, he might try any number of unacceptable ways to persuade it. Beating was the most common tactic, and the arsenal enumerated in the reports on prosecution included not only whips, straps, and

sticks, but also chains, shovels, pitchforks, knives and a variety of other hardware.[23]

Though Lawrence would have assuredly been disgusted with such treatment, one should suspect Lawrence's *special* (as in *species*) selfishness that used symbolic horses to shunt actual horses in a panegyric for a living London. While self-satisfied with his objection to Gerald's egregious cruelty, Lawrence still wants to steal nobility from a cruel system of domestication that steals it from horses. Opposing cruelty to domestic animals without opposing domestication is tantamount to opposing cruelty to slaves without opposing slavery. In both, the obvious incidents of whippings and neglect overshadow the less obvious systemic domination. And while it is more reasonable to oppose the abuse of prisoners (like slaves, another analogue with domestic animals) without opposing some form of prison, being (an animal) is not a criminal act necessitating prisonerlike treatment.

Gerald makes his mare stand and face a train laden with coal from his mines. While we can imagine Gerald's satisfaction at the sight of the train, what exactly is it that bothers the horse? Though Lawrence says it is the train's noise, the movement, size, smoke, smell, or the combined effect of all these might also bother her. Perhaps she is terrified by the train's harsh lines, its metallic opposition, its stillborn movement. Perhaps the mare envisions the train as Lawrence describes it, "a disgusting dream that has no end" (126)—a nightmare—an iron horse coming to kill her, or worse, mate with her. Or maybe she believes Gerald sees her much the same way he sees this train, as a vehicle to carry him and his loads: "I [Gerald] consider that mare is there for my use . . . because that is the natural order" (156). This train would then be her monstrous Doppleganger, a vision forcing her to realize exactly how the rider perceives her—as a machine, not human-made, but one forged by God and Nature and bequeathed to humanity. Would not the mare's theory explain the elaborate equipment pulling at her head, neck, and mouth; puncturing her sides; covering her body; and making her look like a machine? What possible chance could she have to reason with this rider, if indeed (she might wonder) he possessed reason at all?[24]

Never Mind the Bullocks

If an audience ever empowered a performer, the horned bulls before which Gudrun dances are that audience. One event in the chapter "Water Party" inaugurates the crescendo of Gudrun's power and the decrescendo of

Gerald's: Gudrun's backhanded slap across Gerald's face for which the bulls are directly responsible. The events surrounding that slap begin at the nadir of Gudrun's power and the zenith of Gerald's, and are shown most dramatically by Gerald's overpowering of the mare.

At the Crichs' annual party for their colliery workers and the community, Gudrun and Ursula leisurely canoe on the Crich estate's lake. Gudrun assures Gerald of her competence as a paddler, but the watching eyes of Rupert and Gerald make her paddling clumsy and her face red: "The colour flew in her face like a flag" (186). Color Gudrun childlike:

> He [Gerald] watched her paddle away. There was something child-
> like about her, trustful and deferential, like a child. He watched her all
> the while, as she rowed. And to Gudrun it was a real delight, in make-
> belief, to be the childlike, clinging woman to the man who stood there
> on the quay, so goodlooking and efficient in his white clothes, and
> moreover the most important man she knew at the moment. (186)

Gudrun's enjoyment of female, childlike subordination to the important, rich, handsome, male Gerald is fleeting. Gudrun and Ursula paddle away to a nearby sylvan landscape, a gentle, flowery grove roamed only by (as yet unbeknownst to them) a group of bulls owned by Gerald. Upon landing, the sisters become inspired by this new and somewhat natural "little wide world of their own." The sisters, who Lawrence calls "nymphs," skinny-dip; therefore they must be naiads, freshwater nymphs who inspire men and divine the future. But when running naked through the trees to dry themselves, they are like dryads, or tree nymphs. But they can also be seen as Hyads, nannies of young Dionysus (god of fertility and vine some-times worshipped as a bull).[25] Clothed, the sisters sit down to what might look like a Dionysian tea: "sandwiches of cucumber [Bacchanalian ithy-phallus?] and of caviare [fertility?], and winy [Bacchic potion?] cakes" (187). Before long, Ursula breaks into spontaneous song (Orpheus sang of the life and death of Dionysus), causing Gudrun to feel "outside of life" and "suffer from her own negation" (188). Gudrun meekly tries to become a participant: "Do you mind if I do Dalcroze to that tune?" (188) An embarrassed Gudrun has to repeat herself several times before Ursula acknowledges her "scarce moving" lips. Gudrun's weakness is made con-spicuous, but she begins to translate sounds into motion "as if she were trying to throw off some bond" (189). Gudrun gradually so warms to her own "pure, mindless, tossing rhythm," that Ursula becomes conscious of its "ritualistic suggestion" (189). Dalcroze's early-twentieth-century eurhythmics, a movement form akin to Isadora Duncan's bacchantic dances,[26] were inspired by images of ancient Greek dancers. Dalcroze sought "a Greek-inspired reintegration between body and mind through dance."[27] With the help of the bulls, Gudrun will also achieve reintegration and an end to her powerlessness. But in due time.

The bulls appear on the scene and, while they don't advance, they still intimidate. Gudrun, energized from dancing, mocks their presence in an attempt to confront her fear: "'I'm sure they won't [attack],' she said, as if she had to convince herself, also and yet, as if she were confident of some secret power in herself, and had to put it to the test" (190). With Ursula's fear emboldening her, Gudrun now gains "a strange passion to dance before the sturdy, handsome cattle" (190).

Gudrun's dance is ecstatic, "a palpitating dance towards the cattle, lifting her body as if in a spell . . . her hands stretching and heaving and falling and reaching and reaching and falling, her breasts lifted and shaken towards the cattle, her throat exposed as in some voluptuous ecstasy" (190). It might seem strange to dance this way before bulls, or to dance before them at all, but these are not powerful bulls so much as powerful emblems, especially of Dionysus. Dionysus's bacchantic women worshippers, "raging with madness and enthusiasm . . . danced with their heads thrown backwards, with dishevelled hair."[28] But while the Bacchae culminated their frenzy by tearing, eating, and scattering the bulls,[29] Gudrun, the reserved English bacchante, becomes a live wire, "as if she had the electric pulse from their breasts running into her *hands*" (190, my emphasis). When Gerald paddles up and chases his prized cattle away from Gudrun, she is suddenly unplugged and rages at his interference in her energy feed. As her hands were entryways for the power of the bulls, they are also exits: Gerald "recoiled from [Gudrun's] heavy [backhanded] blow across the face" (194). *Shocked,* Gerald can only respond weakly, "You have struck the first blow." But Gudrun retorts as if a prophetic bacchante, "And I shall strike the last."[30] Gerald "did not contradict her" (194), and, in fact, she does strike the final blow. This scene with the bulls marks the earliest instance of Gudrun's ever-increasing contribution to Gerald's demise. And while Gudrun does soothe Gerald by asking him not to be angry, he can only pitifully, or masochistically, reply: "I'm not angry with you. I'm in love with you" (195).

The Dionysian bulls' power (the productive and intoxicating power of Nature), absorbed by the maenadic Gudrun, inaugurates the undoing of

Gerald as Taylorite industrialist, Aryan *ubermensch,* egotistical jerk. As voyeur to Gudrun's dance and as a recipient of her violence, Gerald is a Lawrencian Pentheus. Like Pentheus, who denied Dionysus' divinity and denied the power of Nature, Gerald attempts to deny Nature's divinity. The cold, blond industrialist efficiently rapes the earth for coal, dominates animals, and eventually dies, as if from revenge by Nature's freezing temperatures.

The bull's "strength is in his breast, his weapons are on his head" Lawrence writes in *Fantasia of the Unconscious.*[31] While the breasts of these bulls are never mentioned in *Women in Love,* the bulls are described as "long-horned," with "horns branching into the sky," and "their bare horns branching in the clear light." Horns, like bulls, have a long history as emblems of strength and fertility because most often horns are on strong animals, but also because they are ithyphallic. Lawrence says horns have the "power to create" and the "power to kill."[32] Gudrun can be said to take that horned power and sadistically create a master-slave love affair with Gerald that eventually kills him.

Finally, the bulls in "Water Party" are characterized as "fleecy," and when they run off, their fleece waves "like fire." As Euripides describes him in *The Bacchae,* Dionysus, even in human form, bears some similarity to the bulls:

> *Like frankincense in its fragrance*
> *is the blaze of the torch he [Dionysus] bears.*
> *Flames float out from his trailing wand*
> *as he runs, as he dances,*
> *kindling the stragglers,*
> *spurring with cries,*
> *and his long curls stream to the wind!*[33]

The horned bull's form and flaming torch link Dionysus to the hellfire of the devil, who is also linked to bulls through cloven hooves, tail, and horns. Dionysus, Satan, and sometimes bulls are known for their link to death. Lawrence describes these bulls as having "dark, wicked eyes" (190) and "naked nostrils full of shadow" (189).

What makes these long-horned and flamingly fleecy bulls so exciting to Gudrun and perhaps readers is their ability to kill, and like the thyrsus-bearing maenads and Dionysus himself, and the pitchfork-wielding devil (pitchfork prongs resemble horns), to kill by impalement.

Impalement is a horrid and mysteriously fascinating way to die. Because horns and long slender pointed objects like stakes and thyrsi carry the cultural burden of phallicism, death by impalement might carry associations of rape, or of sadism and masochism. When a *man* is impaled (or gored as in bullfights), a violent homoeroticism might be an ingredient of the male gaze. Nowhere is the well-known link between sex and death so present as in the image of impalement—the bull, especially in bullfights, being the paradigmatic and most potent impaler. The bulls' long horns, then, are historically and physically suited for a transfer of ithyphallic power to Gudrun, who, with her slap, can loosely be said to violate and impale Gerald.

Bulls have long been an almost universal religio-cultural emblem for power. This power is for the taking when humans expose themselves to, subdue, or kill bulls in the temple, arena, or slaughterhouse (beef is said to be real food, male food). While men are said to gain strength from bulls, women usually acquire fertility. When Apis was brought into the temple as a living bull, Egyptian women exposed their genitals to him as a fertility rite. Egyptian princesses were buried with sacred bulls to promote princessian fertility.[34] Monumental ithyphallic effigies in Dionysian festivals and temples were carried as fertility symbols and were also thought to have guarded men's procreative power. Gudrun, however, does not gain fertility. Instead she absorbs maenadic bodily *and* spiritual strength[35] with which she lashes out at Gerald.[36]

There is also an obverse to bullpower. Lawrence's bulls are never called bulls, but "bullocks" and "cattle," words not exactly associable with power. *Bullock* means either a young or a castrated bull. The bulls in *Women in Love* are probably castrated because their long horns indicate an advanced age, a further reason for Gudrun gaining their strength, not their fertility. While castration does not eradicate the bulls' strength, it has made them wary of humans who, by the way, usually castrate without anesthetic. These bullocks are not so much bullish or bullies as they are cowed by Gerald and Gudrun (sexist labels transgressing human boundaries).[37]

In his poem St Luke, Lawrence expresses regret over the transformation of *bull* (a metaphor for St Luke) to *bullock* through being overcome by the physically-weaker Christian Lamb (Christ). But in *Women in Love*, these real bulls will be transformed into Crich's de-theicized (but still emblematic) meat and profit.[38] Why did Lawrence not have a narrator or character express regret or indignation when it came to real castrated bulls?

In addition to "bullocks," these animals are called "cattle." A brief discussion of the word *cattle* is in order before proceeding with analysis. *Cattle* is related to *chattel* and *capital* through the Latin *caput,* or head. Cattle are property (chattel), wealth (capital), and are counted by head (capital, as in top, or literally and figuratively, foremost).[39] According to Engels's *The Origin of the Family, Private Property and the State,* cattle were the first capital, the possession of which contributed decisively to the transition from matriarchy to patriarchy and the chain reaction that led to a double oppression of both women and prisoners of war, the latter forced into slavery.[40] Hunting did not produce the same surplus or capital as cattle herding, which gained an advantage from cattle's ability to reproduce. Male hunters, as owners of non-reproducing weapons and meat, never exceeded the wealth of women who owned the non-reproducing home and its contents. When the new source of wealth—cattle owning—replaced hunting, men, as owners of meat and weapons, assumed ownership of reproducing-cattle and of reproducing-slaves (Engels's theory is that in place of death prisoners were enslaved to tend cattle, a labor-intensive enterprise). The male now became family head, and possessor of reproducing-capital. The one bit of wealth men did not own, children (as laborers), still belonged to the mother through "mother-right." But Engels believes mother-right was usurped by males who became powerful through capital/cattle accumulation, which heralded the *"world historical defeat of the female sex."*[41] If Engels's scenario is cogent, animal property ushered in a triple slavery of animals, of men taken in battle, and of women deprived of owning property or children (children, in Engels's scenario, were chattel even before animals).

Working this long excursus on cattle into the discussion about the cattle in *Women in Love* offers greater import to Gudrun's dance. Gudrun absorbs power from the strong, horned, fleecy cattle, and her slap works toward reversing the *"world historical defeat of the female sex."* But these strong bulls are actually castrated bullocks and cattle (the latter a disparaging term for the masses, about which Gudrun expresses great contempt). Gudrun's power surge from the cattle is therefore limited, and only capable of contributing to the unsettling and eventual undermining of just one already-vulnerable male,[42] arch-capitalist, wage-slaver, cattle-owner, Gerald. As for the bulls, they back off without so much as a charge. It is as if Gudrun, instead of inflaming the power of these bulls through maenadic worship, robbed them of it, the way males had before her, leaving the bullocks even more impotent. While this might remind one of the story of the vampish female stealing potency and strength from vulnerable human males, my goal is quite different—I have been extracting Lawrence's parasitic anthropomorphs from their animal hosts. The trouble is, in the scene with the bulls, one is hard put to discern the difference between them.

Hare Bismarck

Gudrun recognizes Gerald's power, violence, and cruelty when she sees his domination of the red, Arab mare. Gerald is first exposed to Gudrun's power and violence when she dances in front of the bulls. With Bismarck, the rabbit, Gudrun and Gerald recognize each other's cruelty, a trait that constitutes a primary and mutual fascination, one that enables their passionate bondage, and foreshadows, like the bull scene, Gerald's fall: "Gudrun looked at Gerald with strange, darkened eyes, strained with underworld knowledge, almost supplicating, like those of a creature which is at his mercy, yet which is his ultimate victor" (273).

Just as Bismarck is made to show the inflaming attraction of cruelty, the black-and-white Bismarck initiates Gerald and Gudrun into other mysteries. Just as Lawrence, through Bismarck, must reveal how cruelty elicits passion, Bismarck must show the simultaneity of life and death, pain and pleasure, body and mind, blood and consciousness, innocence and ferocity. It is all a rabbit can do to handle being the node at the most violent and mysterious points of meaning; so he does what any such node might do in this situation. He struggles and writhes, flexes and extends as if mimicking the meaning/non-meaning of paradox, as if terrified by the knowledge that any creature pushed into this situation must soon have its blood (ritually) spilled.

Hutch-bound Bismarck belongs to Winifred Crich, Gerald's young sister. Under the supervision of Gudrun, an artist, Winifred wants to sketch the "great" and "lusty" pet. When they approach the hutch door, Bismarck runs furiously around the hutch. Winifred warns Gudrun that Bismarck is a "fearful kicker." Nonetheless, Gudrun plunges in at a moment when Bismarck is still and grabs the rabbit by the ears. "Lunging wildly," Bismarck leaves his signature on Gudrun's body and mind: "Her heart was arrested with fury at the mindlessness and the bestial stupidity of this struggle, her wrists were badly scored by the claws of the beast, a heavy cruelty welled up in her" (273). But just in time, Gerald intervenes:

> Then a sudden sharp, white-edged wrath came up in him [Gerald].
> Swift as lightning he drew back and brought his free hand down like a
> hawk on the neck of the rabbit. Simultaneously, there came the
> unearthly abhorrent scream of a rabbit in the fear of death. It made
> one immense writhe, tore his wrists and his sleeves in a final convul-
> sion, all its belly flashed white in a whirlwind of paws, and then he
> had slung it round and had it under his arm, fast. It cowered and
> skulked. His [Gerald's] face was gleaming with a smile. (274)

Gerald puts Bismarck down in the garden, where the rabbit lies still, then
darts about, and finally settles down to eat. The chapter ends with
Winifred soothing Bismarck: "Eat, eat my darling! . . . Let its mother stroke
its fur then, darling, because it is so mysterious—" (277).

Because this scene and this rabbit *are* so mysterious, some critics have
backed off from Bismarck's mystery as respectfully as Gudrun and Gerald
violently seize him.[43] My project, however, does not allow the sanctity of
mystery when the sacrifice, real or figurative, of an animal is at (the) stake.
Besides, any mystery worth its salt survives snooping.

Perhaps Lawrence chose a rabbit to uneasily balance this burden of
mysterious contradiction because rabbits seem so cuddly, so easily killed;
yet on the other hand, so able to decimate gardens and struggle fiercely to
remain alive (the unfierce Bugs Bunny, who appeared after Lawrence's
time, eludes his hunters with smarts and a command of English). Lawrence
generally equates rabbits with submission and with a fervent yet insolent
desire for death that encourages the killer.[44] The rabbit is also a hackneyed
symbol for fecundity, on which Lawrence capitalizes by calling Bismarck
"lusty." The Lawrencian rabbit might be the locus of both a desire for
death and the "little death" of orgasm. In Lawrence's poem, "Love on a
Farm," a rabbit trapper comes home after a day of work. The trapper embraces his wife who silently equates herself with a rabbit:

> *God, I am caught in a snare!*
> *I know not what fine wire is round my throat.*
> *I only know I let him finger there*
> *My pulse of life, and let him nose like a stoat*
> *Who sniffs with joy before he drinks the blood.*[45]

Because the trapper subjects rabbits to a frantic death in the jaws of a trap it
is understandable why his wife feels ensnared by his arms and lips. *Women*

in Love's Gudrun and Pussum (an earlier sexual partner of Gerald's), because both are initially encouraging and submitting women, are prime candidates for Lawrence's rabbit metaphor and oppositely, lenders of anthropomorphs to Bismarck.

Still, the rabbit is not only a stand-in for human femaleness. The rabbit also corresponds to male characters Halliday and Loercke,[46] but especially Gerald. Just as Gerald's corpse reminds Birkin of a stallion, it also reminds him of a rabbit (543). As in human gestation, where ontogeny is said to recapitulate phylogeny, Gerald's corpse seems to devolve through so-called lesser forms of animal life so that he resembles the lives he dominated. Will he eventually resemble the coal he mined? On the other hand, that his corpse is described as horse and hare might also mark Gerald's resurrection into the animals he abused while applying instrumental reason to nature.

As rabbits are a Lawrencian emblem or mark of the victim, Gerald has the mark of Cain for shooting his brother, supposedly by accident (here, the mark is the fact that everyone knows he did it). The mark of Cain is both the mark of the murderer and a potential victim, a mark designed by God to protect Cain from his fear that he will be slain for killing Abel (Genesis 4:8). Ursula is suspicious of this by-accident explanation of Gerald's fratricide: "'Perhaps there *was* an unconscious will behind it,' said Ursula. 'This playing at killing has some primitive *desire* for killing in it'" (54). From wanting to kill and having killed, Gerald, like a Lawrencian rabbit, comes to both desire *and* fear being killed: "'You [Gerald] seem to have a lurking desire to have your gizzard [an animal organ] slit, and imagine every man has his knife up his sleeve for you,' Birkin said" (37). "'No man,' said Birkin [to Gerald], 'cuts another man's throat unless he wants to cut it, and unless the other man wants it cut. This is a complete truth'" (36).

Birkin's *truth* is finally enacted when Gerald wanders into the snowy mountains after a final fit of hatred in which he delivers two blows to Loercke and almost fatally strangles Gudrun. Having nearly murdered again, Gerald's fear he will murder again is keen: Though wandering alone in the snowy Alps, Gerald senses someone is lurking (Loercking?), waiting to murder him. After seeing a small Jesus atop a lone crucifix stuck in the snow, the someone turns out to be Jesus. Who makes a more desirable murderer than Jesus? Gerald's hatred-borne fear of death also becomes his desire for it: "Yet why be afraid? It was bound to happen. To be murdered!" (540). Murder seems so much better committed by the salvational Lamb, another of Lawrence's analogues for the rabbit.[47] But Gerald, as the lion (he is called a lion, a tiger, and a wolf throughout the novel), fears the Lamb's revenge (ruminated and hoofed to death by a vegetarian?). Gerald, the lion, lies down for the Lamb.[48]

Gerald must indeed be construed as the best candidate for the analogue to the rabbit Bismarck because he is both the weak Lamb/rabbit in his desire to be killed, and the strong Lion: "He's [Bismarck's] almost as big as a lion," says Winifred (269). In addition, like the women mentioned above who submit to (or desire) only a "little death," Gerald is the superior candidate for the Lawrencian rabbit because Gerald desires/submits to both deaths.

The belief in human desire for violent death is problematic (though understandable if we see that displays of vulnerability can seem like asking for trouble, or if a beautiful afterlife is thought to await the murdered), but is even more difficult to assume for animals. First, fewer clues explain animal psychology;[49] second, animals—I overgeneralize—do not display vulnerability when hunted[50] nor submit peacefully to being killed when aware of it; and third, no evidence exists, to my knowledge, that suggests animals conceive of an afterlife. Any theory positing a desire to be victimized, especially one proposed by a victimizer, is suspect.[51] Is attributing to the victim a desire to be murdered a case of metonymy, where the killer's desire to kill and stay alive is transformed into the hunted's desire to die in order to live forever?

The name *Bismarck* draws attention to the fierce side of rabbit behavior. As a tyrannical rabbit, Bismarck can be said to forcefully unite Gudrun and Gerald in cruelty, as Otto von Bismarck, the "Iron chancellor" cruelly united Germany. When Gerald finally sets the rabbit down, Bismarck runs furiously "in a tense hard circle that seemed to bind their brains" (276). But while the ruler of Germany is a chancellor, animals are often *chancellees*. The chancel is the sequestered space surrounding a Roman Catholic altar, and a chancellor is the priest who presides over that space whereon the animal chancellee (the Lamb, now a rabbit) is sacrificed. Lawrence condenses ritual sacrifice and makes the rabbit both chancellor and chancellee of Gudrun and Gerald's initiation into cruelty: "he [Gerald] was initiate as she [Gudrun] was initiate" (276). As judge the rabbit consummates the marriage by clawing both Gudrun and Gerald in a kind of blood brotherhood (*Blutbruderschaft*) like the one Birkin wanted with Gerald (235). And in the same moment, the rabbit is sacrificed as

Gerald's hand swoops "down like a hawk" to seize the rabbit (274). Bismarck is cruelly subdued but not killed:

> "He's not dead is he Gerald?" she asked.
> "No, he ought to be," he said. (274)

Bismarck wounds and is wounded. Gerald and Gudrun "wound" and are wounded. Lawrence skillfully, perhaps too skillfully, makes Bismarck less of a victim. And Gerald and Gudrun have their wounds as trophies.

Blood initiation is an initiation of consciousness for Gerald and Gudrun: "There was a league between them, abhorrent to them both. They were implicated with each other in abhorrent mysteries" (275). The gashes in Gerald's and Gudrun's wrists and forearms (locale of the *Blutbruderschaft*) correspond to the "torn veil of her consciousness" (274) and "the long shallow red rip . . . torn across his own brain" (276). Lawrence declares in a letter from 1913: "My great religion is a belief in the blood, the flesh, as being wiser than the intellect. We can go wrong in our minds. But what our blood feels and believes and says, is always true. . . . All I want is to answer to my blood, direct, without fribbling intervention of mind, or moral, or what not."[52] Flowing in the body, blood is life; spilled, it is death. And what comes most readily to Lawrence's mind when blood is mentioned? Animals:

> But listening-in to the voices of the honorable beasts that call in the dark paths of the veins of our body, from the God in the heart. Listening inwards, inwards, not for words nor for inspiration, but to the lowing of the innermost beasts, the feelings that roam in the forest of the blood, from the feet of God within the red, dark heart.[53]

The string of associations, blood, to body, to beasts (animals), to nature, to knowledge, and God, yields the following: listening to the animal beasts in the forest of our blood is listening to and knowing Nature and God.

But what do Gudrun and Gerald hear when they listen? Gudrun hears little else than Gerald "listening in" on her cruelty: "She knew she was revealed" (274). Gerald, besides listening to Gudrun, seems satisfied with the sound of his own cruelty. After subduing Bismarck, "His [Gerald's] face was gleaming with a smile" (274). Blood-consciousness is violent knowledge and pleasure of a common cruelty, not the common frailty of flesh. This makes sense in light of the name, Bismarck, the leader who by means of his *Kulturkampf,* attempted, but failed, to displace the symbolic blood of the Lamb with the blood brotherhood of the German people.

The rabbit, Bismarck, is "something like a dragon," "beastly," and "fearfully strong." He is also evil, a satanic priest at a Black Mass. The rabbit is "demoniacal," a "demon-like beast," a "devil" "obeying some unknown incantation." Gerald or Gudrun have a "hellish recognition," an "underworld knowledge," and a glimpse of the "unthinkable red ether of the beyond, the obscene beyond" (276). But this rabbit is black and white (not the unbelievable red). The two colors mark the rabbit as dual, but deconstructionist. Lawrence maintained good and evil as necessary and non-dominating complements,[54] and apparently, conceived each pole as mixed with its opposite. Notwithstanding the effects of making a rabbit a devil (recall the effects of conflating the porcupine with the masses), it is refreshing to see fierceness in a creature thought cuddly and harmless, a creature often seen as an appropriate victim.

Bismarck is the most significant animal in *Women in Love*. His mystery is due, at least partially, to the anthropomorphs with which he is infected: Chancellor Bismarck, a priest, a devil, a human conception of fertility, and a human-projected desire for and fear of death. Prior to Bismarck, I discussed the mare plagued by the anthropomorphs of woman, man (penis), Arab (Turk); as well as the mare's association with red, power, and weakness, and her conflation with a machine. I also discussed the bulls infested with Dionysus and man, the phallic symbolism of horns, and notions of power and weakness. When culturally-implanted parasites do their work, a monster—part human-part animal—appears. Lawrence's presentation of Bismarck looks as if a chef had smothered the being of an ontological rabbit in a leftover gravy of fertility and vulnerability made somewhat colorful by sprigs of fierceness and authority. Lawrence's Bismarck, riddled with anthropomorphs, is literary meat that if fully digested will make rabbits seem not so much unwilling victims, but fierce, willing ones.

While taking great care to construct psychologically-complex human characters, the animals in *Women in Love* are props for Lawrence's notions of *physical* struggle. They are anthropomorphized only as object-bodies—they desire, run, fear, bleed, breed, and scream like humans do—but if they are said to think they are all will and no mind (Gerald says this about his horse), or they are said to think exactly what their human interpreters do (see the chapter "Mino" on Birkin's cat). Even Ursula, who most empathizes with animals, only does so in the midst of obvious pain and suffering. Neither the characters nor the narrator expend effort wondering how animals might perceive, or think about a situation differently from humans.[55] Though this is also a form of anthropomorphism,[56]—hard work and guesswork at that—at least the effort might suggest the possibility that some, most, or all animals have, or could have, minds.

Ursula, *Women in Love's* preeminent nature-lover, criticizes the anthropomorphism of which I might be accused after maintaining that animals do, or could, have thoughts. After calling a robin a "little Lloyd George of the air," Ursula catches herself: "After all, it is impudence to call them little Lloyd Georges. They are really unknown to us, they are unknown forces. It is impudence to look at them as if they were the same as human beings. They are of another world. How stupid anthropomorphism is!" (301) But acknowledging that animals might have thoughts is only slightly more anthropomorphic than saying certain animals have legs, desires, and pains even if theirs are different from ours, especially since so many animals have brains and nervous systems. Arguing that animals share similarities with humans need not be pushed to the dangerous absurdity that animals and humans are interchangeable. While complimenting Ursula on her attempt to critique anthropomorphism, I question why it is "stupid" to retain the possibility that birds might have pride. Are humans the only species with something to be proud of? Is pride so sophisticated a mental function?

Ursula's contention that animals are wholly other risks a narcissistic kind of anthropomorphism, where human subjects construct *the human* on the basis of their own image and then impose it on the object (as when it is argued that certain groups, now accepted as human, were not human because they neither looked or acted enough like *us*). If narcissistic anthropomorphism yields no human likeness in the potential animal host (animals as "unknown forces"), the animal-as-object risks deification, or more likely, vilification, and either view easily leads to the object's abstract or concrete sacrifice. To conclude: At one end of a continuum is Gerald, part of whose blatant domination of animals is based on an anthropomorphism that configures animals with baser human qualities. Gudrun is somewhere in the middle. At the other end is Ursula whose anthropomorphism finds in animals an absence of the human replaced by a positive presence of "unknown forces." Even as Lawrence aspires to the example of Ursula, he seems unable to escape Gerald. But neither the modern Gerald or the atavistic Ursula seem to have gotten at the truth of animals that Lawrence seemed desperate to uncover. And even though being made a thing is surely worse than being made a kind of lesser deity, both ends or points of this continuum can be sharp. Imagine this horizontal continuum upended, a stake pointed at both ends: writhing at the bottom, the animal is stabbed or killed; convulsing at the top the animal is mounted or sacrificed.

II
The Forest and the Trees

Where, in chapter three, masses of trees contribute to human fear and, in chapter four, individual trees contribute to human comfort.

3

THE FOREST PRIMARILY EVIL
Deliverance

The forest in John Boorman's film adaptation of *Deliverance* (1972) is an endangered and dangerous place, a place of double mortality. This is not a coincidence—the forest is endangered partly *because* it is perceived as a dangerous place, a locale to be avoided, and one most useful when "cleared," "harvested," or "developed." Fear intensified by representation keeps people away from the forest and precludes concern about what destruction means—except as it directly affects people—to the myriad animals, plants, and elements of and around the forest. Such fear competes with and stands to subvert increasing pleas to save forests, even those with the prefix, *rain-*. Forest-fear offers no obstacle to the chain saws that produce hill-sized mounds of tree corpses and the topographical aftermaths called clear-cuts since that fear overshadows concern about the devastation from noospheric extraction, production, consumption, and disposal. To undermine forest-fear, it must be dragged into the open to see what inflames and fuels it. I survey *Deliverance*'s forest and suggest three fearful locales from which to be delivered: ghetto, Dantean hell, and site (a place where various rites of passage are enacted). These places are mapped and recounted, exposing the dread lurking in *Deliverance*'s Cahulawassee Forest. *Deliverance* may pay lip and eye service to the endangered forest that is prey to predatory development, but this concern is undermined by a not-inconspicuous depiction of a forest full of dangers. Consequently, and against the film's ostensible desire that viewers comprehend the gravity of disappeared and threatened forests, relief or apathy is what persists with the destruction of *Deliverance*'s threatening forest.[1]

Culture's Other Ghetto

The major feature *Deliverance*'s forest shares with an urban ghetto is marginalization, but unlike the urban ghetto that is continually moved away *from*, the forest ghetto, a mere woods, is continually moved *on*, threatened. In either scenario, marginalization produces a place not fit for decent folks, or folks at all, unless destroyed, remade, tamed, by "renewal" and "development." This is because the forest, like the urban ghetto or any locale, becomes implicated in a two-directional synecdoche: The forest turns its inhabitants into degenerates and criminals, and, in turn, its inhabitants make the forest look like a place of depravity. The forest, the realm of nature, is, or becomes, amoral or immoral—dangerous.[2] But in the case of the Cahulawassee Forest, viewers never find out if what is left (if anything) becomes a shunned ghetto or a tempting park.[3] Instead, the camera focuses on destruction—the earthmovers rolling and the dynamited land sending up plumes of dirt. This, with assorted heavy-handed (but often astute) comments by Lewis, is the paltry extent of *Deliverance*'s environmental view.

The Cahulawassee Forest, however, is not a reserve so much as a ghetto because it is likely to be perceived by viewers as a past, poor, and lawless place to improve, escape, or avoid. In *Deliverance,* this second, let us say cultural depiction, undermines the film's environmental strategy. While minimally eulogizing the threatened forest, *Deliverance* portrays an Appalachian forest—with its *bad* (inbred, evil, backward) mountain men—as a *threatening* forest ghetto that, if left standing, could nurture stagnancy, poverty, and violence.[4]

Because a ghetto is viewed as containing a backward, poor, and violent population, its conditions usually get worse before getting better. In *Deliverance,* both a human community and an adjacent wilderness are about to be eradicated because of such views: In reference to the recreation area that will replace the existent town, the taxi driver taking Ed (Jon Voight) and Bobby (Ned Beatty) to the hospital asserts: "Best thing ever happened to this town." His passengers, after all they've been through with "those people," don't object.

Nature in the form of the soon-to-be-disappeared river and its forest environs—to be replaced by a dammed lake/recreation area—draws white urbanites Ed, Lewis (Burt Reynolds), Bobby, and Drew (Ronny Cox), to go slumming in soon-to-be history, and canoeing and hunting in "just

about the last wild, untamed, unpolluted, unfucked-up river in the south."
Nature here is doubly past. First, because little, especially the forest, is said
to be contemporary or to represent progressive time except the forward
march of culture (culture as militaristic) and human history; the as-of-yet
damless, relatively clean river is, by human standards of speed, unchanged,
and therefore evokes a still-present past. Second, the river is virtually past
because it and the surrounding forest will very soon be history, tamed and
domesticated (from the Latin *domus*, to make into a home) by being
drowned under a lake. Pastness is intrinsic to the idea of a ghetto: a place
left behind, a place of arrested modernity[5] where a linear, cultural time
comes to resemble the cyclical, natural time of replicating birth and decay
(since, as with its plants and animals, the next generation lives pretty much
like the last). The ghetto can come to mean a place so past, its inhabitants
so unredeemable, as to be fit for nothing except escaping, dumping, or
bulldozing. In short, for *condemning*.[6]

Sylvan time is thought to be so slow that it is unchanging.[7] Though
leaves grow, turn, fall, and decay, next year's trees will look and do virtually
the same as this year's. Increasingly, people do not expect the same of
clothing and hair, cars and cities. Any music, technology, and architecture
in a consumer society that does not change its approach or appearance is
faster and faster viewed as old or regressive.[8] While the rate at which culture becomes dead continually accelerates, nature looks slower and slower,
a place without style, innovation, or progress, but only discomfort, fear, or
boredom. The forest starts to take on an atavistic appearance like the
abodes of parents/adults to teenagers who keep the outdated at bay with
new posters and music that pound out the dying and decaying culture.

Trees, despite those losing their leaves, indicate an unchanging nature
because trees do not appear to learn or move, because they grow "so
slowly," and because they appear unconscious, possibly even stupid, as in
the term *wooden*. And "those" mountain people living in the forest cannot
escape this drag. People living "close to nature" are seen as moving
slower, deciding slower, changing practices slower; hill folks often avoid
big cities because life there moves too fast. *Deliverance*'s hill people,
remarks Fredric Jameson, are "stuck" in the thirties.[9] The men wear sus-
penders, old-style hats, and overalls, and do not wear watches or glasses.
They chew tobacco; are surrounded by old architecture, tools, and rust-
ing cars from the 1950s; and they speak a dialect unchanged by the
homogenizing speech of media and the influence of coexisting ethnic

groups. The slowness of the forest and its people yields a nature that "is a kind of unconscious synonym for underdevelopment,"[10] and that is synonymous with a nature that is past.

A slow, past forest can only be rescued from torpor by the correct speed or newest trend or development that demonstrate the intelligence of human practice. On one level, nature outings increasingly consist of a drive to and through the forest, skiing or boating through it, making large moving, consuming fires, playing portable music systems, carrying the newest synthetic state-of-comfort camping and hunting gear, or chucking attempts at speed or techno-camping for the more blatant RV.[11]

But camping and even RV experiences become increasingly unsatisfying. The forest must therefore be converted into a more leisure-friendly nature with its speed under human control. Fast-running, rock-filled rivers are made into placid lakes for large motor- and speedboats, and their banks are leveled for roads and homes where one can really bring the speed of convenience—cars, blenders, washers—right to the forest.[12] In a recreation area like the one planned for the Cahulawassee wilderness, people will temper forest slowness and so preclude any need for antiquated outings. The forest will then assume its proper place as landscape architecture, or backdrop for exercises in futurity and speed—since a forest without speed and currency is simply too stressful. Development drives the "slow, dead past" of forest-time into smaller and smaller pockets and with the ever-diminishing influence of forest time, culture's linear and progressive time comes to seem more and more like natural time, namely, the only time. And with the preserved memory of forest-time—nature increasingly becoming a subject for education rather than experience—cultural-time is apt to look progressive.

What makes the past stay past and the ghetto stay a ghetto is partially or even primarily poverty; in the culture of capitalism, no poverty is greater than a capital-less, possession-less state of nature (here, the forest). Though the mountain people in *Deliverance* might seem wealthy compared to animals or the poor in other countries, by contemporary American standards their cast-off, dilapidated, and archaic towns and villages signal unsettling poverty to most people with enough desire or money to attend movies. If mountain/hill people are thought to have any wealth, it is primarily in terms of peace, quiet, and scenery (in the city, a high-priced commodity). But overwhelmingly, poverty moves them negatively toward animality and nature.

Such a view of poverty best characterizes involuntary poverty, but ignores voluntary poverty: a poverty that might more aptly characterize mountain people[13] and which may be chosen because it involves more leisure time, or because the people are simply used to it. In voluntary poverty, consumption is valued less than a certain self-reliant lifestyle. Only Lewis seems to partially understand this because he expects "the machines are gonna fail."[14]

Besides being a place of poverty, the ghetto, like Tennyson's nature "red in tooth and claw," is often thought to be violent with inhabitants uncontrolled by law venting their distress and rage (feelings of abandonment and poverty) on each other and outsiders seen as enemies (which is often the case). Likewise, the tough-talking, gun-wielding mountain men are depicted—like animal predators—as uncontrollably violent, in fact, violent by nature.

If ghetto dwellers understand that they have been left behind in terms of progress and wealth, the dominant culture may fear violence seen as inherent in nature, or the lower class. Frederic Jameson sees Bobby's rectal rape as a *class* act, where proletarian poverty sodomizes bourgeois wealth:

> Being looked at is a rape, being raped is being looked at: such an interpretation suggests the deeper social import of that horrified powerless indignation of Dickey's heroes [canoeists], who are thus seen as though for the first time by a hostile class [the mountain men] which rises up against them as an equal, able to think its own thoughts about you and to see you for what you are with an inexorable severity that puts your own good conscience and your own comfortable images of yourself forever in question.[15]

Jameson's view could use some precision. These mountain men are not necessarily workers or employees at all, and might indeed be happy with their relatively independent, forest lives. Resentment is more likely to come not from wanting to "improve" their conditions or take over the modes of production, but from a threat to their status quo, from the ever-encroaching ways of the city. Jameson's comments have more to do with the economy of mountain communities being threatened by that regressive revolution known as development. Along these lines, the dam, lake, and modernization that Ed and Bobby represent (at the film's beginning, both men are in favor of the recreation area) are an assault on the land and people for which a mountain man's vengeance would be sweet. As "their" land is raped and "their" river will be dammed in front of their powerless eyes, so might the mountain men be said to get revenge by sodomy—an analogous damming and flooding of Bobby's anus—in front of powerless Ed, and by fellatio—a damming and flooding of the other end, the mouth of Ed's "river."

While Ed and Bobby might see the mountain men as closer to animals than humans, the mountain men label their city prey animals before they do them violence. Besides Bobby's transformation into a hog, Ed is asked: "You ever had your balls cut off, you fucking ape?" (castration is commonly practiced on domestic animals, which the mountain men likely own). Ed and Bobby's conversion into animals, which is necessary for their violation by the mountain men, illustrates the fragility of the mountain men's perceived love of nature. The mountain men's relationship to nature is as directly violent (albeit less extensively destructive) as the urbanites' is indirectly violent through invisibly violent and destructive lifeways.

Ghetto, I hope, is a useful term to dramatize the increasing diminishment, marginalization, and imprisonment of nature, especially in the form of forests, and to illustrate the way urban "settlements" often (dis)regard wilderness. But the comparison stops there. No forest, large or small, need be conceived as backward or past, impoverished or violent. While ghetto conditions must end, the forest is improved by not being improved, by being allowed to expand, and by being permitted to challenge and complexify cultural habits of time, acquisition, and violence. The dilemma confirmed by *Deliverance* is that forests can only be reimagined if allowed to flourish, and only allowed to flourish if reimagined.

Woodland (S)Hades or The Dammed

Before *Deliverance*, the forest was already cast as a morally and architecturally appropriate anteroom to hell:

> *When I had journeyed half of our life's way,*
> *I found myself within a shadowed forest,*
> *for I had lost the path that does not stray.*
> *Ah, it is hard to speak of what it was,*
> *that savage forest dense and difficult,*
> *which even in recall renews my fear:*
> *so bitter—death is hardly more severe![16]*

The difficulties of the forest prepare Dante for the hike through the slightly more severe terrain to come; hell also hath its forests.[17] Like Dante, the four campers of *Deliverance* have "journeyed half of [their] life's way" (they are all middle-aged), have a wilderness experience "dense and difficult," and have death as their "companion" (Dante's companion is the dead Virgil). The forest from which these four must be delivered becomes hell in contrast to the relatively paradisaical Atlanta, Georgia.[18]

Ed and Lewis are engulfed by an anteroom forest before their canoe trip through hell. As Lewis recklessly drives in search of a place from which to launch the canoes, he and Ed are shown behind their windshield virtually dematerialized, reduced to specters by a reflected forest cascading across the curved glass. The windshield reflection foreshadows—like the wilderness soon to be drowned by the new human-made lake—Ed and Lewis's struggle against a forest that seems to advance and engulf them.

But hell's more traditional sign is the water snake that Bobby and Ed see just before the rape scene, where snaking tree trunks further evoke Dantean hell. While Bobby is stripping and then squealing like a pig at the behest of his rapist, two long, horizontal, low-lying, tree limbs twist along the bottom of the shot. They hold not only ithyphallic connotations pertinent to the rape, but also indications of Dante's hellish, pathless forest:

> *we began to make our way across*
> *a wood on which no path had left its mark.*
> *No green leaves in that forest, only black;*
> *no branches straight and smooth, but knotted, gnarled;*[19]

At other times, tree parts are positioned between camera and men, especially when the camera moves stealthily, becoming like an animal or a threatening demon. Later, when Lewis shoots the rapist with bow and arrow, a sapling's limbs, like arms extended to comfort a fellow forest-dweller, break the fall and support the mountain man while he bleeds to death. Dante's seventh circle, second ring, does contain bleeding trees but the tree bracing the rapist is not bleeding nor do these trees allude to former suicides. Still, there is evidence to connect the Cahulawassee forest with Dante's infernal one. The whole of the seventh circle that contains The Violent and its surrounding, flaming river, the Phlegethon, resembles a set of topoi and correspondences from which the violation scene in the forest can be assembled. When Dante and Virgil traverse the seventh circle, the centaur Nessus chaperones them. In life, Nessus had offered to assist Hercules by carrying Deianira, Hercules' wife, across a roaring river on his back, but raped her after reaching the other side; soon after, Hercules crossed the roiling river alone, proclaiming, "Let me complete the conquest of the rivers already begun."[20] Upon reaching the opposite bank, Hercules hears Deianira's cries, chases away Nessus, then shoots him through the back with an arrow whose tip protrudes from Nessus's chest. Nessus curses Hercules as the arrow is pulled from his torso.[21] The curse eventually results in Hercules' slow death in which his flesh is torn, "revealing his massive bones."[22] While Lewis-as-Hercules[23] and the sodomite-as-Nessus seem rather obvious (the sodomite's sexual posture is akin to that of certain animals and centaurs the hog screams even resembling a horse's whinnying), it is less obvious that Bobby and Ed are male replacements for the female Deianira.

In addition to these correspondences, Dante's seventh circle contains sodomites. In *Inferno*, however, Dante's sodomite spokesperson is not Nessus, but de' Mozzi, Bishop of Florence, who the Pope exiled from river (Arno) to river (Bacchiglione) where de' Mozzi died and "left his tendons strained by sin."[24] De' Mozzi was from Fiesole, the hill town above Florence, whose people "still [kept] something of the rock and the mountain."[25]

With one mountain man escaped and the other dead, the forest now becomes alarming, resistant to even the canoeists' attempts to bury the mountain man's body (recall that pesky arm Ed can't cover up, likely the same in Ed's nightmare at movie's end). But the river also becomes alarming: Drew, the most haunted of the four, is possibly grazed by a bullet from the escaped mountain man and drowned by the Cahulawassee-cum-hellish river, perhaps the Phlegethon itself (absent the fire). The river, or its demon that lurks below (as suggested by water-level camera angles), appears to destroy the canoe and spill the other three. But the Cahulawassee only kills and maims because these ignorant neophytes—as the Oreean man in the truck said—"go fuck around" with the river's staccato rhythms, obstacles, levels.

When Lewis becomes incapacitated in the spill, Ed, the acolyte, must get himself and the others out of the abyss. With churning white water below, Ed ascends the cliff to conquer the one "demon" who escaped from the sodomy episode. An almost full moon illuminates the treacherous climb. Hugging the cliff, Ed gets a solid foothold and pulls out his wallet to check a photo of his wife and child to urge him the rest of the way. But the photo slips from his hand. Viewers might notice Ed's watch, which is flipped toward his wrist to protect its crystal. With the pictures gone and the watch face not visible, Ed loses a past and present that renders his future more precarious. Ed is threatened by the overwhelming of no-time, hell's all-time. Recall that the forest-cum-ghetto seemed eternally past; now the forest-as-hell seems eternally damned, and without the hope that Dante warned *Inferno* shades to surrender: "ABANDON EVERY HOPE, WHO ENTER HERE."[26] Ed appropriately screams at himself, "Goddamnit, you'll never get out of this gorge alive! Goddamnit!"

But with his head framed against a glowing near-dawn sky, Ed stands atop the abyss as if rising into a less-severe circle of hell. With the killing of the escaped mountain man at sunrise, the blond Ed shines against the horizon as a hero, an archer-god avenging unjust homicide by bow and arrow like Phoebus Apollo, the "golden haired" sun god,[27] guardian of law and civilization.[28] Ed's killing of the mountain man can be easily read as an Apollonian defeat of forest-ways that threaten civilization.

But Ed's journey out of hell is not over. After tossing the gun and broken bow into the river, he uses the mountain man's corpse as an anchor for his rope "ladder" and descends partway before it frays and snaps on the rough cliff edge. When both the quick and the dead fall into the river, the dead mountain man seems to try to drown Ed (though it is Ed's own rope ensnaring him). Ed's reemergence marks a baptismal salvation from an eternally damning fall.[29]

The scene contains elements of Dante and Virgil's last stretch of journey through the seventh circle, again, the realm of The Violent. Virgil, like Ed, casts a "cord" that had been tied for security to Dante's "girdle," over a "steep and craggy bank" into a "ravine" filled with roaring water.[30] The rope is a signal for the demon Geryon, the mountain man analogue, the beast-man "who crosses mountains, shatters weapons," [31] to emerge "like one returning from the waves where he went down to loose an anchor."[32]

Though I would hope viewers would see the mountain men as representatives of culture, *not* nature, I feel these men will be seen as a product more of the forest than of human culture,[33] and further, that the forest forced Ed to be a killer to survive. Devoid the amenities of abundant light, culture, and morality, forests get construed as places of error, darkness, and threat in the cultural consciousness, places that not only nurture, but compel, evil behavior.

Although Ed's journey out of the forest is assured, he must still deal with death: He and Bobby, with Lewis injured in the canoe's hull, paddle out and find Drew broken and dead and drag him alongside the canoe to deeper water where they submerge him. The canoe, homologue of a hearse, also suggests a coffin. Just as boats transport in life, they have long been vehicles to or of the underworld, especially canoes:

> Among certain North American Indians burial customs involving boats and a journey to the land of the dead have been documented. For instance, the typical grave of the Twana and other Coast Salish Indians consists of a canoe suspended on poles or on an elevated platform. . . . According to a Twana tale, the inhabitants of the realm of the dead come in a canoe to claim the newly deceased. Late at night it is said that one can hear their paddles in the water as they come to carry away their new companion.[34]

Because canoes are so often made from trees, they are related to the forest.[35] Virtually all boats and ships were once made of wood and became, at least in Germany, so associated with death that "early medieval German usage of the words *naufus* or *naucus* (ship) alongside *trunkus* (trunk) formerly denoted a coffin."[36] Moreover, the tree is often likened to the human body with its branches and leaves (arms, head, hair), trunk (body, spine), and roots (feet): "The Lakota on the upper Missouri River say that the first man and woman were two trees and that a snake chewed their roots off in order to allow the couple to walk away."[37] The tree might make an appropriate receptacle for the soul, but the canoe, as the moving *corpse* of a tree, is especially suited for a soon-to-be-liberated human soul. The tree's corpse is so changed by its reformation into a canoe (its horizontality, its placement on water, and its new shape) and so overpowered by metonymic association with the human dead it transports, that its identity as a tree corpse—the body of a once living being—is absent. Just as standing trees are perceived as not quite alive (at least not as alive as humans), the horizontal log does not really seem dead. Depriving trees and logs of life and death relegates them to the realm of nature's inanimate elements: rocks and minerals. The point is not only that trees and canoes connect the forest to death and the underworld, but that, strangely enough, it is not trees that make the forest seem alive. Animals do. Instead, trees make the forest seem eerily dead to any culture narrowly associating life with mobility.

At the movie's end, a not-quite-dead arm pushes up from the river of Ed's nightmare as one of the three dead men gains resurrection back into this world through means of the living person's memory. When the ground of the Cahulawassee forest is stripped and the flooding complete, the (t)error and humiliation suffered in the "great outdoors" will presumably continue to haunt Ed, Lewis, and Bobby. *Deliverance*'s forest will remain suffused with evil long after it is gone. Frightening and wretched, this is a place exiting viewers will just as soon shun as bury.[38] Or, with a shiver, enjoy it only from the safe distance of a movie theater.

The Rite Site

A site is a place of enactment, and in this section, of human enactment or rite. Sites refer to nature where humans perpetrate acts that change or mark an area for human purposes, and are distinguished from nature as wilderness. I do not imply *site* as necessarily dystopic, but distinguish it from a place not yet regularly used by people nor with obvious signs of human activity.

The forest in *Deliverance* is a site where the rites of five groups of people are enacted: developers, loggers, earthmovers, mountain men, and canoeists. All are rites of power. What I present in this last section are several views of the forest *as forest*, as a representative of nature more than an allusion to a cultural place like a ghetto or a culturally invented place like hell. Because only the acts of earthmovers are shown in this film and because developers and loggers are completely absent, the next three sections on these workers will be brief, speculative, and much like Toni Morrison's description of her fiction as "a kind of literary archeology: on the basis of some information and a little bit of guesswork you journey to a site to see what remains were left behind and to reconstruct the world that these remains imply."[39] Though it is unusual to take cues from so little information, the need for speculation should soon be clear.

Developers responsible for the dam and recreation area might be imagined as believing that they enact a rite of liberation. The forest and river represent a site where nothing is happening, a place "waiting" to be "developed," an "empty" place where there is little or no sign of people and their artifacts. Trees, animals, rivers, and creeks make conversion sweeter, as a great number of humans and equipment must be marshaled to get rid of these natural entities. These "obstacles," are evidence that developers are accomplishing something big, difficult, and far-reaching. If "tree huggers" or politicians should try to preserve the "empty" forest, developers would be prevented from *accomplishing* (from the Latin *complere*, to fill) something, i.e., from exercising their freedom, and from being fulfilled. To them, preserving a forest when it could be developed might represent an incredible waste of (their) human talent. In this sense, developers welcome the forest as a way to become fashioners of an "unformed" place, of "raw material." As Michelangelo purportedly looked at a block of marble and saw, for example, *David* trapped inside, these developers can look at a forested river valley and see a dam, lake, and development struggling to emerge. For them, the preserved forest is a cage, a shackles on the accomplishment of *objets d'art*(ifacts), while the developed forest is the result of a rite they, at least, see as inner and outer liberation.

Loggers are never shown in *Deliverance*. Their job is already over. But one can imagine their view of logging as harvesting, as collecting nature's bounty. For them, the forest is the site to extract supplies, without which there would be no goods: houses, furniture, paper. The forest is "woods" and "timber"—inert material and human supplies. Its area is *logged*, a word that lexically transforms killing and cutting trees into an act of merely gathering already-lying logs. Areas denuded of trees are referred to as clear-cuts, "clearings," and open areas, which gives an impression (initial, anyway) of land liberated of imposing, dominating trees that make it impossible for anything else to grow, and whose clearing makes it possible for animals—deer for example—to eat what grows back.[40] In this way, dead trees and areas from which trees are taken come to be good for plants, animals, and people. Almost.

Of course, with development there are no clear-cuts, forest animals, or original trees left. Even the memory of them can be eradicated. But that is considered acceptable because removing the forest for dam and development offers not only raw material, but also a place people can enjoy. Anyway, trees are a "renewable resource" and still stand in other places; even animals can move somewhere else. This conception precludes any understanding of the forest as a home, neighborhood, or community of plants and animals (and sometimes people), while harvesting and clearing lose their necessary identification with slaughter, home wrecking, and plunder.

By the time earthmovers arrive, this area of the Cahulawassee is littered with branches and stumps; the former forest now becomes the site for a rite of moving, "cleaning," and evening up. The devastated area is conceived as messy, dirty, with uneven ground, descriptions more befitting completed human settlements and home interiors than wilderness. With their Caterpillars[41] scooping hunks of earth, people in the earthmovers quickly forget (if ever they had such notions) that this was once a teeming, fertile place, a place of life and death important to other groups and individuals now dead or on the run. When dam and development are complete, Lewis's seemingly resonant profundity, "You don't beat this river," will be leaden. The beaten portions of forest and river will hardly be remembered, let alone missed. Developers, loggers, and earthmovers will have seen to that.

Though the camera, at the film's beginning, seems to show the decimation of a nature we often did not see or do not remember when shopping in malls and moving through cities, the camera shows only a small part of the process: an already stripped and artificially contoured land, an area of inanimate rocks and dirt, mere material moved by explosion and machinery. Why did *Deliverance* not show logging engineers and developers planning a slaughter on land reduced to real estate; the government sanctioning it in the name of jobs (and resulting income tax), or for the sake of campaign contributions; or loggers (the engineers' and developers' soldiers or hit men) killing the forest and making refugees of its animals? Why did it show the aftermath of a crime but not the crime itself? Denuded spaces are becoming so quotidian as to seem more natural than the forest itself. The site of a former tragedy, a destroyed village, for example, is far less effective a means of conveying a holocaust than showing the slaughter or corpses of its occupants. This is, finally, the reason it has been crucial to imagine what the film ignored—developers, loggers, and earthmovers—by its perfunctory environmental statement.

Deliverance's mountain men can also be said to engage in rites, secret rites. The forest, because it often represents culture's dark, savage, shameful, and repressed or sublimated natural origins, furnishes a most fitting venue for the performance of these secret acts from a "shameful" natural past.

Homosexual and heterosexual sodomy is judged *unnatural* by many (fellatio much less so). At the same time and by the same people it is regarded as a wild and dirty act, an act without control, and therefore an uncivilized act in a realm outside culture. Sodomy, though called unnatural, is easily aligned with nature by being cast out of culture and having no place else to go (this is also a plausible explanation of *perverse* since its Latin root, *perversus* means facing the wrong way, probably towards nature). In Genesis 18-19, Lot, the spared-because-he-was-good Sodomite who escapes the destruction of Sodom, fled to the mountain (nature) and not the feared city of Zo-ar (culture). There, in a cave, he got drunk and lay with his two daughters.[42] *Deliverance*'s two possibly-incestuous—taking a cue from the "inbreds" at Oree—sodomites, in the site of nature, seem to share some similarity with the incestuous Sodomite, Lot. Their so-called unnatural acts are, viewers might believe, brutal, uncultured, unrefined, and unsophisticated. And a place of brutes (irrational creatures or animals) without culture, refinement, and sophistication is a place thought to be approaching a natural state, or nature itself.[43]

Though sometimes called unnatural acts, incest and bestiality (two sexual practices intimated by these mountain men), sodomy, fellatio, and other "unusual" or "deviant" sexual acts that mountain men *might* practice, belong more to that cultural *idea*, nature, since this culturally-constructed entity represents a freedom from cultural taboo. In this sense these acts that are called unnatural but banished from culture further unite the anonymous mountain men (creatures without proper names are thought to be part of nature) with the forest. Adding rape to the list yields behavior against the law (the law is "sodomized" at the same time the victim is) and outside the law (for example, in the forest, which comes from the Latin *foris*, out of doors or outside). In the absence of any other forest creatures except fish, the water snake, and a deer in Ed's sights—all of whom are silent—the mountain men are, along with the river, rocks, and trees, de facto representatives of the forest. Like a person criminalized for withholding evidence, or a criminal's *hide-out* that is subsequently destroyed, the forest gets implicated in the secrecy and deviancy of these mountain men and seems to hide and possibly even promote such behavior. Perhaps hill people have similar views of the big city, that the metropolis is a Gothic cesspool compared to their forested lakes and rivers.

The forest also hides these mountain men as hunters. We see them kill no animals, but presume they hunt because of their long-barreled guns. Usually the forest is characterized by hunting more than rape and sodomy. Since the mountain men are portrayed as evil, *Deliverance*'s forest can be seen to contribute to the idea that hunting is cruel.[44] But the opposite contention, that hunting metonymically gives the forest a bad name, is also possible. Hunting, while acknowledged as a necessary part of nonhuman carnivorous nature and part of the human archaeological record (the two are not mutually exclusive), is an act noted by many or perhaps most urbanites as a barbarism left over from our days in nature, and increasingly, as an act of destruction instead of a reasonable method for obtaining food.

Remember Drew's comment that he did not know how anyone could kill animals, as well as Ed's inability to kill a deer.

Besides the usual reasons against hunting (most of which are quite good), there is something else about hunting that might contribute to its condemnation. It is an act of secrecy, of lying, and of fraud: acts many of us are warned not to fall victim to or practice. The hunter hides with a weapon that acts at a distance, with no wires or visible connection between the hunter and the animal. To many animals, the weapon might not even seem weaponlike. Nonetheless, many animals have figured out over time that people are deadly at a distance. While the animal hunted by an animal predator has a running or fighting chance, the animal hunted by the human hunter has much less hope in the face of what might seem like inscrutable killing. Fraud's uneven hunting ground makes hunting appear criminal, and a place of criminality is usually a place to avoid or vilify.

The movie camera, a piece of technology, violates by *exposure* the disapproved-of *natural* and *savage* (as in the French *sauvage,* wild) acts of (homosexual) sodomy, rape, and hunting (killing), transforming them into images of light in a dark theater. In psychoanalytic fashion, as the unconscious' secrecy is penetrated to promote cure, so too are these shadowy acts brought to light, into the open. Short of killing the forest (comparable to the analysand's unconscious), the camera (like the analyst) offers the only effective means of surveillance and cure in a beautiful but dangerous forest-site resistant to transparency. And the dark theater, itself a forest of seats with paths between, furnishes, like a dimmed private office, a place conducive to re-accepting such "natural" and "dark" rites.

As psychoanalysis attempts to expose and break the unconscious' disruptive grip on consciousness, *Deliverance*'s camera exposes forest-beauty (the good unconscious) at the same time it cures forest-ugly (the bad unconscious). As insanity, a dis-order, reaffirms the order of culture and reason and ensures the medicalization and commodification of behavior, the disorderly forest reaffirms the order of the city and "settlement." There is even the chance that arguments to save the forest might someday plead that the forest furnishes image-material for the camera—both for the negativized ethico-aesthetic instance of the mad forest (an archaic adjective, *wood,* means insane), and for a positivized ethico-aesthetic example of tranquil(ized) *landscape* and *scenery* (these words imply that people are the normal or unmarked category of foreground and that nature is background). This kind of forest reserve, configured primarily by its relation to humanity, is robbed of its possible meanings outside human relations and is likely to become or remain merely a human accouterment or luxury, an extension of culture.

With the forest as site for the fraud and violence of hunting, and the deviancy and violence of sex, it becomes easy to believe that the mountain men belong to or are produced by the mountains and the forest, and that they need cultural refinement, possibly even psychoanalysis to mend their evil, savage, primitive ways. In this sense, savagery is what the forest does to people: It brings out or aggravates the natural savagery that must be sublimated lest it disrupt civilization. The forest gets implicated by the way the mountain men are depicted because forest influence keeps their behavior shadowy and their thoughts dark. Because the mountain men might seem so different from moviegoing city folk, the former are likely to be seen as virtual foreigners, and the *forest* as a *foreign* (both from the Latin *foris,* out of doors) place enabling moviegoers to relegate such behaviors outside themselves.

If viewers are seduced by the way the forest furnishes a hiding place for evil men with ghastly behavior, even producing or aggravating it, *Deliverance* strengthens viewer apathy about, or desire for clearings, arable land, developments, or trees as crops.[45] In helping to displace evil—as much or more likely to be cultural than natural—onto the forest, *Deliverance* offers comfort that at least we are safer in sites carved out of forest blight: an urban park or lighted city where trees are sparse or the cultured environment of the theater. Thank god, we may feel, that the forest is far enough away that we need not fear its obscenities or dangers. Unwittingly, *Deliverance* makes viewers feel again that nature, not culture, is the real enemy.[46]

After the mountain men, *Deliverance*'s forest is most prominently the site for the four canoeists to enact a ritual, their *rites de passage*. Rituals often involve a "prestige of the body,"[47] and rites of passage, a process of "separation, transition, and incorporation."[48] All four men physically experience a separation from culture, then a transitional ordeal and finally, an ostensible incorporation into nature. In my discussion about the forest-as-hell, I referred to the hero's journey through hell and back as a rite of passage. What distinguishes this portion of the chapter from that underworld journey is a passage into the forest-as-representative-of-nature. Where the message at hell's gate reads "ABANDON EVERY HOPE, WHO ENTER HERE" the sign at the forest's gate is a signal given by the boy-musician on a footbridge over the Cahulawassee River. His mysterious swinging banjo is reminiscent of a certain kind of railroad-crossing sign warning of passing trains. The tick-tocking motion being a *liminal* signal in its double sense of a mysterious, borderline signal and a signal at the borderline. Dante's sign and the boy's signal warn of a heightened anxiety about these places. Both messages also imply an even more intense attachment to the place the travelers left.

At Drew's quasi-funeral, Ed eulogizes, "He was the best of us." Perhaps Ed was referring to Drew's graciousness with the Oreeans, the singer who played a convivial guitar and declared he didn't know how anyone could kill an animal, and the one most visibly stunned by Bobby's rape and the killing of the first mountain man. In the aftermath, Drew is the only one who wants to help the dying man, readily trusts the law to provide a fair trial, and believes in Christian and democratic ideals. Drew might be characterized as a middle-class naïf, a believer, an optimist to the extent that he accepts another cultural tale of the beautiful, peaceful forest as a place to commune, albeit temporarily, with nature. Thus Drew cannot live with the consecutive bombardment of the strangers' violations, the killing, and his friends' decisions to "do the wrong thing" (he tells Ed to "do the right thing" when deciding what to do with the body). These are eruptions in a system where culture runs—like the first day on the Cahulawassee—relatively smooth and level, where even nature has a rough but pervasive goodness. With Drew nearing a breakdown, his pessimism about the forest explodes from its repression and that other cultural story about the forest as evil emerges. Either story quickly ignites with appropriate provocation.

Burying the corpse drives Drew into a fit of "chimplike" behavior and his animality is somewhat enhanced by muteness from the time of the burial to his plunge in the river. Despite the animalization, even his eventual "herbamorphism"—his arm snaps at the shoulder like a tree limb—Drew never reaches the other side of his rite of passage, a living incorporation into nature. He is the only canoeist who dies—like the complacent in so many horror films—probably because he is unprepared for the severe questions that nature, especially as it is associated with the mountain men, poses to culture. Yet, we must remind ourselves, these are not so much nature's questions as culture's, film-culture hunting culture-at-large, tracking down cultural narratives, caging and studying them, letting them live or killing them off. *Deliverance*, however, falls short of the mark: The forest would have furnished an excellent site for culture to bravely examine itself, to operate on its own tumors, and to go back and shrink or remove them in their operable cultural locations. Instead, the forest is forced into stealing the show. It ends up looking criminal, and becomes an accessory to the crime instead of an innocent bystander, eyewitness, or hospitable locale clashing with cultural cruelty. Perhaps *Deliverance* is an instance of a sub-genre that might be designated *vert noir*.

Bobby radiates unexamined cultural confidence and condescension to the "uncultured" in Oree, the last town visited before the canoeists disembark. He speaks with disgust about the piles of auto-junk, and ridicules the Oreeans. He calls the gas attendant "a live one," pokes fun at him—"Mister, I love the way you wear that hat"—and tells Drew to give the banjo player "a couple bucks" out of uncalled-for pity.

Not surprisingly, Bobby's attitude toward these Oreeans matches his attitude about the Cahulawassee River and forest. During the opening voice-overs, Bobby seems confounded that Lewis is so concerned about the disappearing wilderness and asks, "Lewis, why are you so anxious about this?" But when Lewis escalates his tirade against the dam, Bobby lets go of disingenuous bafflement and readily agrees with Ed that Lewis, decrying a "raped landscape," has "an extreme point of view." Looking back from Bobby's rape, we see that early on he was set to fall, a fall from which even his profession of insurance salesman could not protect him.

During the first idyllic day on the river, Bobby is exhilarated by the orgasmic experience of shooting white water: "That's the best—second best—sensation I ever felt." But Lewis, the camper closest to the forest, initiates Bobby's humiliation in nature when he calls him "Chubby," cuts him off from recounting his river experience, and tells him, "You don't beat this river." Bobby attempts a reconciliation and some cultural criticism at the campfire: "There's somethin' in the woods and the water we've lost in the city." Lewis condescendingly corrects him: "We didn't lose it, we sold it." Bobby, humiliated again, decides antipathy to the forest suits him better. The next day he complains about his bites and wants to get off the river as soon as possible.

By the time Bobby is raped by the forest-in-the-guise-of-mountain-men, he might seem to have it coming. As was the case with Drew, Bobby's bodily rite is not so much an incorporation into nature, but "nature," through insemination, in-*corp*orating him. By forcing Bobby to his hands and knees and making him squeal like a pig, the forest would seem to teach him a needed lesson about sexual boasting and urban arrogance. But the difficulty with this reading of Bobby's rape as getting what's coming to him is that next to the mountain men, Bobby, even with his ignorance, is a more sympathetic character. Viewers are safe to assume that Bobby will never venture into the forest again, that he will be glad when the Cahulawassee is inundated. Our tendency, unfortunately, will be to sympathize.

Lewis is Bobby's near-opposite. Lewis trusts the Oreeans with driving the cars and does not condescend to the Oreeans to the extent Bobby does. He is the only one of the quartet passionately against the dam and development, against "smug" suburbanites glad for the electric power, upscale housing, and a recreation area. Lewis seems to truly love the wilderness. Yet somewhat suspect is the way Lewis acts on his objection to its destruction: by having a last fling in it. No indication is given that he took the smallest action to protest it. And the speed and recklessness with which Lewis barrels through the forest is an early tip-off that his feelings for wilderness are more complex than reverence.

It soon becomes apparent that Lewis loves nature as an adversary in a game of survival; he does not destroy or plunder the forest like developers, loggers, and earthmovers but feels that the forest, by its very presence, is challenging him to a duel. His weapons are simple: a bow and arrow (even if high-tech and fiberglass) to hunt his food and a canoe to carry it in, and to conquer walking-speed and distance. He does not kill for ego or excitement and wants to keep the river unpolluted from noise, gas, and oil; in this way the forest is maintained as a worthy adversary rather than destroyed as an unworthy victim. Lewis makes it clear that the adversarial relationship is not one where nature gets beat—"You don't beat this river"—but one where he wins by staying alive or surviving. Because the forest is a place to prove and strengthen self or subjectivity, Lewis's comment when he first sees the river, "Sometimes you have to lose yourself before you can find anything," fits less what seems to be his view of forest experience than does his earlier assertion at Oree, "I never been lost in my life" (which might also explain why he doesn't lose himself in alcohol).

Lewis loves the forest primarily because he sees himself fit to take it on. While viewers might construe Lewis's rite of passage as nature's lesson in the dangers of overconfidence and of risktaking, they are likely to feel nature's lesson is severe. This can be countered with recalling that Lewis did what he set out to do, lead these mostly-inexperienced men down a river of which he had no knowledge. *Deliverance* is too subtle about the fact that Lewis, even as a sympathetic character, did get what was coming to him. By movie's end, viewers are more likely to remember nature's cruelty far more than Lewis's recklessness.

Ed's rite of passage is the most complex, and apparently, the one most favorable to the forest. Ed is *Deliverance*'s composite character: a combination of the aesthetic Drew, the socially and economically comfortable Bobby, and, in physical prowess, a wannabe Lewis. Ed also mediates Drew's naiveté, Bobby's apathy, and Lewis' environmental radicalness with reasonable caution (indicated by his pipe). Because Ed is the hero, he is *Deliverance*'s most alluring and therefore treacherous character.

At the film's beginning, voice-overs reveal that Ed supports the dam and development as "a very clean way to make electric power, and those lakes up there provide a lot of people with recreation. And my father has a houseboat up on Lake Bowie." When Lewis retorts about landscape rape, his radicalness—not Ed's excuses—are justified by sequences of earthmovers tearing up land.

While driving to Oree, Ed, with his "little bit" of insurance, becomes squeamish about this canoe trip and wants to go back to town and play golf. He is afraid of Greiner, the mechanic Lewis gets to drive the car, and of snakes, and wants to use a map, or the Greiners, to find the river. But despite the hesitations, Ed apparently has gone on many such survival trips with Lewis. While fishing, Lewis asks Ed why he goes on these trips. Lewis knows that Ed, despite his suburban life, is naggingly dissatisfied.

While a successful hunt is often "a passport into adulthood"[49]—in Ed's case, a passage into self-reliance and bravery—Ed gets off to a shaky start when he cannot shoot the deer, and is humiliated because he cannot equal Lewis's ability (Lewis says that Ed's bow needs repair and is "losing glass," probably from neglect). Still, Ed must feel that hunting is important because he keeps trying. This might explain his dissatisfaction: he can support a family, but he cannot fulfill the other part of a chronic American male dream. Ed's sense of inadequacy, even with all the forest outings, has not been cured. As long as Ed travels with the superior outdoorsman, Lewis, Ed's rite of passage will likely be precluded.

Initially, Ed is readied or made susceptible to cure after he is threatened at gunpoint, after Bobby is raped and the mountain man is impaled, Drew jumps overboard, and finally when Bobby and Lewis become helpless. It is now Ed's "turn to play the game," Lewis's game. Ed undergoes a rite of passage on the cliff: His body is bloodied by his fall, disfigurations often performed on the body in such rites. Furthermore, Ed has a tone of authority he did not have before. Ed even takes on a Lewistic appearance, a vest without a shirt and hat, which he wears while steering Lewis's canoe. And where Lewis decided to bury the first mountain man, Ed buries the other. Ed tests his own mortality, kills someone, and leads two men out of the gorge. Unlike the other survivors, Ed is not broken by the forest; finally it has made him strong. He has become "one with nature" as Lewis was, united in a fair fight with the worthy adversaries of river, mountain man, and forest. Would Ed *now*, like Lewis did, oppose dam and development?

Ed's forest rite, however, does not so much incorporate him into nature as much as reincorporate him into culture. Not only has he finally succeeded at being incorporated into the much-coveted, culturally-constructed male ideal, but his "exaggerated reversal of roles and behaviors emphasizes the goodness of social structures which are returned to with a sense of refreshment after the liminal period [the period in nature]."[50] When Ed returns from the trip and sees the cars, his posture and gestures suggest he worships them and the culture they represent, and his quiet somber tone as he is treated in the emergency room sounds like a meditation on the grace of cultural amenities: "That's nice. Chromium, paper tissues, hot water. It's nice." Ed, after such a harrowing experience in uncaring nature, is glad to be back in caring culture.[51]

At the film's beginning, the unnecessary destruction of a beautiful, bountiful wilderness seemed primary; however, at the end, and long after seeing the movie, that message might hardly be recalled. Instead, a vague recollection of a forest full of danger will likely usurp memories of *Deliverance*'s cursory environmentalism. The film's end subverts its beginning and the characteristic foibles of culture—error, ignorance, oppression, and perversion—risk being foisted from men onto nature. Perhaps the viewer's own nightmare is less vivid than Ed's vision of the arm rising from the river, but it might go something like this: In a forest with no signs, words, people, institutions—nothing to particularize or emphasize human existence—the forest gradually becomes a source of hellish error, frustration, humiliation, and anger that seems to move toward us and close in for the kill.

Waking from this nightmare, the *panicked* (meaning fear of Pan, the therioanthropomorphic god dwelling in the mountains of Arcadia) dreamers set out to alleviate an inchoate humiliation brought on by fear of nature or the "indifference" of nature. Nature will, dammit, recognize us, even if we must concoct a desperate contradiction to nature's unsettling indifference:

nature with a human telos. Those of us intoxicated with a certain cultural tall tale, will, by argument or assertion, claim ourselves as nature's ultimate or highest realization, all the while contradicting this claim with another claim that nature is indifferent to us. This contradiction—nature's indifference to humans and nature with a human telos—is usually resolved by scoring or inscribing nature with our human signature, trans-forming it into a testament of our existence and our importance. Such a "nature" seems less (in)different and, at its core or its teleological reaches, human. The dam and lakeside recreation area on the Cahulawassee become that "nature" recognizing us, created by (the) people, for (the) people. However, as in the micro-rituals of the canoeists, the macro-ritual of dam and development only unites us with culture, not nature. Nature thus remains at a distance from culture, a ghetto, hell, or site to ritually challenge humanity to a duel. This human "solution" to the "problem" of nature— this inscribing of an immense cultural fortress against nature, both literal and figurative—cannot be taken lightly by environmentalists. Try as it might *Deliverance*'s cursory environmentalism is helpless against both this bastion of development and its more prominent message of a fearful forest. In fact, the film comes off as reconciled with those behind the parapets of development instead of those at the barricades of revolt. Nothing exemplifies this better than the film's title. For, in the end, the best answer to the question—From what are these four urbanites delivered?—is regrettably a nexus of associations implicating the forest as primarily evil.

4

A PECULIAR ARBORARY
Beloved

A good reason not to see the forest for the trees has to do with a politics of number: Fear often haunts large numbers, especially a mass entity like the forest. Just as the individual loses integrity with the use of mass nouns like *crowd, horde, masses, mob,* and *rabble,* trees can get lost in *forest*[1] (from the Latin, *outside* from which *foreign* is also derived, a word that has negative connotations), and especially *jungle* (from the Prakrit *jangala,* a rough, waterless place). And just as one can get lost in and fear the crowd, one might also become lost in and fear the forest for what it hides, or what hides in it. This fear coupled with the perception of sheer number and abundance contributes to devaluation of individuals, and facilitates shooting into a crowd or killing trees on "timberland" and in "woods" (not unlike calling living persons "organ donors" or "meat") which seem inexhaustible and reproducible, and which hide dangerous animals and people configured as a kind of "lurking class."

There seems no way to understand what it means to be a tree in or out of the forest or to reliably ascertain a tree's point of view (or the absence thereof). In terms of *being*, outside or inside the forest, it is humans who are the "forest," the *outsiders*.[2] One might theorize that people's inability to "get inside" is *the* reason trees are easily viewed as the living dead, and thus ethically easy to commodify, damage, and kill. Though *Beloved* makes little attempt to endow or imagine trees in or out of the forest with subjectivity,[3] it most often refuses views of the forest as place of fear or mere material. Its archmethod does not deduce trees from a forest, but induces a forest from trees. As the first chapter on *The Silence of the Lambs* followed that film's bestiary, this chapter resembles a walk through a peculiar kind of arboretum or, on the model of the word, *bestiary,* an *arborary* in which not only kinds of trees are given a common (and species) name, and where individual trees themselves earn proper names, but where trees mean something more than material. In *Beloved*, the alleged Enlightenment-importance attached to the human individual comes to the forest as the attention paid to this or that individual tree, kind of tree, or stand of trees, and most importantly the relationship of trees to that "peculiar institution," slavery.[4] While Enlightenment-thought—despite drawbacks of greedy (capitalist) individuals run amok at the expense of the group—is a necessary complement to the importance of the (communist) group, Enlightenment-individualism applied to trees is a rare occurrence (despite the fact that tree-greed poses no threat). When Enlightenment is visited upon trees, as it is in *Beloved,* there is some cause for celebration.

Beauty and the Backtree

Sethe (pronounced Seth-uh),[5] *Beloved*'s main character, is an escaped Kentucky slave living in a rural community with her child, Denver, (and sometimes others) on the outskirts of Cincinnati. Partially motivating her escape is a punitive whipping across her back while she is pregnant. The gashes form an unintended pattern that Amy Denver, a white girl also on the run, notices:

> It's a tree, Lu [Sethe]. A chokecherry tree. See, here's the trunk—it's red and split wide open, full of sap, and this here's the parting for the branches. You got a mighty lot of branches. Leaves, too, look like, and dern if these ain't blossoms. Tiny little cherry blossoms, just as white. Your back got a whole tree on it. In bloom. What God have in mind, I wonder. I had me some whippings, but I don't remember nothing like this. (79)[6]

Amy massages Sethe's swollen feet and cares for Sethe's burning back just after Sethe's escape: "Amy returned with two palms full of [healing spider] web, which she cleaned of prey and then draped on Sethe's back, saying it was like stringing a tree for Christmas" (80).[7] Amy, by comparing a pattern of torn flesh to a member of the cherry tree family, seems to try to lessen Sethe's pain. Cherries do have a heap of sweet, gendered symbolism:

> Cherries symbolized love and beauty in literature. Helena's lips in Shakespeare's *A Midsummer Night's Dream* were lusciously described as "kissing cherries" and Robert Herrick's poetic lovelies were all cherry-lipped with teeth like pearls. In European religious

paintings, cherries routinely represented the sweetness of life . . . in Chinese art, cherries symbolized female beauty and sexual power. . . . *Cherry,* presumably also from its short-lived lusciousness, entered English as a slang term for "young girl" sometime around 1850. . . . From cherry, young girl, came cherry, virginity, and cherry, the hymen, and—inevitably—the practice, designated as 'low and raffish' by Eric Partridge, of cherry popping. . . . By 1393, John Gower, a friend of Chaucer, had coined the phrase "For al is but a cherry faire," a sentiment that survives today as "Life is just a bowl of cherries."[8]

But Amy is no soother. Upon seeing Sethe's swollen feet Amy recalls, "I know a woman had her feet cut off they was so swole"; Amy even sibilates a saw's "Zzz Zzz Zzz Zzz" cutting off these human *limbs,* a further coalescence of tree and Sethe (34). These scars must indeed look like a chokecherry tree.

Why a cherry tree? Because Cherokee women use(d) "cherry-bark tea to alleviate the pain of childbirth?"[9] Cherokees, before being pushed onto reservations in western North Carolina, lived in the southern Alleghenies of Virginia, near the border of Kentucky across which Sethe escapes. And Sethe's baby is born the day after Amy describes the backtree.

But this cherry tree is *Prunus virginiana,* a chokecherry, given its common name for its astringent drupes, which are an acrid disappointment to those associating cherries with sweetness or female genitalia. The Latin, *Prunus* means burning or burning coal, surely for the deep red of its fruit, and *virginiana* means virgin or maiden, although the scientific nomenclature actually refers to the tree's Virginia locale. As to Prunus, the narrator does describe "the fire in her [Sethe's] feet and the fire on her back" (79). Add the pain of Sethe's burning birth canal and you get *Prunus virginiana,* only somewhat tendentiously translated as *burning maiden,* or Sethe herself.

The chokecherry tree's bitterness does not stop with the fruit. Its twigs have a disagreeable odor and taste, and its wilted leaves can poison animals. These aspects might allude to the bitterness of slavery, Sethe's whipping, for instance. Or perhaps the *drawing* (as in both figure drawing and drawing blood) of the cherry tree on Sethe's back connects to the "bitter" ink Sethe made from cherry gum, bitter because it was the same ink schoolteacher (the slavemaster) used to observe and "write her up" the day she was whipped (6). And just as Amy strings Sethe's backtree with web,

"Tent caterpillars *(Malacosoma)* often construct their silver webs on the branches of this species."[10] With Amy's description of Sethe's lacerations as the trunk, branches, and buds of a chokecherry tree, these unspoken homologous and analogous traits make the choice of trees appear markedly calculated, if not uncanny.[11]

As Amy's chokecherry figuration might have comforted Sethe, trees, on another occasion, also soothe Sethe's pain:

> Although there was not a leaf on that farm [where she was a slave in Kentucky] that did not make her want to scream, it rolled itself out before her in shameless beauty. It never looked as terrible as it was and it made her wonder if hell was a pretty place too. Fire and brimstone all right, but hidden in lacy groves. Boys hanging from the most beautiful sycamores in the world. It shamed her—remembering the wonderful soughing trees rather than the boys. Try as she might to make it otherwise, the sycamores beat out the children every time and she could not forgive her memory for that. (6)

On one hand, the chokecherry reflects slavery's bitterness, and on the other, its beauty occludes it. The beauty of the sycamores and the chokecherry acts as barrier to cultural history and promotes a soothing revisionism of cultural memory. Not only are the trees considered beautiful, but their filtration of memories connects them through the useful to the beautiful. If the forest often represents the past, as it did in *Deliverance*, it is here a past before or without humans. The "soughing" trees call Sethe to leave behind the bitter portion of her past. The oneiric revisionism the trees suggest cannot be wholly condemned: If Sethe had heeded the ability of the trees to buffer the past, she might not have killed her children to save them from a slavery that might indeed have been worse than death.

Trees' beauty, coupled with their ability to promote forgetfulness of (often negative) cultural memory,[12] alludes to Sethe's general or underlying sentiment: Trees are beautiful partially because they are not human. To Sethe, trees might seem so vastly different from people—notwithstanding anthropomorphizing—that it becomes hard to construe them as monsters.[13] Trees neither enslave nor brutalize, and unlike humans whose comfort lies in proximate real or figurative warmth, a tree's comfort furnishes a coolness seldom turning cold (shade). But even in the beauty of trees, Sethe cannot shake the nagging cultural memory that hangs about trees like a specter: Beautiful trees can hide evil people. Among beautiful trees, white people perpetrate the atrocities of slavery. For Sethe, whites are such an overarching evil that not even arboreal beauty can prevent the association of trees with whites—"there was not a leaf on that farm that did not make her [Sethe] want to scream" (6). Beautiful trees (and everything else) are put at risk by this kind of linkage.

Amy's naming of the chokecherry implies knowledge of trees—at minimum, leaves, flowers, and overall shape. Though this might be Amy's particular expertise, knowledge of trees in the more rural 1850s was probably more widespread than today.[14] This is not because rural and urban people seldom see trees, but because when they do, trees merely line streets or property boundaries, occupy medians, and stand in well-delineated yards or parks. Because trees are often killed when they obstruct architectural and landscaping plans, trees are most often understood as marginalia to the text of streets and buildings, as decoration or subliminal suggestion, and are seldom noticed except when flowering, leaving, or changing color. The same beauty that saves trees from the chain saw (however subliminally this beauty functions) also results in general arboreal commodification, topiary, and laboratory breeding and experimentation. Beauty of trees, as of women, slips easily into trees-as-artifacts and trees-as-possessions, and makes being, itself, into a kind of artifact (subtext to the still widely-believed human telos of nature). Westerners, at least, are so oriented to artifactualism that it becomes difficult for many of us to imagine trees serving purposes of their own, purposes overriding ours.

Beloved's frequent identification of plants and especially trees—sycamore, pine, chestnut, aspen, hemlock, mulberry, etc.—throws a subtle wrench in the machine's representation of trees as artifacts, commodities, and timber. While classification is often a tool of oppression (South Africa's melanin classifications, for example), dendrologic taxonomy seems designed less with humanity, than with trees in mind (in spite of preoccupation with visual, sexual reproduction, and scientific naming often based on human boundaries and discoverers).[15] Knowledge of differences in families and individual trees indicates trees as more than decorative, as important enough not to kill for convenience or taste, and as important enough to be studied/appreciated/understood rather than just aestheticized. Knowledge of trees, evident throughout *Beloved*, nudges readers toward understanding the purpose and existence of trees as their own, a purpose and existence at odds with the status of commodities.

The Sacred Clearing

Baby Suggs, Sethe's mother-in-law, is a former slave. As community preacher for other freed slaves, Baby Suggs sermonizes in the Clearing, which is described as "a wide-open place cut deep in the woods nobody knew for what at the end of a path known only to deer and whoever cleared the land in the first place. In the heat of every Saturday afternoon, she sat in the clearing while the people waited among the trees" (87). Her sermon to the community of former slaves is a cult of the flesh:[16]

> "Here," she said, "in this here place, we flesh; flesh that weeps, laughs; flesh that dances on bare feet in grass. Love it. Love it hard. Yonder they do not love your flesh. They despise it. They don't love your eyes; they'd just as soon pick 'em out. No more do they love the skin on your back. Yonder they flay it. And O my people they do not love your hands. Those they only use, tie, bind, chop off and leave empty. Love your hands! Love them. Raise them up and kiss them. Touch others with them, pat them together, stroke them on your face 'cause they don't love that either. *You* got to love it, *you!* And no, they ain't in love with your mouth. Yonder, out there, they will see it broken and break it again. What you say out of it they will not heed. What you scream from it they do not hear. What you put into it to nourish your body they will snatch away and give you leavins instead. No, they don't love your mouth. *You* got to love it. This is flesh I'm talking about here. Flesh that needs to be loved. Feet that need to rest and to dance; backs that need support; shoulders that need arms, strong arms I'm telling you. And O my people, out yonder, hear me, they do not love your neck unnoosed and straight. So love your neck; put a hand on it, grace it, stroke it and hold it up. And all your inside parts that they'd just as soon slop for hogs, you got to love them. The dark, dark liver—love it, love it, and the beat and beating heart, love that too. More than eyes or feet. More than lungs that have yet to draw free air. More than your life-holding womb and your life-giving private parts, hear me now, love your heart." (88-89)

If any part of a person is thought natural, most resistant (so far) to culture, it is flesh, notwithstanding implantation, amputation, piercing, tattoos, and prosthetics. Baby Suggs therefore chose well when she chose the Clearing for bodily liberation, as it is a place distant from cultural control of the body and in the case of slavery, ruthless control. The Clearing is a site apparently free from body-shame, a locale filled with (naked) plants stretching and animals exercising limbs and trunks.

The Clearing is important not because its trees are eradicated but because it is deep in the forest, a space surrounded by trees. As character Janey Wagon says, "I never went to those *woodland* services she [Suggs] had" (254, my emphasis). The forest has a long history as a sacred wood:

> Gothic architecture was widely regarded as an attempt to reproduce in stone the branching of a forest walk. When it returned to fashion in the 1750s, so did the view of woods as primitive churches. Those "oak priests," the Druids, it was said, had frequented groves because they felt the religious awe which ancient trees engendered. "It is natural," thought Alexander Hunter in 1776, "for men to feel an awful and religious terror when placed in the centre of a thick wood." To worship a venerable oak was idolatry, admitted William Cowper, but it was "idolatry with some excuse." In the Romantic era the analogy between groves and ecclesiastical architecture became commonplace. It was no accident that Coleridge's Christabel went to pray beneath an old huge oak tree or that in *The Rime of the Ancient Mariner* the "hermit good" lived in a wood. For Wordsworth no moral philosophy could match "one impulse from a vernal wood," while in nineteenth-century America the Transcendentalists would see the forests as "God's first temples." "In the woods," thought Emerson, "we return to reason and faith." "If we do not go to church as much as did our fathers," wrote John Burroughs in 1912, "we go to the woods much more."[17]

Comprising the walls of the forest-cathedral are an unspecified species of the genus *Quercus*, or oak (90).[18] Since the Old Testament, oaks have stood for strength and longevity. The English oak, *Quercus robur* (from Latin meaning either strength or oak, as in *robust*), was the species worshipped by Druid "oak priests."[19] Also along lines of strength and longevity, the oak leaf cluster is a U.S. military decoration pinned on top of another decoration, and signifies a second honor for valor, wounds, or service. Finally, oaks are known for their vulnerability to lightning: "The mighty oak gets blitzed by lightning more than any other tree, which unfortunate faculty, some scholars theorize, led the ancient Greeks to consecrate oaks to Zeus, a notorious hurler of lightning bolts, and the ancient Norse to associate them with Thor, the obstreperous god of thunder."[20] The oaks (perhaps even *Quercus robur)* that surround and overarch the Clearing lend Baby Suggs's words of courage and endurance a long history of sacredness, strength, and longevity, and bestow Zeus's lightning and Thor's thunder on Baby Suggs's litany of limbs, apertures, and organs.

The other tree comprising this forest is the horse chestnut, member of the buckeye family from which Ohioans—these Cincinnatans in the Clearing—get the label, *buckeyes.* The best-known American horse chestnut is *Aesculus glabra,* Ohio's state tree commonly known as the Ohio buckeye. Thrice in *Beloved,* mention is made of "thunderous feet and the shouts that ripped pods off the limbs of the chestnuts. With Baby Suggs's heart in charge, the people let go" (94, see also 164, 261). This links buckeyes with the formerly-enslaved Ohioans who let go of hatred of their own flesh and hatred of whites as slavers. If the Buckeyes are implored to let go of slavery-engendered self-contempt, then the buckeye pods are letting go of their tree, *Aesculus glabra (Aesculus,* Latin for oak, and *glabra,* for young male slave). Baby Suggs asks the Buckeyes (buckeyes) to let go of slavery (the tree). Falling buckeye pods become not only proof of ardor in the arbor but an analogue for continual liberation from slavery's ongoing effects.

Besides *Aesculus glabra*'s name, the horse chestnut has another characteristic that aligns it with slavery. *Glabra* refers to the smooth bark of this tree in comparison to other horse chestnuts (*glabra* in *Rhus glabra, Carya glabra,* and *Pinus glabra* refers to the smooth bark of species of sumac, hickory, and pine, respectively). The bark's smoothness is tied to a boy's beardless face—*glabra,* again, means young male slave. But its other common name besides *American horse chestnut* and *Ohio buckeye* is *fetid buckeye,* named for the unpleasant odor of its crushed leaves and twigs, flowers, toxic bark, and poisonous buckeyes. If the tree, *Aesculus glabra,* stands for slavery, then the dropping seed-pods herald a kind of castration, an attempt to render both the tree and slavery impotent. But the metaphor also breaks down since seeds are potent and can germinate and become new "slave trees."

Aesculus glabra's distasteful and defensive chemicals (chemicals that cannot, however, defend it against being made into furniture, floors, and musical instruments), open it to associations with offensive slavery. Not exactly apt. But *Beloved,* even while producing a problematic metaphor at the expense of *Aesculus glabra*, produces a somewhat complex view of not only oak and horse chestnut, but all trees, from which can be inferred detailed knowledge that does not simply objectify, but that understands trees as distinguishable, with names rich with history and character, trees that might be more resistant to massing, objectification, commodification, and logging.[21]

Brother and Related Trees

Of all *Beloved*'s characters, Paul D, another escaped slave, is most intimate with trees, in particular a barely described, unclassified tree called Brother. During an attempt at sex with Sethe, Paul D muses on trees as he ponders Sethe's already described backtree:

> And the wrought-iron maze he had explored in the kitchen like a gold miner pawing through pay dirt was in fact a revolting clump of scars. Not a tree, as she said. Maybe shaped like one, but nothing like any tree he knew because trees were inviting; things you could trust and be near; talk to if you wanted to as he frequently did since way back when he took the midday meal in the fields of Sweet Home. Always in the same place if he could, and choosing the place had been hard because Sweet Home had more pretty trees than any farm around. His choice he called Brother, and sat under it, alone sometimes, sometimes with Halle or the other Pauls, but more often with Sixo, who was gentle then and still speaking English. Indigo with flame-red tongue, Sixo experimented with night-cooked potatoes, trying to pin down exactly when to put smoking-hot rocks in a hole, potatoes on top, and cover the whole thing with twigs so that by the time they broke for the meal, hitched the animals, left the field and got to Brother, the potatoes would be at the peak of perfection . . . . Now *there* was a man, and *that* was a tree. (21-22)[22]

Sixo is also connected to trees in other ways: he "melts" into, and often dances in the forest (25), frequents a place called High Trees (59), and, while Sixo is tied to a tree, the slavemaster unsuccessfully tries to burn him alive with wet hickory wood (finally, he is shot dead). Like hickory, the hottest of burning woods, which is one of the toughest, Sixo is indeed tough (these characteristics led to Andrew Jackson's nickname, Old Hickory).[23] Not only is Sixo the most rebellious and savvy slave at Sweet

Home, he laughs while slowly burning at the stake—the last laugh at what his murderers think is punishment but what Sixo perceives as liberation from slavery. Sixo's correlation to trees, especially to Brother, and Paul D's characterization of Sixo and Brother as ideal beings, makes Sixo a refreshingly favorable representation of the woods dweller or legendary wild man.

Brother is not classified (is he an everytree?), and garners little description, except that "he" must be pretty, and is "old, wide, and beckoning" (221). What can be inferred from a tree known only by a proper name, specifically *Brother*?[24] A proper name humanizes the tree but another's knowledge of a proper name (including a tree's) is a snag in the veil of privacy and anonymity, a pointing at foretelling a potential for repression or destruction.[25] On the other hand, knowing a proper name can grant a live-and-let-live treatment to the named; in Brother's case, worthy of not chopping or cutting.

Brother, a male name,[26] is used possibly because the tree is named by males, because of its massive and immovable trunk and limbs, and because it marks a gathering site for males.[27] But what seems more important than the name's maleness is its genericalness—any male can be called "brother." In fact, *Beloved* concatenates maleness and genericalness in the names of males: Hi Man, schoolteacher, Here Boy, Mister, Paul A, Paul D, and Paul F. *Beloved*'s females, on the other hand, do not have generic names. While generic proper names indicate individuality and gender, genericalness also devalues individuality. Perhaps male slaves were pinned with generic names because they were undervalued since they would not breed by the master's economic-sexual raping. Or Brother could have inherited a generic male slave-name simply because he was named by male slaves with generic names. This suggests that by being on the slaveowner's land, Brother is also enslaved; he is the slaveowner's property (not the property of the namers) and susceptible to the owner's whims.

Only one other tree is singled out with the same kind of attention paid to Brother: the aspen sapling Paul D loves while he is a slave in Alfred, Georgia:

> His little love was a tree, of course, but not like Brother—old, wide, and beckoning. In Alfred, Georgia, there was an aspen too young to call sapling. Just a shoot no taller than his waist. The kind of thing a man would cut to whip his horse. Song-murder and the aspen. He

stayed alive to sing songs that murdered life, and watched an aspen that confirmed it, and never for a minute did he believe he could escape. (221)

While fragile, the aspen is green with possibility, a creature Paul D visually possesses to guard against losing his mind since he has already lost his body (he is always shackled in Alfred). Aspens, also called poplars, belong to the genus *Populis* and are "said to derive from the Roman use of the trees as the sites of public meetings—hence *Arbor populi,* or 'people's tree.'"[28] Both Brother, and to a lesser extent, the aspen, are variations of family trees and a related notion of trees as support structures. Amy Denver leans on an ash tree for support while nursing the pregnant Sethe back to health. Massaging Sethe's swollen feet and singing, "Amy sat quietly after her song, then repeated the last line before she stood, left the lean-to and walked off a little ways to lean against a young ash" (82). Yggdrasil, Eddic mythology's cosmic ash tree or *Axis mundi,* has this legend: "The fruit of the [ash] tree placed in fire is good for women in childbirth. What was within then comes out, such might has the tree for men."[29] Short of throwing ash-tree fruit into a fire, Amy-cum-midwife, who is probably unfamiliar with Icelandic myth, serendipitously finds the next best thing in leaning on a young ash that is presumably too young to bear fruit. The leaning seems to work: The subsequent birth, despite Sethe's abject physical condition, is successful.

The family tree appears in *Beloved* in at least two variations. The traditional sense is expressed by, "Ax the trunk, the limb will die" (242), the trunk referring to Sethe, and the limb to Beloved. Unlike family tree charts, where successive generations proceed downward, here offspring less arrogantly and more hopefully, proceed toward the tops of trees.[30] Treetops are also literal sites for children: Before Sethe was at Sweet Home, the slave women at her former plantation "use to hang their babies in the trees—so you could see them out of harm's way while you worked the fields" (160).[31] And on two occasions, Sethe imagines or dreams seeing parts of her sons Buglar and Howard hidden in the leafy tops of trees as if playing in a tree house. Kids and trees are conjoined because the former often climb the latter, partially, perhaps, to climb out of smallness and to feel tall, or in Howard and Buglar's case, to escape an earth overrun with the slavery that drove their mother to kill them. Or considering the evolutionary theory about early *Homo*'s pre-erect, arboreal days, perhaps children's tree-climbing is an atavism from, or attempt to get back to that supposed halcyon existence.

In sum, Brother and the aspen sapling are portrayed as living beings; the ash and family trees serve as trustworthy supports or locales of human genealogical history. Such depictions of single trees are capable of subverting notions of trees as timber or mere scenery, especially if the portrayals are reinforced by representations in the world outside the novel. But could these images go further, since with all of these related trees, importance is manifested by conceptual or proxemic connection to people. What if these connections are interrupted or should fall away?

This is the subtle flaw in *Beloved*. On no occasion are *Beloved*'s trees imagined useful or pleasurable to themselves or to other plants and animals, or rendered important because trees are individuals that represent a fascinating and crucial variation on existence. Such perspectives would render each tree, flower, and weed *autovalent* or important enough to itself so that taking it means dispossessing it; and *extravalent,* or meaningful to multiple species, so that taking it or killing it means depriving other species of its benefits.[32] A conception of trees as humanlike (our brethren, friends), or exclusively for human benefit (as timber, air filters, food producers, decoration) lessens the possibility of representing trees as valuable to themselves or to a host of others.

Perhaps there will be those who say that imagining a tree as autovalent sends us back into a regressive anthropomorphism, the kind where, in this case, trees are simply imagined in the image of those most excellent autovalent beings, humans. Anthropomorphism, it is true, is not only difficult to escape but to embrace, even if it is less a problem than construing plants and animals as so utterly other as Descartes did with his description of animals as mechanisms.[33] I offer two suggestions for making anthropomorphism more viable. First, step up the accuracy of comparison. For example, since we (and other living individuals) have defense mechanisms, why not imagine that a tree's defenses (heavy bark, poisonous chemicals) indicate that if they had the ability—if they don't already—they would communicate their desire to not be attacked. The second suggestion is to seek out or create acentric anthropomorphisms that avoid anthropocentrism and produce obstacles to the usual battery of uncontested anthropocentric notions. For example, trees could be imagined just as alive as people, since trees usually live much longer, reproduce and produce far more abundantly, draw sustenance directly from soil and sun, are usually larger than people, heal themselves, and remain standing and growing despite attacks from weather, animals, other plants, and humanity that would kill people in the same circumstances. Positing trees as autovalent is, accurate or not, less a problem for verification than *assuming* they are not fully alive, or that their meaning can be summarized primarily as material for human use. Presently, it is dangerous to assert arboreal autovalence because it risks sounding insane or sentimental. But to ignore the autovalency of living organisms, such as plants, is the same as attempting to preserve the forest, especially the trees, solely for humans and animals (e.g., spotted owls) or because trees maintain the ecological infrastructure, or some other extravalent reason. This is similar to the rather uncommon and extravalent argument that humanity should be saved for, say, the sakes of domesticated animals and urban infrastructure. Perhaps such extravalent arguments result from living in a technosphere where nearly everything we experience is produced by and supposedly exists for the sake of people—an artifactual sphere without autovalence (at least for now), with an extravalence only in relation to people. Those of us operating from the headquarters of the technosphere, still, long after Newton, overextend mechanism to all of nature, to even fifth world plants and animals, organisms-cum-mechanisms construed without autovalence. These remain, like artifacts, entities to be preserved primarily on the basis of an extravalence for the first four worlds of humanity, and only more recently with the specially (as in *species*) endangered animals of worldnature. *Beloved* shows readers a way it can be beneficial not to see the forest for the trees. Still, the weight of the old cliché also holds true, and indeed may be taken further. Just as it is a problem when we are unable to see the forest for the trees, it is a disaster when we are unable to see the tree for its limbs, or its flesh, or its shade, or its beauty, or its soil-holding roots, or its rich rotting leaves for the forest floor, or its . . . .

Conclusion

Beloved's promising representations of individualized trees have a purpose other than the characters' cathexis in real trees or trees as a leitmotif. They separate good guys (blacks) from primarily bad guys (whites). In *Beloved*, blacks love trees. In addition to Brother, Sethe's backtree, the trees around the Clearing, and the emerald closet, beautiful and comfortable trees or their parts are mentioned: sycamores at Sweet Home, leafy shoes comforting

Sethe's swollen feet, the mulberry tree Beloved sleeps with her head against a day and night after being reborn. In white hands, however, trees either become the enemies of slaves, or whites the enemies of trees. On several occasions, whites lynch slaves from trees and schoolteacher, the slavemaster, beats the Sweet Home slaves "in the prettiest trees you ever saw" (197). When Baby Suggs walks through a white part of town, sick, twin chestnuts stand in the yard of uppity whites named Tucker, from the Old English *tucian*, to torment. A white sawyer's lumberyard is right outside the carnival where the smelly, dying roses are planted to "take the sin out of slicing trees for a living" (47).[34] Another problematic white man, the owner of the restaurant where Sethe cooks, has the surname Sawyer. Conversely, black characters do not violate trees (they do chop and burn wood for their stoves). In fact, through white (especially male) instrumentality, unity develops among those deemed property; Africans befriend and love trees. Such affect might be called tragically sentimental—things with sentiment feeling for things without sentiment—affect thrown away on unappreciative, deaf and dumb trees. This is somewhat justifiable because trees probably do not *give* oxygen, shade, food, and wood; oxygen and shade are *used*; some food and all wood is *taken* from living trees. But notwithstanding trees' self-interest, *Beloved* shows that sentiment need not be a transaction: Things can be loved or respected and allowed to live and flourish for what they are as well as what they return.

Slaves and trees are so close in *Beloved* that at certain points they merge: Sixo "melts" into a forest of trees, Sethe has a tree on her back, Denver smells like leaves and bark, and the slavemaster barters one of Baby Suggs's children for lumber. Flesh and cellulose shockingly coalesce when Sethe, in the novel's most important scene, kills her children in the *woodshed* to save them from being sold into slavery. Sethe's daughter, Beloved, is "mercy-killed" by the *handsaw* Sethe drags across her throat, and appears later, in magic-realistic fashion, after a carnival sitting on a *stump* just after being reborn from stream water.[35] (Recall also Amy's "Zzz Zzz" when alluding to *sawing* Sethe's feet off.) These acts indicate one last analogy: the one between trees and slave children. Already mentioned were Sethe's children hanging or playing in trees, Denver in the emerald closet, Beloved under the saw, and Baby Suggs's unnamed child exchanged for lumber (slaves treated as children is also implicit). Perhaps the reason children, trees, and slaves become juxtaposed at all, through either intimacy or similarity, is their status as property, which allows for disposition and disposal of trees as wood, and of humans as laboring bodies.[36] Perhaps this is Morrison's ever so reserved criticism of Sethe: viewing her children as property allowed Sethe to kill one of them. This is a variation on the obscenity of making people into property in slavery, and I would add, the abominations of turning plants and animals into property.

Through personification of trees—coalescing their beings with those of enslaved and freed blacks—and through naming, knowing, loving, and *individualizing* trees, *Beloved* points the way, perhaps sets a precedent, for how trees may figure as a prominent part in a rich ecology of representation. And through corporeal mergings of tree bodies and enslaved human bodies, *Beloved* exposes the dilemma of viewing people and trees as mere extensions or the property of ascendant humans, a predicament that may someday be understood when dragging a saw, not only across beloved flesh, but beloved trees.

III
For Land's (Not Property's) Sake

Where, in chapter five, stolen land is hoarded, and, in chapter six, liberated land is shared.

5

THE DEED AND ITS UNDOING
The Conservationist

In Nadine Gordimer's *The Conservationist,* owning is dying. Or, to put it less aphoristically: The practice of real estate—where owning enables responsibility or control, and not owning encourages disowning of responsibility or control—results in the demise of a particular owner/disowner. Gordimer's version of *Homo dominus* is a wealthy, white South African industrialist, named Mehring, who is involved in owning and disowning, acts manifested in his attempt to own (control) his four hundred-acre farm on the outskirts of Johannesburg and disown responsibility for the corpse found in one of its pastures. The corpse is a black South African, perhaps murdered, for whom Mehring accepts the police's cursory burial (no coffin, memorial, or funeral). Mehring's owning of formerly-black African land, and disowning, especially of any responsibility for the murdered black African, set in motion Mehring's asymptotic demise.

Mehring cannot seem to master his farm nor successfully disown or disregard the decaying-yet-resilient resident. The land and all its live occupants, and the dead man Mehring tries to disown, are beyond his control: Mehring's land partially burns and mostly floods, its human, animal, and plant inhabitants seem cavalier or indifferent about his attempts at regulation, and Mehring's disowned dead man rises from Mehring's memory and the inadequate grave, haunting him with intimations of the kind of death born of owning and disowning real estate.[1] Gordimer's rather religious notion of owning—that the owner/disowner suffers a demise—offers the other side of an environmentalist notion that real property meets its unmaking in private ownership, especially where individual and corporate ownership dominate land by regarding it as mere resource.[2] In *The Conservationist,* the owner/disowner is less resilient than his four hundred acres that finally rebloom after seven years of drought, fires, and a flood.

And the disowned corpse, a modern-day vegetation god, "rises" from the earth as plants take nourishment from his decaying body. While dangers to nature under the notion and practice of real property are less pronounced than those to Mehring as owner and disowner, they exist to the extent it will be beneficial if they are teased out. In general terms Mehring, as owner, haunts; Mehring, as disowner, is haunted.

If one is to believe the strange notion that owning real estate equals (results in) demise or death for the owner, then the "boundaries" or "shape" of the notion of real estate had better be drawn with dangers clearly posted. A study of Mehring's owning and disowning entails elucidating three ways by which nature (and more) is trans-formed or trans-ideated into property: commodification, labor, and occupation/defense. I undertake this analysis in the hope that the noun *real estate* and its accompanying verbs of *owning* and *disowning*, especially with relation to nature, will not only expose the reciprocal dangers of property, but cut a hole in the fence large enough for a competing notion and practice of nature to slip through.

Commodification

Commodities are exchanged and owned property. While commodities are a form of property because they are owned, property need not be a commodity since it might never be exchanged.[3] Mehring's land is both commodity and property because he buys and takes possession of it. The transaction of buying and selling (commodification), more than other acts like occupation or marking, is the primary means by which land or any entity becomes an object of human possession. Mehring generally likes to pay for and invest in certain objects because such acts enable control, whether it be over his teenage son to whom he doles out money and of whom he tries to keep custody after Mehring's divorce,[4] or over a prostitute he pays. Nothing but access to money, it seems, could obstruct Mehring's will to commodify people and nature.

He pays a high price for his four hundred acres, but his monetary discomfort is somewhat mitigated by the farm's appreciation in value and a tax deduction for any losses the farm incurs. But these advantages are themselves a problem since Mehring notes that "A farm is not beautiful unless it is productive" (23). Only as long as Mehring can operate the farm at a loss will it be a tax shelter, albeit one less "beautiful" or productive than he would like. He opts for the less beautiful, more-but-not-too-productive arable tax shelter because he hasn't the time to make the farm a going enterprise.[5]

Mehring's proof of ownership is a deed, a sheet of paper that represents something done, a document ensured by tradition and enforceable by the Johannesburg Police. However, at the time of this novel, 1970s South Africa, it can be argued that a deed is a mere sheet of paper, something as easily undone as done. Mehring's lover makes the point: "That bit of paper you [Mehring] bought yourself from the deeds office isn't going to be valid for as long as another generation. It'll be worth about as much as those our grandfathers gave the blacks when they took the land from them. The blacks will tear up your bit of paper" (177). Images of flimsy documents and torn paper recur throughout the novel. One of Mehring's farm hands, Witbooi, has several recommendations from previous employers that have not helped him find work. After the floodwater dampens Witbooi's possessions, Mehring sees that: "Witbooi's references from previous employers were spread on stones to dry, weighted at all four corners under smaller stones. Drops blown from the trees and dangling crystals from the fence shook down to magnify, then blotch still farther, the lettering TO WHOM IT MAY CONCERN" (238). Blurring indicates that "IT" concerns no one. Just as Mehring's lover predicted, the domain of whites' paper, at least officially, does not last the generation. If Mehring lived long enough to witness the end of official apartheid, he might today be struggling to keep his farm, or have abandoned it to indigenous residents come to take back the land from which they were thrown off.

In order to become a commodity in the form of real estate, Mehring's land undergoes a process of parcelization. Parcelization necessary for commodification turns land into parcels of land, units of exchange similar to packages or objects bought, sold and transported. Rather than packaged with paper and cardboard, however, land is "wrapped" by borders or fences, and just as with packaged personal commodities, more expensive packaging often wraps more expensive land.[6] But unlike a fungible commodity, land or a place cannot be moved or possessed in the same way personal property can. Still, land is made into real property by means of a similar kind of possession: What is on the land is conceived of as, and made, manipulable—movable, changeable, acquirable. This includes animals, plants, watering places, soil, topography. The possession and manipulability of biological creatures and topographical features—part of which are not, strictly speaking, owned (like non-domesticated animals)—allows land to be referred to with possessive pronouns. Reciprocally, creature and feature possession, through manipulability, reinforces the owning of land. Parcelization of land is the practice of breaking a preexisting continuity and tearing a place from a preexisting context, then placing it into a usually narrower (human) continuity and context, made apparent by bound(aries)s.

Parcelization alone, however, does not lead to commodification; the act of exchange is also necessary. Parcelization promotes exchange, and exchange promotes parcelization. Parceled and exchanged plants and animals, and land in the form of soil, stones, minerals, and water, become so fungible as to seem personal property, and so comparable that a document and a parcel of land can both be called *tracts*. Such parcelization and exchange of land's creatures and features also enables the purchase of rights—logging, drilling, mining, grazing—to land owned by another. Virtually all the planet's plants, animals, and land fall within the purview of parcelization and exchange and under the potential and actual whims of human owners. This condition is a property dictatorship, where each owner is an imperialist despot presiding over a domain she or he seeks to increase beyond what can be defended with the owner's *own* strength and smarts.[7] To the owner and others who recognize themselves as potential owners, the owner is absolute over his or hers. The rights of ownership enable manipulation, which can take the extremes of creating, preserving, or destroying across vast domains like Indian gods Brahma, the Creator, Vishnu, the Preserver, and Shiva, the Destroyer. Every owner belongs to a kind of royalty (and divinity) because everything owned is an imperial subject. With modern ownership—and not just of land—this royal privilege is acquired by virtually all humans, although in vastly differing degrees. But while such ownership continually results in a terrible disparity between "have lesses" and "have mores," it is often more calamitous for indigenous or already-occupying plants, animals, and land bent to the purpose of property (especially development).

Perhaps it is accurate to say that when the Boers enslaved South Africans—before the introduction of extended documentation and widespread commodification of land—Europeans thought Africans had, if anything, territory, not property. By most traditional white Western definitions of ownership, Africans, because they lived close to nature, belonged to the land; the land couldn't belong to them.[8] Because Africans were not owners in this Western definition (in fact might have been seen as the property of nature which belongs to anyone who takes it), then just as land, plants, and animals could be owned, so could Africans. If this theory is even partially true, then according to colonial Europeans, Africans, who were little different than animals in their land ownership, could also be treated as animals, with little or no respect. Africans can be enslaved, displaced, relocated, and exterminated as coldly and calculatedly as animals and plants, even be restocked with aesthetic or economic commodities and "proper," or property-owning, Europeans.

Mehring's four hundred-acre domain of previously populated territory is quite large as far as commodity ownership goes. His commodified subjects are protected or dispatched according to whim and capitalist or taxpayer logic. The land is internally fenced into three pastures grooved by irrigation ditches and partitioned into living areas. Indigenous unexchangeable plants deemed *weeds*[9] are killed off to make way for Mehring's monocultural fields of commodified plants: alfalfa, teff, rye, and wheat, all of which are *crops*, whose verb form means to cut down). The struggle between crops and weeds is not a war with nature because nature does not attack; it is a slaughter in which culture dominates portions of nature, domesticates it into *agri-* (Latin for field) culture.[10]

Prior to Mehring's tenure as owner, larger and commodity-threatening animals such as jackals were exterminated or forced off the land, enabling Mehring to safely graze several hundred cattle (commodified oxen). Mehring somewhat laments this loss because jackals keep the land "clean" (249). One or more of those slaughtered jackals could even be part of Mehring's kaross of black jackal skins. Yet he makes no association between his "nicely-made" kaross of dead jackals and a stretch of land without live jackals, or with corpses of slaughtered jackals. Commodification's subjection and objectification would seem to obliterate Mehring's ability to link a spread of land with a (bed)spread of skin.

Wild guinea fowls, which Mehring hopes will repopulate his land, do not quite become commodities but they are the brunt of commodity-thinking, probably because elsewhere they are commodified as food. Mehring counts the guinea fowl like stock and thinks that if they increase "too much" he will kill them for the table (109). "Too much," given no rationale, appears arbitrary since guinea fowl neither eat crops nor damage other species of plants or animals. Perhaps Mehring's "too much" comes from his training in business where value is apt to decrease as quantity increases. Or perhaps it is a psychology of number where beyond a certain point a group becomes a crowd making the skies seem crowded in terms of a certain human aesthetic.

Mehring's farm is largely a commodity factory and warehouse for plants and animals understood as plant material, brute matter—where plants are material and brutes are matter—(potential) "stock," his stock. As stock, they are stocked, kept stock of, stockaded, placed in stocks, pushed around, altered, or dispatched according to will. But another perspective also fosters such manipulations: conceiving nature as a commodified spectacle parceled by frame or stage, access to which is bought and sold, and production of which involves economic investment. Mehring's conservation efforts are largely a matter of visual aesthetics, less the aesthetic of nature's rejuvenation than of nature as spectacular or beautiful, filled with trees and birds and clean of litter. Mehring feels driven to make such "improvements" because he bought "A landscape [the farm] without theatricals" (24) and "a dirty piece of land, agriculturally speaking" (22).

Planting two chestnut trees is an extended example of Mehring's spectacularization effort. He thinks it would be better to plant an indigenous species but he has romantic memories of New York City's roasted chestnuts and likes that the chestnut trees are European imports, just like himself and his forefamily. Once he gets the trees to the farm he cannot figure out where they would *look* best, either at the entrance to the driveway or the house. He is apparently molded by memories of artifactual landscapes, not thoughts of functionality or the trees' or land's best "interests."[11] But a tree's or land's "interests" might seem absurd to Mehring who sees his nature as an arranged or staged spectacle, where an increase in investment toward visual beauty usually leads to a rise in ticket prices at the box office, gallery, or real estate office.[12]

Mehring's four hundred acres of creatures and features become virtual parcels, objects of aesthetic arrangement and commerce. They are conceived of and treated like commodities because they appear and are placed on commodified land. And conversely, land gets commodified by having commodifiable creatures and features. The site where land, plants, and animals become commodified property is the place where nature loses otherness, becomes engulfed by culture becomes a mere cultural extension, no longer nature but culture, agri-culture.[13]

Commodification also enables disowning. As Mehring feels he owns and is somewhat responsible for children and women, by paying for them he is also able to disown responsibility for unknown girls and younger women who he has not paid for: The Portuguese girl he "fingers" on the plane is another adult's property, and the young woman he picks up on the road is another man's property, or her own. The corpse found on the farm is disowned, not simply because Mehring does not know him or because Mehring is a white racist, but because the man was never invested in or paid as an employee, and because Mehring will get no return on a monetary investment in the burial. Mehring believes the corpse belongs to the State since the dead man is, dead or alive, a kind of trespasser or lawbreaker belonging to the State. The dead body is also the State's because it is within State boundaries and subject to its policies or manipulations (the State-subject is a kind of commodity, that is separated from its family or community and exchanged or dispatched according to political whim). Or the dead man belongs to Nature since death is thought to be natural, and to nature since the corpse is decomposing and becoming food for animals and plants in a wetland. Or because even living dark-skinned people are routinely associated in the white psyche with nature. Yet, how reconcile the fact that this corpse is part of the State yet also of nature and Nature? Only because the corpse is so problematic to Mehring can the State be allowed to temporarily intrude, and nature to acquire its other role as Nature, owner of humanity, which is easy since this human is already dead. This is only to say *nature*, the word, is large, and contains all definitions.

By the same token—that he has made no investment—Mehring disowns (his responsibility for) the gold-mining dumps he passes to and from his farm. Mehring's profession is mining and metals, one of the most destructive anthropogenic activities, not only on mine workers but on nature.[14] The most visible results of South Africa's gold mining and processing industry are pyramidal heaps of cyanide slag.[15] The commodified mining lands are probably the distant result of his work (which might be maintaining or opening foreign markets to gold) but since he does not personally own these slaglands, he believes they are not his concern. Yet apparently, disowning the slagheaps is not so simple. To disown them, Mehring must also see the dumps anew, as spectacle. One day he drives by and looks at them; this leads to an erection:

> What is really holding his attention strangely for a few moments is the wide, flat-topped pyramid of a mine-dump to which he has deliberately turned his gaze as another normal landmark. There: has it not even a certain beauty? There are beautiful, ordinary things left.

> People say they are unsightly, these dumps, but in some lights . . . .
> This is a firm dump, that the rain has not softened in substance and
> outline, but that the wonderfully clean sunny air, sluiced by rain, gives
> at once the clarity of a monument against the glass-blue sky and yet
> presents curiously as a (remembered) tactile temptation—that whole
> enormous, regularly-crenulated mountain seems covered with exactly
> the soft buffed yellow and texture of a much-washed chamois leather.
> That's it. It is *that*—the imagined sensation of that lovely surface
> under his hand (the tiny snags of minute hairs when a forearm or
> backside cheek is brushed against lips)—that produced, unbidden by
> any thought that normally prompts such an unconscious reaction
> (God knows, his mind is far enough from these things, this morning)
> the familiar phenomenon in his body. It's not what the doctor calls a
> "cold erection" though: pleasureless, something prompted purely by
> a morbidity in the flesh, what they say happens when a man's hanged.
> It's more like warmth coming back to a body numbed by cold or
> shock. Subliminally comforting. (253, ellipsis in original)

Through conceptual beautification, or spectacularizing, Mehring can disown the blight these lands are, and own them through his eyes. When the
dumps are idealized into a beautiful monument, then into the feel of fine
cloth, and finally the feel of a woman's buttocks on his lips, the dumps
become entities he would own, has owned.[16] In this sense, disowning is a
way of owning, of getting control over a thing, a person, a situation. After
mentally laundering these dumps into, finally, a sexualized female body
part, Mehring is able to reassimilate them, even get a warm hard-on.
Mehring has rid himself of the dumps by erecting in their place an ownable
spectacle: a huge (commodified) female body.[17] Who says aesthetic
endeavor has no function, is mere play, when through it titillation (acceptance) replaces or competes with disgust (rejection)?

Just as Mehring benefits from detaching himself from control and
responsibility for the corpse and the mine dumps, he also benefits from
disowning commodified nature. When Mehring hears the howls from
what he apparently conceives of as a dog-as-property, he assumes the dogs
are being beaten by farm hands (dogs are owned by the laborers largely
because money and labor are expended on them for food and restraining),
and he ultimately feels he cannot meddle. Though Mehring *can* partially
own the black African farm hands by owning their labor and housing, the

dogs remain their property. Mehring's literal disowning is accompanied by figurative ones, such as his rationalizations: Blacks cannot be changed, are by nature dog-beaters, and anyway the dogs probably stole meat thereby bringing it on themselves. Property ethics reinforce figurative disowning and vice versa. Owning up, disowning, being on one's own, and holding one's own are notions anchored in and stretched further than mere property relations.

Mehring attempts to silence the dogs' howling in his head by turning them into someone else's commodified property. This process is aided by the dogs' inability to speak a language people understand, or worse, some people's dubious and self-serving claim that dogs have no language, no thoughts, no consciousness. Perhaps readers know the ACT UP motto, Silence = Death. In the case of dogs, the literal and figurative silencing of plaintive howling is enabled by commodifying or "propertizing" them, a kind of Silencing = Death. Dogs-as-property can then be easily ill-treated or beaten, or almost as easily, killed without much concern by either dog owners or disowners. Even when dogs, property, are well-treated, it can be because their demise would mean a setback to the owner's domination and value.

If even dogs can be silenced by being imagined as property,[18] then land, since it does not howl, is easier to silence, and think of as silent, dead. While I would not make a case for the aliveness of dirt particles, let alone for their language or voice, I do propose that commodity ownership is partly based on the kind of silencing or silence of propertied stuff, things, and objects. But land's silence is not stuff's since most land is suffused with sounds and voices of a living multitude. These sounds and voices are *non-disembodied*, I would add, so as not to confuse them with disembodied or representational media. And if people do not listen or cannot hear these emanations, they might be imagined. A person already imagines what other people would think or say about a certain action, even if *people* is a non-particular abstraction. Because land does not speak, except figuratively, it might be particularly difficult to imagine what land would say about a certain attitude or action of ours: Land's voices are difficult to imagine amongst the din of other people's remembered or imagined voices, namely one's own voice(s), the cultural voice(s). If Mehring could imagine or would listen to the loud land, perhaps his own possessive voice might have difficulty with the *volume* in even one acre of land, let alone four hundred.

Labor

Not just the investment of money, but the investment of work or manipulation establishes property. A feeling of ownership often comes over those who work (on) something—persons, plants, animals, land, or artifacts. Since the work is usually considered an improvement (i.e., "improved" land), there is an often inchoate notion that the worked object owes those who put work into it, or that in return for investing work in the object, the object is indebted to work: Parents tend to think children owe them respect; farmers think farms owe them fertility; and makers and fixers think machines owe them proper functioning. This could explain some of the hostility shown toward people, nature, and artifacts when relationships between them break down, break off, break up, when artifacts break, and when investment of work is deprived of return.

But Mehring owns his farm less through (his own) labor than through his money. He primarily visits the farm on weekends and a greater share of the work is done by the black African laborers he pays in wages and services. Herein lies one tension prevalent throughout the novel, the one between whether money or labor (including its results) is the more powerful proof of ownership. If money is, Mehring is the owner. If work is, then the laborers are. This tension surfaces as the workers take more control of the farm's affairs, especially when Mehring cannot get out to the farm for two weeks after a flood washes away part of the road. Mehring's absence is likened to death. The farm hands, especially Jacobus, make decisions during the flood and successfully ensure that animals and plants are not destroyed. Mehring, because he believes the workers cannot *manage* without him, is pleasantly surprised but also realizes that he is replaceable and unnecessary.

But Mehring does, in a loose sense of the word, labor to make the farm his. His work is conservation, mostly in the environmental sense.[19] His litany is, "Soon there will be nothing left," and in one passage he continues: "In the country. The continent. The oceans, the sky" (11). In addition to Mehring's conservation effort regarding guinea fowls, he keeps a close eye on litter, prevents the farm's eucalyptus trees from becoming firewood, and, while this is not strictly speaking, conservation, he also plans to plant a hundred trees. The only glaring inconsistency in this fairly conservative conservation effort is his killing of the rock pigeons on his land for sport, which is unexplained in the novel. Perhaps this is a conservation act similar

to killing or relocating non-indigenous species[20] in order to return an area to a theoretical original or former (and therefore better) state of nature, a well-meaning example of or last-ditch effort at meddling with nature instead of the culprit, culture.

But there are more subtle ingredients to Mehring's environmental concern. First, his conservation activity seems like those of an investor who expects substantial returns for an investment (recall the appreciating value of the land). Second, they resemble operations befitting a stage designer, a landscape painter, or a director of *mise en scène*, where nature is not so much conserved than it is arranged or constructed like spectacle (recall the chestnut trees). Third, as farmer and miner, his role in environmental devastation contributes to Mehring's weekend conservation, in which he is voluntarily dominated *by* nature. Perhaps this is a response to his weeklong industrialist and agricultural domination of nature, not unlike the executive who hires a dominatrix to alleviate his guilt of daily controlling others.[21] That land is gendered female in this novel seems no coincidence.[22]

There is one final way Mehring labors. He studies his land. Using field guides of wildflowers and trees he identifies wild lilies and distinguishes indigenous trees from foreign trees. By knowing the names, taxonomy, and nativity of flora, he gains a bit of knowledge about his land. While knowledge can lead to domination—destroying non-indigenous species, buying commodified indigenous species to repopulate the area, and killing animals who might destroy his plants—no evidence exists to show Mehring's green study will lead him down such a *beaten* path. Instead his study looks like a partial antidote to the dubious and meager manifestations of his conservation, and a means toward understanding the beats of other drummers.

Yet his study might be said to drive him toward a too-extreme conservation ethic, one where nature becomes an outdoor museum, where plants and animals become exhibits or displays, examples of this or that species, structure, taxonomy, or behavior. After identifying wild lilies by the river, Mehring wants to make sure they are not destroyed by blacks gathering them for medicine: "Jacobus [the farm's superintendent] ought to be told that medicine or no medicine, these bulbs mustn't be taken" (175). Though the harvesting of these plants for medicinal purposes takes a toll on individual plants, hand-collecting them for medicine is not likely to decimate their species. Mehring's distanced exploitation of nature by lifestyle—his urban consumption destroys nature at a remove—precludes him from accepting local exploitation even on a small scale for good reason. Everyone knows someone like Mehring, a person who would never kill but has no compunction about hiring someone else—especially lower classes forced by economic circumstance into being hit men—to do their killing (slaughter) for them.[23]

Presumably, Mehring is able to disown land in which he has invested no labor.[24] There is no example of this in the novel, yet none seems needed. Mehring does, however, disown the corpse, which relates to disowning land one has not labored on. He is partly able to disown the dead man because Mehring does not know him, and knowing someone is a kind of social labor, especially when knowing someone is a *chore*, when one must put *work* into a relationship. Because Mehring has invested no social labor in this dead man (nor the dead man, in him) Mehring can tell himself he owes him nothing (I presume Mehring would have buried someone who worked for him or someone he had known). By the same token, it is easier to disown land not experienced firsthand. Actual experience of a place as social labor is perhaps a strained or problematic notion, but it might contribute to understanding how lands known *about* but not *known* can be psychologically shunted, how people might care far more for their (kn)own surroundings or environment, past, present, or even future. Being in a location involves having a relationship with it, and having a relationship is a kind of labor—satisfying and dissatisfying. Without having performed this labor of being in places, their development (destruction) might garner no more than passing interest. On the other hand, having had a (pleasurable) experience with many places might make one concerned about the loss of any place. Decreasing wilderness, however, makes such contact increasingly difficult, which results in a vicious cultural circle. And some say nature is vicious.

Occupation and Defense

The oldest methods of possessing land are occupying and defending it. These are the ways by which animals and plants also "own" land. But these methods were, and to a lesser extent are, ways by which all humans also "owned" land, notwithstanding the debate about whether in such early ownership the land belonged to people, or people to land. This older form of ownership is not hard to fathom since it is common with found objects: They are ours if we occupy them (find and keep them) and defend them against takers. Occupation/defense is the oldest and most enduring form of possession. Depending on time, place, defender and defendee, it can also be the most effective. An owner, by title and labor, cannot easily remain owner if unable to occupy and defend what is owned.

In the sense of occupation/defense ownership, indigenous South Africans lost their land because they were unable to defend it against European weaponry. Now, in post-apartheid South Africa, whites have more trouble defending and acquiring land. This is partly because there are many more indigenous South Africans to occupy/defend the land. The rather common-sense notion, partially based on observing animals, that more people need more land, surely has something to do with the ethical issue of whether one person is en-titled to four hundred acres, while whole communities are en-titled to far less. This is only to say that ethics might be a result of observing nature, as well as spontaneously springing full-fledged from the head of culture.

The proper names of Mehring's black employees indicate that Mehring has little right to occupy not only so much land, but this land.[25] The workers have primarily Old Testament Hebrew, or Hebrew-sounding, names like Jacobus, Phineas, Izak, Solomon, and Simon, all of whom are descendants of the patriarch Abraham.[26] The Old Testament states that God gave Abraham and his seed Canaan (Palestine) forever.[27] As ancient Hebrews believed, or now, Zionist Jews believe that Palestine is theirs, Gordimer is probably alluding, by analogy, to the rightful ownership of Africa by Africans. While it is debatable that Jews have as much, or any, right to Palestine in the same way Africans do to Africa, the linking of black African and Hebrew/Jewish struggles is a convenient allegory. The novel's unstated prediction is that Mehring's workers, especially Jacobus, will supplant Mehring (*Jacobus* is Hebrew for the supplanter) as the land's rightful occupants (many of them even belong to the sect of Zion). This is the right to occupation by virtue of tradition of history. But it must be said that as far as the effect on wild plants, animals, and land, people are more or less people, which means that while whites may be arch-exploiters, other groups also show such aptitude.

Mehring believes he is entitled to a vast stretch of land, not only because he paid for it, has a deed to it, and has worked on and cared about it, but because it is occupied with his house—though no one lives in it—and because all the tools, animals, and laborers he pays for also occupy the land. By Western standards, the land would still be Mehring's without any of these, that is, without any occupation; deed or title would be sufficient as long as these were enforceable. Nonetheless, Mehring's things—his house, car, tools, animals, crops, and hired help—lend themselves to a psychology of ownership since most people assume that if someone's stuff is on the land, the land is probably theirs, even without proof of a deed or evidence of work done on it. Likewise, it is usually assumed that a room is someone's simply because it contains their stuff.

However, it is not quite enough that Mehring has a deed, directs the labor performed on his farm, and has occupied it with his stuff, since area-residents still trespass in order to use the farm as a shortcut; fences and a gate do not keep them out. Mehring decides to put up a sign, "a yellow board with black lettering, baked enamel on steel, clamped to two iron poles painted shiny black and sunk in concrete ... the message three times over, in English, Afrikaans and Zulu. NO THOROUGHFARE GEEN TOEGANG AKUNANDLELA LAPHA" (140). Though the sign seems strong, emphatic, and thorough, Mehring expresses his doubts to his son about the sign's effectiveness:

> As if anything'll keep them out. It's a constant parade, all weekend especially, cutting up through the farm to that shanty town over beyond the vlei. And old De Beer and Nienaber, too—a short cut for their damned milk trucks. It's the fire-risk that bothers me. You [Mehring's son] nod; and to what are assenting? The signboard's absurd, a hopeful claim that can never be recognized? Or that it's not a sense of possession but concern for the land that has set it up? (140)

These kinds of words on a sign stuck in the ground at the edge of a piece of real estate are so much like well-placed urine—territorial markings that are, however, apprehended by sight rather than smell. The sign exerts control without constant need for defense, the latter a form of labor. Mehring's money, time, and labor devoted to active defense might, by this sign, be saved. What No Trespassing signs say, is not "You cannot come in" so much as "If you come in you will be at risk." Mehring cannot hope his sign will work unless there are other "signs"—like dogs or guards—that people will suffer harm or humiliation if they cross his borders. He has none of these signs, and "Sure enough, there are Sunday visitors tramping along the private road" (141). It takes a lot of effort or money for one man to privatize four hundred acres, which indicates that land is better suited for the many than the few. Or the one.

The reason behind Mehring's desire to keep out trespassers—his "concern for the land"— is likely his comforting delusion, since occasional foot- and truck-traffic seem to involve little fire risk. Mehring's sign is a paltry attempt to maintain control when he knows he is losing it. A signboard without backup is the mark of a comfortable, propertied, unfiercely ideological capitalist, not a tenacious imperialist. Mehring only exerts control at a distance, when control is only obscurely or obliquely repressive and not too much trouble. This is the key to his conservation efforts. Mehring's brand of conservation takes little physical effort, little conviction. Therefore he could not do as his lover suggested: "Why not just buy it [the land] and leave it as it is," (22) because, it would, while taking little physical effort, require too much anomalous conviction. A sensible man like Mehring must visibly occupy his land but avoid the cultural extremes of either armed compound or nature preserve.

A stereotypical idyllic farm is both nature and culture, but a not-too-imposed or occupying culture. Thus, armed borders are less than bucolic. Agricultural weapons such as farm implements, machinery, and engineered projects on the other hand seem pastoral largely because of their setting; they would hardly look pastoral outside such a middle landscape; even a dishwasher might seem pastoral if seen *en plein air*. Farmers like Mehring might appear to be stewards of nature, but *steward* probably meant keeper of the house or of the sty, both of which need upkeep because they neither generate food nor reuse waste. Nature, unlike home and sty, needs no taking care of (which is not to say that it doesn't need caring about). Mehring knows this: "Nature knows how to use everything; neither rejects nor wastes" (245). But he is overwhelmed by his cultural impulse: "It's ridiculous just leaving land to turn back to swamp" (245). What makes swamp intolerable to Mehring is perhaps not that "it can't take care of itself" but that it *can*, and that it shows no signs of human occupation. It is said that nature abhors a vacuum. Culture should know. A pronounced or inchoate fear and loathing seem to engulf places culture cannot or does not occupy.[28]

Farmers might seem close to nature because they are outdoors in fresher air more frequently than most people, but a great deal of the plants and animals surrounding them are as artificially imposed (*introduced* is the euphemism) as buildings, sidewalks, and streets. The farmer eliminates and keeps nature at bay as summarily as the developer. If it does not appear so, it is only because animals replace animals and plants replace

plants. The fact that the replacements are commodities rarely causes friction with the idea of farms as nature, especially alongside the existence of
urbs and suburbs often stripped of nature, stocked with culture. But farming, no matter how comparatively peaceful and close to nature by
(sub)urban standards, is an occupation, and the farm is occupied territory.
While farming is less involved in defending against external cultural-
encroachment, internally the farm is all about a constant offensive on
plants, animals, and land.[29]

Mehring's farm, however, less apparently exhibits the occupation of
land or nature per se than occupation of African land. Mehring neither
acknowledges that this land should belong to indigenous Africans nor
admits that his conservation efforts are dubious in nature. This denial of
the problems surrounding his occupation and the disowning of his various
practices—especially his denying the corpse a respectful burial—haunts
him and the farm.

If he would own up to being a trespasser himself, he might be less
haunted and would not have to watch his control slowly seep away. But his
inability to own up allows the corpse to gradually possess the land. The
laborers and their families will not trespass the third pasture where the
corpse lies, and when Mehring goes there he is disturbed by thoughts of
the corpse. Mehring's slow isolation, the allusions to his corpselike status,
and the infertility surrounding him contrast markedly with the land around
the barely buried corpse, which has bloomed after seven years of drought,
the decaying life-giving body rising from its insufficient pit-ock.

Mehring is losing his land, or dying, in three ways: through his isolation, his infertility, and intimations of his death. He is gradually isolated
from everyone and everything he knows: wife, lover, son, workers, land.[30]
His infertility is rife—the land has undergone seven years of drought; his
old friends, Kurt and Emmy are childless; his only son, the androgynously-
named Terry is gay; his wife and lover leave him; his stud bull Nandi
(Shiva's bull, symbol of fertility) cannot mount females; his sexual flight
with the young Portuguese girl is "digital," (he "finger-fucks" her, 126-32);
and, except for a last sexual adventure, he seems not to have had sex for
almost a year (the length of time from the corpse's discovery to its burial).
There are also allusions to Mehring's infertility through stone eggs, an egg-
like marble, and wild guinea-fowl eggs that children play with and that
"will never hatch" (257).[31] Perhaps the most developed example of failed
fertility is Mehring's planting of the two chestnuts, which, in the Old

Testament, spur cattle fertility: "And Jacob took him rods of green poplar, and of the hazel and chestnut tree. . . . And he set the rods which he had pilled [peeled] before the flocks in the gutters in the watering troughs when the flocks came to drink, that they should conceive when they came to drink" (Genesis 30:37-39).[32] But Mehring's Spanish chestnuts seem unlikely to survive. Rootlets snarling from dried-out European packing dirt are "limp and brittle" (225), and once the saplings are set in their holes that smell like a "violated tomb" (226), the pitiful things look like "branches children have stuck in sand to make a 'garden' that will wither in an hour" (226). Mehring is afraid his two hundred rands have been wasted on European or "family" trees, near-dead on arrival.

Land and fertility are also linked through an analogy between women and land throughout the book. For instance, there are the winter landscape of the riverbank—"the bony hip of an Amazon torso"—with river flowing from the "rump," completed by pubic reeds (76); desert "dunes" in ana-grammatical relation with beach "nudes" (103-4); desert and beach sand piled up around *Haus Wusten Ruh,* or Calm Desert House where Mehring remembers having hard-fought-for sex as a boy; and the "soft lap after lap" of desert sands that Mehring's plane crosses while he explores the "lap" of the young Portuguese girl. If Mehring's land complements fertile and eroti-cized woman, fertile due to the corpse's nutritive decay, then sand—as both nude beaches or torsoed deserts—likely indicates infertile sexual activity as it is always present in the same textual locale as sterile sex with women or, on one occasion, when Mehring imagines his son masturbating. Mehring's impotency is not only indicated by infertile desert sands, but is mirrored by his long-lasting inability to make things grow on his four hundred acres and the sterility resulting from his industries' ravishing of African lands.

To nail the lid on isolation and infertility there are repeated references to the groove Mehring's life is stuck in, perhaps creating a riff on *groove* and *grave* or simply making a connection between stagnancy and death. The wet quicksandlike ground even sucks him in, almost whole. When it finally lets him go he "feels like a part of himself is still buried" (228). He seems only good to the land if dead, and nutritively decaying like his "brother," the dead man.[33]

While Mehring is getting closer to the earth through death and senti-ment, the dead man seems to be passing him in the trance (the passageway connecting the realm of the dead with that of the living) coming the other way. Mehring's disowning of the corpse results in alienation from the land he increasingly comes to love. At the same time, the decaying corpse, like a slain vegetation god, enables the land's rebirth through a series of events. The corpse is found in late autumn. A fire then torches the wetland reeds near Mehring's land. Though there are yearly fires in the area, the reeds where the corpse lies shallowly-buried have never before burned and, on the other hand, never has the rest of Mehring's land remained so unharmed. Did the corpse, by burning its nest of reeds make itself appear? Did it protect most of Mehring's land? Does the fire lead to eventual germinations as after a forest fire? Mehring wonders what has happened to the corpse: Is "it consumed as if in a furnace, your whole dirty, violent, threatened and threatening (surely), gangster's (most probably) savage life—poor black scum—cleansed, down there? Escaped from the earth in essence, in smoke?" (110-11). While this smoke rising from a former picnic site— there is an altaresque fire ring of stones where Mehring once roasted a *sheep*—might be diaphanous evidence of the released sins of this "gangster" corpse communicating with a fertilizing rain divinity, the thread of smoke issuing from Mehring's cigarette throughout this scene is infertile because it results in nothing except Mehring's bad health and perhaps even his infertility.

After the fire exposes the area around the shallow grave, the flood then destroys the grave itself, allowing the corpse to rise like Jesus (Mehring indiscriminately denies just about everything immediately after the corpse reappears[34]). Because of the flood, Mehring is unable to drive to his land for two weeks. Several white people are even killed driving on a washed-out road, perhaps in an allusion to the Flood. The only difference is that now it is not the woefully-fallen human race that is destroyed, but members of the wicked white race. Meanwhile Jacobus, Phineas, Izak, and the other farm hands manage perfectly well without Mehring. When Mehring finally returns, he surveys the area around the corpse:

> A stink to high heaven: the burned willows have grown again and the reeds have become thickets of birds, the mealies have stored sweetness of lymph, human milk and semen, all the farm has flowered and burgeoned from him [the dead man], sucking his strength like nectar from a grass straw. (251)

According to Frazer, sacrifice in autumn (when the corpse was found) practiced by ancient agrarian people probably meant that the sacrificed "divinity [was] an embodiment of the earth or of the corn."[35] Mehring's land with its rows of mealies (corn) gains its strength through this dead black man. But it could have been any black African. Solomon himself, another farm hand, almost becomes a corpse in the same pasture. After being beaten up and left for dead, Solomon is discovered barely breathing and with a strange mouthlike wound in his forehead. Another vegetation figure, Hyacinthus, died from such a wound and was later reborn as a flower.[36] Black Africans, in contrast to the white African, Mehring, are shown as fertile. Black children appear in countless places on Mehring's land although they have no active role, speak no lines, and go unnamed and unaccounted for. Black African children open and close *The Conservationist* and seem to be the real occupants and the eventual inheritors of these lands. There is even a reference to one child's dusty penis, an ingenious analogue to that other fertile member, the green thumb.

The corpse is not only the fertile occupant of South African lands, but the rightful one, the one who will set the earth and Africans free to flourish. As such, this corpse is not only like Jesus and Hyacinthus, but also Moses, deliverer of Gordimer's Old Testament African laborers—the corpse was found in wetland reeds (bulrushes) by a river, the same environment where Moses was recovered by Pharoah's daughter in a bulrush basket.[37] Gordimer's corpse is potent deliverer, of race, (blacks and people of color are largely conceived of as mere labor by whites, especially by industrialists like Mehring), of class[38] and of nature. Indigenous Africans and nature, as opposed to European imperialists and their imported culture, are the future of this land. This is not the negative association of blacks and nature Arendt spoke of in volume two, *Imperialism,* of the three-volume, *The Origins of Totalitarianism*[39] but nature and black occupancy as inevitable steps, and as progress. The burgeoning of nature thus represents a nexus of future (the past somewhat redux) and of liberation. That is why Mehring decays on his feet. As he disowns his part in the future (and the past) of this land and *its* people, their traditional and less-destructive occupancy hastens his infertile rotting and the corpse's fertile decay (Mehring's status as dead-living and the corpse's status as living-dead). If Mehring would have respected this dead man enough to have given him a proper burial, he would avoided being another linchpin in apartheid,[40] a prong in the domination/stewardship of nature, and less an example of the need for a new South Africa and for a new practice, or no-practice, of nature. Mehring's audacity and insensitivity results in his demise at the hands of a black population and nature that comes to take him down and possibly out.

In sum, occupancy that is non-imperialist, historical, traditional, and occurring within conditions where nature flourishes wildly, where plants, animals, land, and people are not disenfranchised or decimated by greed or privilege leads to the most unassailable forms of "ownership." Imperialist occupancy—property rights as parcelization and exchange, as labor expended on an object, as occupation by fences, artifacts, gates and No Trespassing signs—becomes death. While property represents only the figurative death of owners, it often results in the real death of the franchise and lives of people within or displaced by an owner's entitlement. *The Conservationist* heralds, instead, an open state where no one can be denied rights of either occupation or access to land and its fruits, and where land, itself, enfranchised for the many, escapes being dominated (through agribusiness, development, dumping, weapons testing) by the few.

6

OWNING UP TO BELONGING
Daughters of the Dust

In *The Conservationist*, land stolen from Africans by white Europeans was put into wealthy white hands, hands like those of the industrialist Mehring who owns a four hundred-acre estate worked by dispossessed farm hands. In the early days of the United States, the analogues of Mehring were European whites who stole land from American Indians and forced dispossessed and chattelized Africans to work as slaves. This similitude makes it possible to imagine *Daughters of the Dust* (1991) as the sequel to *The Conservationist* despite the fact that the events in *Daughters of the Dust* occur in 1902 and the events of *The Conservationist* occur seventy years later. In *Daughters of the Dust*, African blacks own land, which in *The Conservationist* they had been deprived. Here, then, is a chance to see how land fares in a particular case of black ownership and occupation—land that belongs to Gullahs in the Sea Islands off the southern coast of South Carolina. The film also provides an opportunity to examine how land is represented or "possessed" by the writing and direction of Julie Dash and cinematography of Arthur Jafa, in the first nationally-distributed feature by an African American woman.

While the twenty-four-hour diegesis in *Daughters of the Dust* shows neither people-as-property, nor their transition into owning property, the memories of Nana Peazant (Cora Lee Day) and Bilal Muhammed (Umar Abdurrahman)—the sole former slaves in *Daughters of the Dust* —warrant an introductory discussion on the relationship between real and chattel property, especially focusing on the first community of freed slaves during Reconstruction. Therefore, preceding a "closeup" of *Daughters of the Dust*, I will use an extended historical and philosophical "establishing shot" to summarize the postbellum events in the Sea Islands—those events relating to the interconnection of slave property and real property—and will compare these events to the history and philosophy of wage slaves and private property in Europe. Following this background, I will pay attention to the primary text and show that though Sea Island Gullahs *own* themselves and their land, their ownership is tempered by *belonging* to themselves, to one another, and most importantly for *Green Cultural Studies*, to the land they own.

Coming into Their Own
The Violent History of Property

In the opening moments of *Daughters of the Dust*, the only Sea Island Muslim, Bilal Muhammed, inaugurates the day with a prayer to Allah. African Muslims were not only an anomaly within Sea Island Christian/West African religious syncretism, but were also somewhat uncommon among exported slaves. Muslim, Senegambian Mandingas, who spread Islam from east Africa, were the first to meet Portuguese sailors in the fourteenth century on the upper west coast of Africa to trade European goods for African hostages (distinguished from criminals) captured because they would not convert to Islam: "European demand for slaves exacerbated a process of ethnic displacement already occurring in Upper Guinea . . . by Moslem Fula, Susu, and Mandingas."[1] While those captured were primarily non-Muslim, Muslims themselves were not immune from becoming property:

> Besides the slaves which merchants bring down, there are many bought along the river. These are either taken in war, as the former are, or else men condemned for crimes, or else stolen, which is very frequent. . . . Since this slave trade has been us'd, all punishments are changed into slavery; there being an Advantage on such condemnations, they strain for crimes very hard . . . every trifling crime is punished in the same manner.[2]

Perhaps it is surprising that the Nation of Islam rooted itself in American soil: Not only were fewer Muslims sold as slaves, but enslaved Muslims would likely have thought twice about a religion whose members had sold them into slavery.

Many West Africans thus suffered twice in relation to land. First uprooted and driven toward the Atlantic littoral by westwardly expanding Islam, African unbelievers and criminalized believers were forcibly deterritorialized.[3] Second, as property, Africans were removed, shipped as cargo, and set on land they could neither own or territorialize, nor—because they could be sold—possibly even occupy for any length of time. If Africans were generally thought to live closer to nature in the white mind,[4] now they became legally identical with nature: As with plants, animals, or land, they became not only subject to the caprices of owner-ship, but were prevented from owning and territorializing land.

As owned-nature, Africans lost benefits of both wild nature and culture and were declared (a piece of) private property whose offspring would also be property. Those whites who believed themselves separate and above nature thus came to own those perceived as nature. Perhaps if Africans were not first conceptualized as nature by Europeans, they might not have become commodities to such an extent that even the offspring of slaves were—"by nature"—property.[5]

The Gullahs in *Daughters of the Dust* are comprised of both former slaves and the first generations born free. Yet for them slavery has not lost its galling bite. While weaving a basket, Nana Peazant, the Peazant family/clan matriarch, reweaves her days of enslavement: "This was the worst place to have been born during slavery. Our hands, scarred blue with poisonous indigo dye that built up all those plantations from swampland. Our spirits, numb from the sting of fever from the rice fields. Our backs, bent down forever with the planting and hoeing of the Sea Island cotton" (105-6).[6] Scarred hands, numb spirits, and bent backs coincided with scarred, denuded land, bent to the purpose of capital accumulation. But Sea Island Africans were matched to the land even before being forced to work it, or more precisely, matched to the farming of the crops imposed upon the land:

> Most Africans possessed no rudimentary English and had no experi-
> ence with white society. Their value was a long familiarity with plant-
> ing and cultivation of rice and indigo [in Africa], the quality of which
> was said to have surpassed that grown in Carolina. This meant that an
> extensive "breaking in" period and close agricultural supervision of
> "new" Africans was minimal. Thus while Upper Guinea Africans
> may have been preferred because they were tall and considered more
> manageable, evidence also suggests a more sound explanation:
> knowledge of agriculture made these Africans particularly sought
> after in coastal Carolina.[7]

These West Africans, "BaKongo peoples of Kongo-Angolan origin, followed by Upper Guinea Africans of the Senegambia and Windward Coasts,"[8] while matched to the work, were destroyed by its abundance and its dearth of reward. Because slave women were worked to the point of sterility and death, frequent replenishings of slaves became common. From the film we know that Bilal Muhammed came over on the last slave ship, the *Wanderer*, in 1858, over fifty years after importation of slaves became illegal. The constant demand for more African slaves ended up preserving African culture in the United States: Postbellum, Sea Island freedmen and freedwomen and their recent descendants were not only former slaves, but were likely to know those born and raised in West Africa—Nana Peazant, whose mother was likely from the Congo-Angolan region, linked country to person when she said that as a child she "saw Africa in her [mother's] face" (106). Perhaps it was partly the remembrance of freedom in Africa that made slavery so untenable to the generations of Nana and her mother. But whatever the case, it was these generations who experienced the transition from being property to owning property. This transition, absent in the film, is recounted below.

On November 7, 1861, forty-one years before the events in *Daughters of the Dust*, Confederate whites, attacked by Union ships sailing into Port Royal Sound on the southern coast of South Carolina, fled their Sea Island estates. Many slaves refused to follow. Instead, they destroyed cotton gins and, along with Union soldiers, looted mansions. When the sacking ended, Union forces declared the runaway slaves "contraband of war": No longer slave or chattel property blacks became property seized as the result of the South's "criminality" (secession), and plundered for Union advantage.[9] The slave's redefinition as a new kind of property was the first stumbling toward The Port Royal Experiment, a project designed to make citizens and property-owners of former slaves in Port Royal, South Carolina.

Dash's magnificent filming of *Daughters of the Dust* portrays the Sea Island setting of The Port Royal Experiment some hundred years after slavery:

> Few lived long in the islands without responding to the somber spell of the great live oaks with their festoons of Spanish moss. In spring the islands became intoxicatingly beautiful, alive with lush greenery and the color and fragrance of yellow jasmine, roses, and acacia blossoms. In the fall the scarlet cassena berries gleamed along the roadside

hedges with the white tufts of the mockingbird flower. The creeks abounded in fish, oysters, and crabs; on the outer islands wild deer and game birds grew fat and plentiful. One asset the visitor never failed to note was the remarkable song of the mockingbird.[10]

Contrast this description with that by Austa Mansfield French, abolitionist and educator, one of Port Royal's first teachers. Seeing the Sea Islands for the first time, French wrote: "Slavery is written upon the shore, the trees, the sky, the air. . . . The enormous black hawks, with their screams, seem to be its very spirit. No wonder they caw, caw, over this land—mean vultures, waiting for blood."[11] As in some readings of the Fall, nature falls because humans do and comes to look as if it sanctioned slavery.

Agostinho Neto—poet, leader of the socialist MPLA[12], and president of independent Angola (1975-79)—describes a contemporary Africa branded by slavery and struggle, memories of which are kept alive by the poem's "we" that stands for Africa's exiled Diasporic sons and daughters:

> *They live*
> *the grieved lands of Africa*
> *because we are living*
> *and are imperishable particles*
> *of the grieved lands of Africa.*[13]

Neto's Africa is marked by grief and is kept alive by the "imperishable particles," some of which are the successive generations of daughters of the dust.

Statements by Nana Peazant, Agostinho Neto, and Austa French, indicate that land marks and is marked by occupants, that land impresses and is impressed upon. Peazant's African land in her mother's face conveys the fresh indignity of enslavement. Neto's African land empathetically grieves for or becomes its grieving exiles. French's Sea Islands become complicit, through indifference or wickedness, with slavery. Such associations through metonymy (land contiguous with people) or through synecdoche (people as part of land) characterize the statements of Peazant, Neto, and French. Even at the risk of making too much of tropes, land tropically shackled to human affairs is literarily—but not literally—enslaved, subject to the vicissitudes of affirmative or negative association. Imagine an opposite figuration where people are tropically shackled to nature: in the fully flora-ed and fauna-ed Sea Islands, slavery looks natural. Or, in the landscapes of Hiroshima and Nagasaki shortly after the bombs, its people—disfigured or not—are shunned because they are associated with obliteration.

Back in the Sea Island setting, the contraband of war—the generation of Bilal Muhammed and of Nana Peazant in events before the time of Dash's film—rebel against the driver-led, gang labor system (a holdover from slavery) that was reinstituted by Port Royal experimenters in April 1862. Two landless laborers refuse to work the cotton for the required four hours and one draws a knife on the white boss. Without further incident, a new labor arrangement is instituted: Each black family is now assigned a portion of land to garden as it chooses, and in addition, individuals work the whites' cotton crop for wages, and decide the length of time they work.[14] This new work arrangement conforms to no clear classification of property relations. Instead, it combines particular features of communism, feudalism, and private property. The plan at Port Royal resembles communism because the Union's representatives more equitably redistribute the land. The plan also resembles feudalism because the serfs or *peasants*—who in *Daughters of the Dust* become *Peazants*—are forced to remain on the land they control, owe their bodies as soldiers to the *lord* (the Union), and have access to the *commons* (land unoccupied by people).[15] Finally, The Port Royal work plan resembles a system of private property because it is only wage labor that allows access to both private land and money, otherwise rendered off limits. All in all, Port Royal's plan of syncretized property relations is noteworthy because under a dominant system, more interesting and equitable arrangements are possible, even if at the cost of a little struggle.[16]

The Union's seizure of southern property by violence and blacks' access to property through threat of violence indicates that dominant forms of property relations are changed most profoundly by violence or its threat. John Locke's 1690 observation that "where there is no property there is no injustice"[17] inspired the following statement from Jean-Jacques Rousseau in 1754:

> The first person who, having enclosed a plot of land, took it into his head to say *this is mine* and found people simple enough to believe him was the true founder of civil society. What crimes, wars, murders, what miseries and horrors would the human race have been spared, had someone pulled up the stakes or filled in the ditch and cried out to his fellow men: "Do not listen to this impostor. You are lost if you forget that the fruits of the earth belong to all and the earth to no one!"[18]

In the late nineteenth century, Paul Lafargue also grounded property in violence: "Jurists, politicians, religious and socialist reformers have repeatedly discussed the rights of property, and these discussions, how interminable soever, have always come back to the initial point, to wit, that property had been established by violence, but that time, which disfigures all things, had added grace and sanctity to property."[19] What kinds of violence underlay the "grace and sanctity of property"? Lafargue says, "on the one hand it [feudalism] grew out of the conditions under which the village collectives evolved, and on the other it sprang from conquest."[20] But even Lafargue's evolving conditions were violent, "forced appropriation." In general, forced appropriation arose from the inequality of the village's clan or family allotments: In order to pay regressive, fixed taxes rather than taxes based on crop yields, people with less borrowed from people with more. When villagers did not pay increasing debts, their land was taken by creditors. As a result, more land and the fruits thereof increasingly fell to fewer owners, creating a vicious acceleration of borrowing and loss.[21]

Especially ignominious was the transition in England from feudalism to private property. While serfdom disappeared toward the end of the fourteenth century, most of the population would continue to work the land. The first peasant evictions came when burgeoning wool industrialists were faced with more foreign markets than wool to supply them. To get more wool, industrialists offered landed-lords money to turn their peasant-worked arable land into pasture, or "sheepwalks." The numerous peasants who had worked the land were evicted from these sheepwalks and were forced to become cheap labor for the wool industry.[22] Evictions came again with the enclosure acts of 1709-1869: Through parliamentary law backed up with force, peasants were thrown off land they worked and forced into the cities to look for work. The lucky ones sold their labor cheap. Others starved or became thieves or beggars.[23] Against these latter two groups, cruel legislation was passed.[24] This was justified on the basis of increasing the wealth of the nation, or what Americans call the economy or the GNP.[25]

But back in Port Royal, violence is largely a background issue. After the two-man revolt of April 1862 there was little actual violence leading to black ownership until March 9, 1863, eighteen months after Union troops forcibly confiscated southern property.[26] About seventeen thousand acres of land was sold at a dollar an acre and blacks bought two thousand acres with pooled savings from one year's wages in whites' cotton fields. The sale rendered these contraband of war de facto citizens six years before the Fourteenth Amendment (1868).

From there, almost two years of political and social struggle passed before any more land was allotted to freedmen and freedwomen. The next move, however, was summary: General Sherman's Special Field Orders No. 15 (January 1865), designates the whole of the Sea Islands, from Charleston, South Carolina, to the St. John's River in northern Florida, and thirty miles inland, "for exclusive Negro settlement" (328). By mid-1865, forty thousand blacks were settled in the Sea Islands. A contemporaneous reporter described it this way: "He [Ulysses Houston, a black minister] and his fellow colonists selected their lots, laid out a village, numbered their lots, put the numbers in a hat, and drew them out. . . . It was Plymouth colony repeating itself" (331). But this celebratory scene was countered by another where thousands of black war-refugees finally reached the Islands only to die of exhaustion, disease, or hunger since "freedom means death to many" (332).

Two months after Sherman's Orders, the Freedman's Bureau Act was passed in March 1865, "legalizing the military action taken by Sherman" (338). Property seemed secure in the hands of blacks, that is, until a month later when Andrew Johnson, friend of dispossessed Confederate white planters, became president. Johnson immediately attempted to get whites back any unsold land (most of the Sherman land was only claimed) and in February 1866, vetoed even a heavily compromised bill that allowed blacks possession of the Sherman lands for only three years. Betrayed for the umpteenth time, many blacks were either forced to work as wage slaves for returning exslavemasters or be kicked off the land altogether by the Union's occupying forces. To compensate for this new round of white coercion, blacks worked at a leisurely pace or worked only on the newer Yankee-owned estates; as a result southern planters had difficulty finding productive workers. On some estates, blacks still had claim to a few acres where they raised a multiculture of tomatoes, okra, huckleberries, and watermelons, which caused southern planters to complain that blacks worked too little on the planters' cotton. Finally in July 1866, five months after blacks were betrayed on the Sherman lands, Congress overrode Johnson's February veto of the Freedman's Act, but not before the act had been compromised: "The Negroes who had been ousted from the Sherman lands would get no more, it was now clear, than permission to lease twenty-acre lots in other government-owned lands, with a six-year option to buy" (374).

The incidents at Port Royal constitute a history of land relations that differ from those that Marx, Lafargue, and Polanyi explicated and enumerated regarding England. In Port Royal, land was confiscated by the forces of internal central authority (the Union), distributed to people-as-property (contraband of war), and eventually given or sold at a low price to people-no-longer-property. This is an infrequent instance of a positive transition to private property, to private property as substantial freedom (because it does not involve forced labor); in the European transition from conquered, to feudal, to private property, landowners, and those having any access to land, decreased.[27] But in the extant case, Sea Island slaves were neither evicted from the land nor forced into cities for anywork at anywage, where theoretically they might regain access to land through a lifetime of labor (most former slaves were not so lucky).

And what of the violence done to the land itself? By the 1870s Willie Lee Rose describes the South Carolina coastal country as "suffering":

> The amount of land under cultivation in Beaufort County had fallen from 259,543 acres in 1860 to 150,000 in 1870. Some land was idle because of the cost of restoring the expensive system of dikes for flooding the rice lands, but other land was in disuse because many Northern investors had failed at cotton planting. Many old owners who had regained their land could afford to operate only with small acreages. In the three years before the war the Sea Island cotton crop had amounted to 54,904 bales; but in the three years between 1870 and 1873 the total output had only amounted to 23,207 bales. (381)

Former plantation lands plummeted in value and "most of the freedmen who retained farms were living—in the years just after the war—at a subsistence level raising vegetable crops with enough cotton to produce a little ready cash and pay the taxes" (382). After a tidal wave in 1893 and boll weevils in 1918 "the long-staple cotton crop disappeared, making room for new crops better suited to the new institutions of freedom and small landownership" (407).

Rose had called these Sea Islands of the 1860s and 1870s a "suffering" region with "idle" land. But by 1890, when three-fourths of the land in Beaufort County, South Carolina was African American-owned—and still "idle"—his tune changed: "The freedmen had become self-supporting, if not wealthy. They paid their taxes, and they took care of their local troubles with aplomb" (408). With a change in labor relations, a decrease in labor, and a narrower gap between excessive wealth and extreme poverty (slavery), the soil-enervating monoculture of cotton decreased (indigo and rice production waned earlier), liberating greater areas of land for wild plants and animals. People and land went from destructively productive to productively idle.

To a subsistence laborer, even when the laborer owns the land, land translates into work less than wealth. Locke believed that before money, more property meant more labor, which prevented excessive land expropriation: "Right and convenience went together; for as a man had a right to all he could employ his labor upon, so he had no temptation to labor for more than he could make use of."[28] The lack of temptation to expropriate increasingly-larger areas of land pointed to agriculture as violence against the body of the laborer, a violence not lost on Lafargue and Rousseau. As Lafargue asserted, "Agriculture, which led to private property in land, introduced the servile labour, which in the course of centuries has borne the names of slave-labour, bond-labour, and wage-labour."[29] Thus, agricultural labor is like Adam and Eve's original toil that was a major element of their punishment and subsequent sorrow. Former slaves would be especially well-acquainted with labor-as-violence, not only the backbreaking kind associated with work, but the backlashed kind following the refusal or inability to work.

Besides punished bodies, Genesis 3:17 also indicates agriculture's connection to punished or cursed ground[30]—not only the land's forced fertility (and sometimes resulting sterility) by agriculture, but the propertization of land, its *bounding* by walls and fences. Rousseau contemplates how violation of body led to violation of land:

> What man would be so foolish as to tire himself out cultivating a field that will be plundered by the first comer, be it man or beast, who takes a fancy to the crop? And how could each man resolve to spend his life in hard labor, when, the more necessary to him the fruits of his labor may be, the surer he is of not realizing them? In a word, how could this situation lead men to cultivate the soil as long as it is not divided among them, that is to say, as long as the state of nature is not wiped out?[31]

Wilderness—Rousseau's "state of nature"—is "wiped out" by enclosure. The end of wilderness is not necessarily destruction of land per se, but the end of an ideology of land as no one's/everyone's, the opposite pole of private property. While some would rightly object that even animal territory is a kind of proto-property,[32] the ideology of territory is substantially different. Establishers of territory might put it this way: The land whose boundaries I/we mark must be constantly defended ("because" there is no such thing as property). Acknowledgers of territory might say to themselves: Moving beyond these markings involves some risk, but nothing and no one is preventing my entrance. These statements point to property's absence, and offer a vision of occupied yet unbounded land upon which unbounded movement is still possible. Whether the difference between territory and property is deemed a matter of quality or quantity, property is an egregious form of territory that keeps out most people, animals, and even plants even when they represent no threat.

In The Port Royal Experiment, former people-as-property coming into their own by owning themselves and the land off which they live is a movement toward a twofold liberation of people and land. In this historical introduction, the emancipation of African slaves has been interwoven with an emancipation of land—some land freed from all agriculture, other land partially freed from the intensive monocultures of rice, cotton, and indigo. The increased liberation of Sea Island land under freedmen and freedwomen, however, gives no reason to call emancipated slaves proto-environmentalists or nature-lovers. More liberated land under the control of West Africans and their descendants is less about having a progressive (African) vision of land, than not having a regressive (Western) mythology of progress. While white Euro-Americans primarily looked at or treated land as abstracted national wealth or personal property, Africans viewed land as a place from which to obtain food and shelter, and in the case of Sea Island slaves, a place to get away from whites, and their work "ethic." Although not a political vision of nature per se, the African vision of land-use furthers a politics of nature without expressly invoking it, is more centered on liberating human activity, or culture, than land/worldnature. Thus land and worldnature gain not only from culture's reinvention of its concepts of nature, but from culture's reinvention of itself.[33] Or, in the case of Sea Islanders, reclaiming the African cultures of which and from which they were robbed.

Coming to Belong

By 1866, Sea Island freedmen and freedwomen were freer to choose between African and American cultures. *Daughters of the Dust* depicts Africa looming larger in the lives of first-generation freed slaves, Nana

Peazant and Bilal Muhammed, than in each successive generation: Viola's mother (Geraldine Dunston) remembers few African words, the younger Haagar (Kaycee Moore) downright scorns African ways, and her daughter, My Own (Eartha D. Robinson), wants to be "a new kind of woman" on the mainland. The loss is somewhat slowed in 1902 when the Sea Islands are revisited by those who have experienced mainland culture or feel the allure of Sea Island African roots: Yellow Mary (Barbara-O), Viola Peazant (Cheryll Lynn Bruce), the photographer, Mr. Snead (Tommy Hicks) and Trula (Trula Hoosier). Of these four, only Trula returns to the mainland, and she leaves for reasons more complex than not being a Peazant.[34] On that day in 1902, the loss of African culture was also interrupted by those who chose to stay on Dahtaw (Gullah for "daughter") Island, and those who foresaw the struggle on the mainland: Eula (Alva Rogers), Eli (Adisa Anderson), and St. Julian Last Child (M. Cochise Anderson).

The threat of mass departure by the Peazants forces a kind of second freedom after the first freedom granted by the Emancipation Proclamation and the Thirteenth, Fourteenth, and Fifteenth Amendments. The second freedom allows the Peazants to choose between mainland Euroculture and island Afroculture, and between culture and nature. Whether all the Peazants know it as well as Yellow Mary, the choice is also between once again between being owned—this time as wage slaves by racist whites—or owning oneself and one's land. The fact that so many of the older main characters decide to stay on Dahtaw Island who previously had planned to go (Eli, Eula, Yellow Mary, Viola, Mr. Snead), and that those leaving seem somewhat unaware of what awaits them (especially Haagar), puts Dash firmly on the side of those choosing to stay and remain owners of a greater measure of autonomy, of Sea Island African culture, and of access to land or nature.[35]

The decision to retain or own self, culture, and land, however, is marked by its participation in, and appearance of, belonging to self, culture, and land. Because owning and belonging are interwoven, and because *Green Cultural Studies* focuses on figurations of nature, land being its broadest category, I will show the way to an interweaving of owning and belonging. There are three means in *Daughters of the Dust* through which people can belong to land: through photography, through belief (myth/religion), and through dwelling (leisure, labor, and social organization).

Photography

As Viola represents Western religious culture, her photographer, Mr. Snead, represents Western scientific culture, a culture skillful at entrapping an entity in order to know and reproduce it, especially in photography. Snead comes to Dahtaw Island primarily to do a job, to photograph the Peazant exodus from—as Viola would have it—ignorant nature to enlightened culture. However, most Peazants choose to stay; not even the non-Peazant, Snead, returns. What takes hold of this man of reason, this photographer whose profession is centered around trapping evanescence and creating history? Perhaps it is African culture, since Snead is always inquiring about "the old ways." But if Snead is an aesthete first, and an African second then perhaps the beautiful Sea Island context—as well as the African text—contributes to the attraction Snead develops to African ways and history, to the Peazant family, and to making pictures that incorporate "beauty, simplicity, and science"?[36]

For Snead's first shoot, he leads the Peazant men across a beach glistening in pink light. Filmed at high angle and in long shot, the group moves away across the lower right corner of the screen. Except Snead, that is, who disappears frame-right.[37] Such technical choices show men getting smaller (even disappearing in Snead's case) in relation to landscape—those central characters of sand, sky, and ocean. While it is unclear who owns this beach, the men searching for the proper setting and lighting to photograph walk here and there "like they own it," but seem, cinematographically, to be controlled by or belong to it. The diegetic search on the beach reproduces the film crew's own experience:

> Due to environmental restrictions, we couldn't take a four-wheel-drive vehicle on the nature trail or along the coastline, so all the equipment had to be carried in each morning. We also couldn't bring in a generator, so A.J. [Arthur Jafa, Director of Photography] decided to shoot with natural light—sunlight—only. Therefore we needed to squeeze in as much shooting time every day as the sun would allow. Often we would be in the middle of setting up or shooting a particular scene when the sun would suddenly cast perfect and beautiful light in another spot. We would hurriedly change directions and capture the unscheduled scene with only a moment's notice. Sometimes this would work, sometimes it failed comically; but we kept shooting (10-11).

Cast and crew, surrendering to limited technology and natural light, experienced a belonging or contented subjection that contributes to the film's atypical treatment of nature and culture: *Daughters of the Dust* is shot almost completely out-of-doors (unique for anything other than a nature documentary), with few props, and with landscape occupying a large area in most framings.[38]

In one scene, Snead, while trying to photographically capture the Peazant men, is himself captured, not only by beachscape but by the Unborn Child, phantom daughter of wind and ocean, who appears only in the viewfinder of Snead's camera. This child of nature who takes possession of Snead's camera later holds a stereoscopic viewer which, in her hands only, makes photos come alive, cinematic, more like nature/reality. In *Daughters of the Dust,* phototechnology setting out to capture landscape becomes itself captured and animated by a child of wind and sea.

In a second photo shoot, Snead stumbles backwards into a bog. Not realizing he is being metaphorically and humorously overwhelmed by these islands, he instead worries about being swallowed by gators. In another photo shoot he tells the whole Peazant clan, "Look! Look up! . . . And remember . . . Ibo Landing!" (149) because it is the place, perhaps as much as its people, that has captured his senses, imagination, enthusiasm.

Snead is helped in his decision to not return to the mainland, by the Island that sets everything—the people, the culture, even himself and especially Viola Peazant—"in a good light." Island sensuousness becomes Sneadian sensuality: Twice Snead boldly grabs and kisses the chastely-Christian Viola when Island-inspired desire overwhelms cultural propriety. The photographer capturing scenes and light becomes captured by Sea Island African ways and people set within the sensuality of land and light that holds everything within their "camera."

Nature as photographer? Niepce labeled his early photography, "heliography" (sun writing). Fox Talbot called the camera "the pencil of nature." Daguerre called photography the "reproduction of the images of nature."[39] Snead progressively moves from being a photographer to a figure in nature's own camera. Surely he realizes that remaining on the Sea Islands will limit his photographic pursuits. Supplies will be a problem. If Snead finally puts down his camera altogether, it might indicate that he belongs to land more than landscape belongs to him, and that he belongs to natural evanescence more than spectacular permanence belongs to him.

Belief

People take hold of photographs that, in turn, possess them. If the mind can be said to carry and summon images, remembered photographs are surely part of the stuff of remembered images. Another way to carry images is by way of religious, mythical, and historical narratives that connect people not only to people, but to land.

As a result of Nana Peazant's memories, a viewer might think that because of slavery African Americans tend to connect negatively with the American south, and by metonymy, perhaps even with the land itself. Africa, on the other hand, with its associations of freedom and autonomy before the fall (slavery), is more apt to produce a positive reaction, perhaps even to the land itself.[40] If, to the Africans who worked it, southern land itself seemed to enchain them, memories of African lands comfortingly linked exile to exile, and exile to homeland. When freed slaves took up residence in the Sea Islands, they, in many ways, went back to Africa in the way they lived on the land they owned. Their ownership was less a matter of agitated accrual of land and objects, and more about satisfied subsistence, an ideology of land that moves away from debasing it as property.

One of the few sources of inspiration for land as something other than property blew in with the ships crowded with enslaved West Africans, people themselves turned into property and eventually freed. While the people and religions of West Africa are many, certain tendencies of belief concerning land are shared. I cite some of these overgeneralized notions in the hope they will complicate the Western stock of attitudes about land.

Let a turtle lead us. Recall the film's turtle with the symbol (see figure on next page) painted on her shell, the one handed from a young boy ("Ninnyjugs") to an elder ("Daddy Mac"). The turtle, it is said, carries his home on his back. Here the home is decorated with a BaKongo or KiKongo symbol of the sun's movement around the earth. The scene with the turtle suggests several comparisons: animal to human, youth to age, creature to home,[41] and in the symbol itself, earth to sun (the outer circles represent solar positions around the inner circle, the earth). Earth and sun are tied even more intrinsically because the daily relationship of Earth and sun correspond with the cycle of earthly life:

> Using the sun through its course around the earth, the BaKongo pointed out the four stages which make up one's life cycle: (1) rising— meaning birth, beginning, or regrowth, (2) ascendancy—meaning

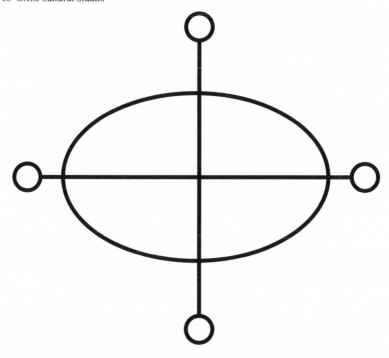

maturity and responsibility, (3) setting—implying death and transformation, (4) midnight, indicating existence in the other world and
eventual rebirth. Life was a continuum and the sign of the four
moments of the sun symbolized "spiritual continuity and renaissance"
via its spiral journey.[42]

The sun that does not die, that is reborn every morning to Belial's prayers,
indicates or reflects a human life disappearing behind death only to reappear on the other side as birth and infancy. The continuity of the dead with
the living is what Nana tries to implant in the young, specifically that the
Unborn Child lives with the ancestors in the infinity of light, wind, and
ocean.[43]

In addition to extraterrestrial belonging, there is the metaphysical way
people belong to the land in which they reside. The film's Gullah legend of
the Ibo walking across the sea to West Africa tells not only of a proud people who refuse slavery, but of a people so attached to homeland that water

presents no obstacle to their Christlike walking. The Ibo's African homeland is a continuum of people, land, and nature established especially through burial: "Here [in Iboland] nature is typified more concretely by the 'land'—the abode of man, plants, animals and all other living creatures as well as the earth, which is the abode of the spirit of ancestors and the place where all dead members of the community are buried."[44] Taken from their homeland, the enslaved Ibo would lose the land's protection, that continuity between themselves, guardian ancestors, and the land in which their ancestors are buried. Edmund Ilogu describes Ibo religious belief as "ontocratic," as: "having an understanding of reality in terms of a total order of harmony between nature and man, between the spirit world including one's ancestors (to state it in Ibo's cosmic terms) and the natural world of men and their society."[45] Within this weblike totality, it is difficult to draw a clear line between possession of, or being possessed by the land/nature.[46] This belonging—the living to the dead to the unborn to the land to the cosmos—yields an African stewardship ethic:

> Of all the duties owed to the ancestors none is more imperious than that of husbanding the resources of the land so as to leave it in good shape for posterity. In this moral scheme the rights of the unborn play such a cardinal role that any traditional African would be nonplussed by the debate in Western philosophy as to the [very] existence of such rights. In the upshot there is a two-sided concept of stewardship in the management of the environment involving obligations to both ancestors and descendants which motivates environmental carefulness, all things being equal.[47]

While Nana's sentiments and ideology might make her seem owned by the past, she is also owned by the future. Eli and Nana's conversation in the graveyard about the living's debt to the ancestors is intercut with children playing a game on the beach: "Here comes another one just like the other one," the children say while a young girl blows a bubble pipe from which issues a continuous chain of connected spheres that suggest successive generations. Past and future so connect as to become conflated in Nana's assertion: "The ancestors and the womb . . . they're one, they're the same" (94).

Nana, however, is not owned by the past as some of her descendants think; after all, she mischievously takes Eli's gift of tobacco at the grave of her husband who forbade her such pleasure. Neither is it correct to say that Nana does not understand the symbolic nature of objects that indicate the ancestors. She clarifies her understanding to Haagar: "Nobody ever said that the old souls were living inside those glass jars. The bottle tree reminds us of who was here and who's gone on" (148). Nana's West African perspective does not entrap the living in the past or future, but cradles them in a time that owns all things, time that competes with N/nature for a notion of totality. A West African time/nature totality disrupts a Western religious notion of nature as time past and culture as nature's development, telos, and future. In most West African world-views, world-nature and human culture are, at all times, indissoluble from each other and from past-present-future. Nature is not a past to overcome or escape with progress. Nonetheless, an afterlife is super-natural, which points to a culture not fully accepting its belonging to temporality/nature. Not accepting itself as mortal, a culture may constantly have to prove to itself its eternality by living as large and as long as possible. On such proving grounds, individual plants and animals are subjugated.

Dwelling

Dwelling is the most pervasive way people belong to land. Dwelling precedes the agreement, contract, and deed, and with them, exists coextensively. Heidegger's work inspired the title for this subsection because his version of *dwelling*, while mostly related to *building*, is larger: *"Only if we are capable of dwelling, only then can we build."*[48] He continues, "Dwelling, however, is *the basic character* of Being, in keeping with which mortals exist."[49] Building, Heidegger means, should only be the result of dwelling, not dwelling's cause or proof. In this subsection I will discuss how the Peazants belong to or dwell on/in the land. I will proceed from activities less involved with ownership to those most involved with it: from leisure, to labor, and to social organization.

Leisure: There is much resting in *Daughters of the Dust*. In what might seem the exact antithesis of cinema (from the Greek *kinema* meaning motion), especially in decades dominated by the action flick, resting does retain another crucial aspect of cinema: the spectacular (from the Latin, *spectare*, which means to look). Numerous scenes in *Daughters of the Dust* reveal characters resting near or in trees. Some shots depict trees enthroning the resters.[50] But *thrones* is anthropocentric. Jafa respects that these trees are not props, not even for a movie (prop being short for property). He usually situates people within the tree, rarely pushing in so close to a person that the tree is off-frame. Actually, the opposite is far more frequent:

The camera is positioned so that human action is contextualized. Recall St. Julian Last Child in the magnificent oak: The camera, in long shot, slowly pans back to extreme long shot as Last Child virtually disappears in arborific immensity and fullness, and as Iona—reading St. Julian's love letter to her in voice-over—chants, "Signed, St. Julian Last Child. Son of the Cherokee Nation, Son of these Islands we call Dahtaw, Coosa, Edisto [etc.]" (91). The camera seems to add, "Son of Oak Trees." Not only does Last Child belong to this tree and these islands, but the islands become ancestors themselves, as the status of the buried is carried over by metonymy to the soil of burial. This close relationship between soil and ancestors foreshadows the end of the film when Last Child undermines Iona's departure to the mainland. Despite her *proper* (from the Latin *proprietas*, meaning peculiarity, ownership) name, Iona (I-own-her) will not allow herself to be owned by her mother who wants to kill off the family tree through leaving the Sea Islands. Iona will, however, belong to a man who in turn believes he belongs to ancestral land.

In another scene, Eula talks to Yellow Mary and Trula who rest in a stunning tree festooned with epiphytic Spanish moss (this moss resides on these trees without owning/destroying them). Even while Yellow Mary berates the "backwater" and "desolate" character of the Sea Islands, and Eula tells of a girl drowned by a slavemaster and of her own longing for her dead mother, these weighty events are overshadowed by this massive tree, which no matter how close the camera gets to the people, is always in or dominating the shot, rendering human concerns details in the life of this tree. Trees, here and in others scenes (the family photo, the newlyweds together, the final gathering the day before exodus), own this film, its characters, and perhaps the sentiments of a large percentage of moviegoers.[51]

Two other activities somewhere between labor and leisure are worth mentioning, hair-braiding and mapmaking, correlated not in the film itself, but in the script's directions: "PEAZANT MEN map out on a piece of paper the roads and trails that will lead them North. The hairbraider borrows the pattern of the roads and trails being etched out on paper by the men; she creates a hairstyle that is a map of their migration north by parting, sectioning and braiding an elaborate hair design" (87). There could hardly be a more powerful icon of belonging to land.

Walking is another leisure activity in *Daughters of the Dust*. On several occasions a group of actors walk away from the camera and *into* the landscape in long shot. Yet the most literal scene of "into-ness," appears only in the script where the film's ending illustrates the film's title in a walking scene. Eula, Nana, and Yellow Mary walk on a beach across the center of the frame in long shot and slow motion and then walk offscreen at the right. However, the script reads: "while they are walking, each woman individually turns to dust and blows into the burning sun" (164). In the script, the three more substantially approach the eternal in the sense that their substance fuses with land's. Here, it is not soul or spirit that is continuous, but the opposite, substance especially of bodies and land.[52]

Through such instances of dwelling—resting, mapmaking/hair-braiding, and walking—land, is spared. Heidegger argues that

> Real sparing is something *positive* and takes place when we leave something beforehand in its own essence . . . when we "free" it in the proper sense of the word into a preserve of peace. To dwell, to be set at peace, means to remain at peace within the free, the preserve, the free sphere that safeguards each thing in its essence. *The fundamental character of dwelling is this sparing.*[53]

Heidegger's frequent use of *in* implies that people belong to land more than land belongs to people. While nature as a realm only of peace is too sentimental, and while resting does not *actively* preserve, set free or spare, it is by these leisure activities, more than any other human activity, that land retains more of what it is or has. Land remains a valued entity in being spared, and in land's otherness or difference people have, through leisure at, in, on, or within a site, the best chance of becoming part of land, belonging to it.

Labor: On the other hand there is dwelling as labor, or what Heidegger calls building (I expand its definition to encompass not only architecture but agriculture). But when seeing people toil on the land or in a setting that bespeaks nature, dwelling is not what comes to mind. Laboring is only thought to be dwelling when people live on the land they work. Dwelling usually connotes staying—especially with stability—in a more leisurely fashion. For example, one is said to dwell on a problem when meditating, thinking, or concentrating, activities that resemble a body at rest even though the mind could be either busy or resting. The upshot is that if more friction exists between laboring and dwelling than between leisure and dwelling, people who attempt to dwell on, with, or in the land will need to dwell on making labor more like the leisure depicted in *Daughters of the Dust.*

Indeed, the film shows more leisure than labor.[54] Virtually all the film's labor is shown in the diegetic past (indigo dyemaking, rice husking, and farming). The exceptions are Eli blacksmithing, the men gathering Spanish moss, and women preparing food—the lattermost activity resembling leisure more than labor because it is done while sitting and conversing outdoors. As a result of so much leisure, some viewers had the idea the Peazants worked very little. In a lengthy conversation with bell hooks on labor and leisure, Julie Dash says:

> Early on I received criticism from people, including a lot of black folk, because they wanted to see this family, the Peazant family toiling in the soil. They wanted to see them working. If they didn't see them physically working, then they didn't understand how they lived, how they had food, how they survived. And I kept telling people, look, you don't work on a Sunday, the day that you're saying good-bye to your great-grandmother. (43)
>
> They [the viewers] could not accept the fact that this family had food because they were able to sustain themselves from what they planted and what they pulled from the sea. Now, I kept saying this in the dialogue, but still people kept saying, where did they get that food, that beautiful food? (45)

Siding with viewers, there *is* little about the Peazants working in the diegetic present. Most work is in the diegetic past. Yet siding with Dash, it is hard to believe that most viewers would think the Peazants did not fish and farm for food, even if such labor was not shown. Haagar's remark about the exoticism of Yellow Mary's gift of store-bought biscuits indicates that the Peazants labor for their food. The film also infers that subsistence has been challenging from the time the Peazants first claimed this monoculturally-damaged land to the day of this plentiful picnic in 1902. Recall Nana's flashback where dust blows from her open hands as she asks her husband, "Shad, how can we plant in this dust?" Shad replies, "We plant each and every year, or we're finished!" (158) And Nana asks her progeny: "How can you leave this soil . . . this soil. The sweat of our love, it's here in this soil" (154).

So while the Peazants are skilled leisurers, they also labor for food, clothing, tools and shelter. In Marxist terms, they are nonalienated: They follow food from source to table, follow iron to tools, and trees to homes. Not only is each worker likely to see production beginning to end, but the community is likely to grasp these processes. Here, boss-less laborers live together with consumers. There is little need for transportation systems to move materials to producers, or products to consumers.

Most labor on Dahtaw Island is surely measured in "humanpower." It takes one unit of humanpower (St. Julian Last Child) to move a wheelbarrow of Spanish moss from trees to home. If work is done by humanpower, as in the flashback of Shad Peazant planting with an African heel-toe method, no animals are forced into servitude, no land is destroyed by domestic grazing, and there is insignificant impact on the area's soil, air, water. Further, ground that cannot be farmed by limited humanpower is not forced under the plow. And the space dedicated to shelter, since it is also built by hand, will likely be more modest.

It is these methods applied to culture, not nature (in other words, not to a separate policy of preservation or conservation of nature) that allows wild nature to reoccupy more area. Though the Peazants and Last Child seem to be even less vitally concerned with a politics of nature than the modern day environmentalized citizen, there is little need. Island practice shows that what is most necessary for a politics of nature is a politics of culture, in this case, practices that have left the Sea Islands relatively undeveloped even today. As late as 1975, seventy-two years after the Peazant picnic, forests and wetlands occupied three-quarters of coastal Charleston County, within which are many of the Sea Islands.[55] As a result:

> The landscape is pastoral and mysterious compared to inland areas of the United States. Most islands are characterized by graceful palmetto trees, expansive green terrain, and atmospheric haze. The landscape in fact bears a striking resemblance to the topography of such coastal countries as Nigeria, Ghana, Angola, and Liberia, the tropical homelands of the Sea Islanders' ancestors.[56]

Through labor that retains a village or community dimension, uprooted Africans have rescued many of these islands from European-Americans and re-created an African America.[57]

Social Organization: The Peazants appear to own their land as a clan or family, rather than as individuals. It might be wise to begin this discussion with Africa as care or stewardship of African land is a matter that affects the dead, the living, and the unborn. The same is true of ownership: "[T]he land, the most fundamental means of livelihood, belongs not to individuals but to whole clans, and individuals only have rights of use that they are obligated to exercise considerately so as not to render nugatory the similar rights of future members of the clan. The clan itself is thought of as consisting of members living in the world of ordinary sensible experience, those living in the post-mortem world of the ancestors and those yet to be born."[58] In the African traditions preserved on the Sea Islands, the extended family is also the norm:

> Most islands are sectioned off into family communities, where all members of one family, their close relatives, and people remotely related live or have a right to live as long as they can satisfactorily show evidence of kinship. Land is not normally sold to family members but is passed on through an unwritten contract called "heir's land"; if land *is* sold to relatives, the charge is only one dollar to fulfill "legal tenets of the state."[59]

While such a system could run into the uneven distribution problems of inheritance, the amount of Sea Island land is small and in proportion to comfortably subsistent living. In addition, such a system ensures that all people born on these islands will be able to provide for themselves on the land, obviating absolute dependence upon jobs, money, and development. With this version of heir's land, people gain an automatic livelihood, a means of self-reliance and autonomy from uncontrollable economic systems that transforms people into commodities (workers) consumed by employers.

Communal or familial responsibility for land is accompanied by community respect and responsibility for its members. In the Sea Islands "common-law marriages are as valid and stable in the eyes of the community as those marriages contracted under law."[60] In addition there is community child-rearing:

> Some children are reared by sisters, aunts, uncles, or even distant cousins. It is not unusual for a child to reach adulthood living not more than a block from the natural parent but residing with another relative, who is perhaps childless or more financially secure. Even children born out of wedlock generally know who their fathers and grandparents are. These children are given the same respect in the community as legitimate children and are as likely to be reared by the paternal side of the family as by the maternal side.[61]

If considered property at all, land, children, and spouses are considered communal property.[62]

Kwasi Wiredu sees African communalism as an improved politics of culture and nature: "What communalism adds is the increased readiness of the individual to empathize with demands for communal welfare over an expanding field of [individual] interests."[63] Taking Wiredu further: Subjecting so-called private demands to community temperance and welfare might also foster a subjection of private—even communal—demands to nature's temperance and welfare, to the subsistence needs of plants and animals with whom land should be shared.[64]

Epilogue

Sharing, however, does not quite suffice as a land ethic. Sharing still implies owning: One shares what one owns individually or communally. Aldo Leopold's land ethic does not get around this: "When we see land as a community to which we belong we may begin to use it with love and respect."[65] The idea of land as a community of which we are part is an improvement over land or nature as say, raw material or obstacle to development. But land/nature as a community is a fairy tale that turns land/nature into an intentional and cooperative system. Intention and cooperation, however, only characterize individualized communities within nature, especially animal communities. If Leopold thought of nature as a community, it was not because its members regularly kill and eat each other in the name of community harmony.[66] Leopold's notion of a land-community sought to render a complex worldnature into a simpler, kinder entity, an entity, however, that encouraged more outdoor recreation instead of reformations of culture that release nature from humanity's grip.[67]

An ethic that allows nature's wild flourishing must still be searched for which Kirkpatrick Sale maintains, is part of the problem:

> The issue is not one of morality ... but of *scale*. There is no very successful way to teach, or force, the moral view, or to insure correct ethical responses to anything at all. The only way people will apply "right behavior" and behave in a responsible way is if they have been persuaded to see the problem concretely and to understand their own connection to it directly—and this can be done only at a limited scale. . . . Then people will do the environmentally "correct" thing not because it is thought to be the *moral*, but rather the *practical*, thing to do.[68]

Perhaps Gullah life, notwithstanding the series of governments overarching it, is motivated by the practicality—not morality—Sale and Wiredu advocate. But Gullah communities are under pressure, and the many African communities that lived on a Salean scale were destroyed partially by the lure of wealth (property as commodities, land, and money) but predominantly by force. Wiredu hoped communalism would increase empathy for others in the community, and I extrapolated, perhaps even empathy for nature, especially for land outside the boundary of territory and property. But subsistence communalism is fragile, subject to the freedom of private interest (increasingly, transnational corporations) to trample on or bribe those who would interfere with the huge profits accruing to the extravagant few.

Not only has private property flattened nature, its pervasiveness has overwhelmed the history of private property as a recent development (1789 in France and the 1830s and 1840s in England) where because of industrialization and invention, people were pushed off their land, rebelled, were forced into factories, and rebelled some more. The right to own private property can only now be called a freedom because it was our forebears who were robbed and denied access to land they owned or controlled as a community, as a family, or through exchange for feudal services.

While access to land is natural—"We might as well imagine his [humanity's] being born without hands and feet as carrying on his life without land"[69]—the private ownership of land was a coercive development whereby dwellers and their progeny were deprived of land and its fruits, entities nearly as intrinsic to human functioning as limbs. Adding insult to injury, these essentials were sold back to the people at the cost of working as wage slaves for the entities (industry) that had robbed their ancestors in the first place. Imagine not being able to walk, talk, or manipulate objects until our right was earned through fifty years of demeaning, unsafe, and long, tedious labor. How far is this condition really from slavery? In both, one's land and autonomy is stolen and then returned at a nearly impossible price.[70]

An awareness of ourselves as prey to a system of wage slavery that we were born into every bit as much as slaves born into slavery—a system that robs people of land and forces them and their descendants (ourselves and our children) to toil to get it back—will enable an understanding of the similar plight of "enclosured" wild plants and animals captured, dislocated, or slaughtered by a tyrannical human minority.[71] The four worlds of humanity share with the fifth world of nature a disenfranchisement of land and exploitation that while less-fatally devastating for most humans, is disastrous for worldnature. Acknowledging the history of land stolen from people, plants, and animals is essential to generating the resolve to get nature back and get off the back of nature.[72]

But this is just half the story. Even though we are the offspring of those robbed of land, we are also, especially in the United States, over-privileged and gluttonous, a nation whose impoverished population is even privileged in comparison to third- and threatened fourth-worlders who lack access to effective shelter, waste disposal, inexpensive processed foods, affordable appliances, cheap energy, and a seemingly-endless supply of cheap disposable items. This bounty is produced on the backs of increasing numbers of first-world poor people and the even poorer people of poor nations, made poor by first-world colonizing in the guise of free trade agreements. If having is cheap, it is only because it is so expensive. Not only is mounting first-world poverty a privileged condition compared to mounting poverty outside first-world nations, it is obscene when compared to the lives of plants and animals whose subsistence falls far below upwardly refined standards of human subsistence.[73]

Daughters of the Dust is unique in picturing beautiful subsistence of a small society that labors less yet with ample reward; a community with access to not only food, clothing, and shelter, but land, leisure, and nature; a people without the mainland's endless effluvia of commodities and commodity-culture (and the attendant miseries of wage labor and environmental devastation). This example of living small yet well should inspire a society of owners to own up to belonging to themselves, a community, and a land that should be everyone's—and this includes plants and animals— because it is no one's.

IV
Nature, in Theory

Where, in chapter seven, culture is brought up to the level of nature and, in chapter eight, nature is brought up to the level of culture.

7

AN ENVIRONMENTAL IMPACT REPORT
Of Grammatology

The deconstruction of the nature/culture boundary in Jacques Derrida's *Of Grammatology* is inadequate. Its critique of metaphysics lacks sufficient grounding in the physical and political reality of fifth-world (nonhuman animals, plants, and elements) decimation. Derrida's task is to rescue culture, especially writing, from the way Rousseau (who, for Derrida, represents a strain of traditional metaphysics) casts it as a fallen or corrupt deviation from Nature, and then to place culture on an equal footing with nature. While Derrida rightly seeks to lower the status of Nature to nature, he gets entangled when he perhaps unwittingly construes nature as a metaphysical Nature calling forth culture as God's Word called forth the universe (including culture, or at least humanity). Attempting a nature/culture parity by deprivileging nature, Derrida's solution or deconstruction privileges the *relationship* between Nature and human culture. As such, Derrida's tale of culture's fundamentality for nature's existence necessitates an environmental-impact report to account for potential reverberations in the fifth world.

Because poststructural blurrings of the nature/culture boundary can, at their extreme, render the fifth world as mere extension of culture—a strategy illustrated by the now-common practice of placing *nature* between quotation marks—I offer two similar yet distinct caveats about deconstruction. First, radical questioning of hierarchy and separation of oppositional terms through problematizing differences between them runs the risk (though crucial) of pushing difference into identity, essence, and oneness that connote Origin and Truth, the very fruit whose rottenness Derrida warns against. Second, as a result of the first precaution, indiscriminate deprivileging, or identitization of substantive difference or hierarchy, can paralyze substantive choice.[1]

My critique begins with Derrida's notions of the cultural nature of Nature and the natural Nature in culture, that is, the first instance where difference risks sameness:

> The supplement [human imagination, culture] to Nature is within Nature as its play. Who will ever say if the lack within nature is *within* nature, if the catastrophe by which Nature *is separated from itself* [producing culture] is still natural? A natural catastrophe conforms to laws in order to overthrow the law (258).[2]

"Decriminalizing"[3] culture by including it within Nature is one of two simultaneous steps in which Derrida makes culture and nature approach each other to the point that they risk becoming indistinguishable. Culture, depicted as "play" and no longer outside the "laws" of Nature, becomes a naturalized incurrence easily interpreted as no less natural than hurricanes and earthquakes. My quarrel is neither with the politically-provocative characterization of culture as a virtual catastrophe, nor with culture's inclusion *within* Nature (or nature), which carries the implication that culture is not superior to it. But the notion of culture as a *natural* catastrophe ignores at least three differences between natural catastrophes and the catastrophe(s) of culture: first, the *motivated* fabric of culture (it is doubtful that tornadoes have motives); second, the widespread awareness of what these cultural motives are and how to avoid such catastrophes (even while it might be naive to hope that the commercialization of everyday life should be easier to stop than earthquakes); and third, the speed, extent, and duration of much culturally-perpetrated ecocide (sudden, large-scale disruptions exist in worldnature, but rarely are these perpetrated on a global scale by the land's own residents simultaneously committing swift ecocide and prolonged suicide).

What might result from Derrida's depiction of culture as the natural "play" of Nature—a play akin to hurricanes and tidal waves? Culturally-perpetrated destruction of the fifth world can look either like Nature's intention or natural selection, or as God's will. If readers want to justify or avoid complicity in fifth-world exploitation, they can turn to Derrida to justify their resignation or fatalism. This is the risk of culture naturalized as mere play, culture decriminalized.

Derrida's other strategy that serves as complement to decriminalization is "supplementalization."[4] Derrida correctly reads Rousseau's Nature as a metaphysical, non-supplemental entity, pure and self-identical,[5] from which imperfect human law and norms issue. It is this imperfection which burdens culture with a supplemental/substitutional status:[6] "One can no longer see disease in substitution when one sees that the substitute [culture] is substituted for a substitute [Nature]" (314). Rousseauist philosophical tradition casts Nature as metaphysical occupier of the inner sanctum of the normative, infallible, and incorruptible. Derrida re-casts Nature as a substitute like the other substitute, culture, which was construed by Rousseau as a fallen outer supplement to Nature or as sorry substitute for Nature. In this way, Nature loses its capital N and becomes—like culture—moralled or normed, fallible, and corruptible.[7]

Nature as supplement? To what?[8] Nature as substitute? For what? For an always, already culture?[9] Nature might be seen as culture's substitute when a tropical forest comes to look like some eerie facsimile of Disneyland or Biosphere 2, or when pets replace people or artifacts as objects of affection, but it is hard to imagine Nature, let alone nature, as a substitute (aspects of nature having existed always, already, and probably, forever). Before, Derrida had recast the supplemental essence of culture— culture as something extra, as something Nature does not need—as virtually identical to the status of natural catastrophes (decriminalization). Now, with supplementalization, the Rousseauist non-supplement, Nature, is reformulated by Derrida as a kind of supplement (to culture). Brandishing decriminalization (culture as natural) and supplementalization (Nature as cultural), nature and culture not only approach identity, if not confusion, but risk a reversed hierarchy.

It is critical to notice that it is a cultural representative, Derrida, who decriminalizes culture while transforming Nature into at least as supplemental an entity as culture. Suspicion should be aroused when anyone proclaims himself and his boys guiltless, as just doing their job, just makin' a living, or just followin' orders in a system that, though corrupt, cannot be bucked. Likewise, suspicion should be aroused when cultural representatives (people, even brilliant ones) declare their culture natural, while the larger system (Nature) itself is deemed flawed, corrupted, or supplemental.

This brings up the question: How does Derrida accomplish the decriminalization of supplementarity? By improving the image of supplementarity itself. Derrida notes that the supplement, in order to be a supplement, must share something with the interior, that which is non-supplemental, here, Nature. In other words, culture (the exterior) must share features with Nature (the interior) in order to be Nature's supplement. Still, this is hierarchical thinking that Derrida wants to avoid because the interior (Nature) remains superior to the exterior (culture). But one might ask, how can this be if interior and exterior share features to such an extent that one can be substituted for, or supplemented to the other? To ask the question differently: If Nature, as the interior, contains within it exteriority, then what is wrong with exteriority and supplementarity? According to Derrida, supplementarity is neither quite interior nor exterior, neither good nor evil: "I show the interiority of exteriority, which amounts to annulling the ethical qualification and to thinking of writing [which is emblematic of culture] beyond good and evil" (314). This statement is aimed at Rousseau's notion of speech as part of Nature, as non-supplemental, intrinsic, interior, and therefore good; and at his notion of writing as part of culture, as supplemental and exterior, and therefore evil and corrupt. Derrida problematizes Rousseau's hierarchy and ethical assumptions; he decriminalizes culture and supplementalizes nature which causes the virtual whole of juridical ability to collapse beyond a question of good and evil. This then is Derrida's third step, "acriminalization."[10] With acriminalization, culture, as de-ethicized supplement, *maintains* its Rousseauist supplementarity, while Nature *becomes* demoted to a de-ethicized supplement, that is, nature with a lowercase *n*. Both culture and nature now reside as equals in a supplementarity which is not exterior to anything, and is therefore invulnerable to a Rousseauist accusation of corruption or evil.

While it may be easy to see the concept of supplementarity (Derrida's specific example is the supplement, writing, and the non-supplement, speech) beyond good and evil, what of seeing culture beyond ethics, beyond good and evil? Perhaps the idea or the existence of culture, as with writing, can be construed beyond good and evil, but surely not each and every practice of culture. Virtually all cultural acts are ethico-political because they impact inhabitants of all five worlds. It is difficult outside a zone of metaphysical concepts to imagine most cultural acts as exempt from a historical and contextual *better and worse* (since we are aware that notions of metaphysical good and evil, God and Devil, should have atrophied long ago).

Derrida proposes an even wider-ranging supplementarity than that applying to speech and writing, one whereby any self-sufficient, self-identical origin (such as speech) in its correlations to the Word, God, Truth, the Good, or Nature, inexplicably divides and gives birth to a *fallen* supplement—writing, humanity, the false, evil, or culture respectively. Derrida announces the death of fallen supplementarity, itself, for most of philosophical thought: "yes above all, in as much as we designate the impossibility of formulating the movement of supplementarity within the classical logos, within the logic of identity, within ontology, within the opposition of presence and absence, positive and negative" (314). Here then is the fourth process, namely "de-supplementalization,"[11] by which the supplement within the above contexts no longer exists as a pure supplemental entity because no self-identical entity (God, Nature, Presence) is purely itself and not also mixed (Rousseau would say "tainted") with its other. Derrida's point is that Nature cannot be purely itself. It must always contain culture, either as possibility or fruition. He maintains that culture has always been within Nature, that there are no unadulterated, non-differentiated entities, and that entities prescribe their difference, which is also their corruption: "[Rousseau's] text twists about in a sort of oblique effort to act *as if* degeneration were not prescribed in the genesis and as if evil *supervened upon* a good origin" (199). In this statement, things contain within them their own demise,[12] and good involves evil. Further, entities do not just prescribe or suggest supplements but aggressively *call for* them: "Placing representation outside, which means placing the outside outside, Rousseau would like to make of the supplement of presence a pure and simple addition, a contingence: thus wishing to elude what, in the interior of presence, *calls forth the substitute, and is constituted only in that appeal, and in its trace*" (312, my emphasis). The fifth and final step in Derrida's narrative of the supplement (or substitute), states that something cannot be what it is without not only *being* what it is not, but *needing* what it is not. I call this process "de-essentialization,"[13] to mark a general move not only beyond the bipolarity of good and evil but to a point where dichotomous terms become what they are because they are *not* what they are, because they contain within them their difference, supplementarity, and demise. Thus, Nature cannot be Nature unless it "calls forth" its difference, its supplement, its demise, namely culture; Nature cannot be Nature unless it is also culture. While the process of deconstructing nature and culture allows for maintaining their separation, the result of the process might be construed as a de-essentialized entity, an almost homogenous brew that subverts "divisive" categories of nature and culture, speech and writing, interior non-supplement and exterior supplement. In this kettle, rendering nature into an *also-culture*, and culture into an *also-nature* produces a whirled where differences become nondivisible unities. Pointing out this process is less a criticism of Derrida, than of potential Derrideans, attracted to a Unity risking the totalitarian, a oneness without the challenge of opposition.

Before moving on, I should summarize the steps of Derrida's deconstruction of culture and Nature (à la Rousseau). In step one, culture is decriminalized by becoming natural (like a natural catastrophe). In step two, nature is supplementalized by becoming transformed into an entity containing the *fallen* aspects of culture. In step three, supplementality is acriminalized. Neither nature nor culture, even when categorized as supplements, are fallen. In step four, supplementality is de-supplementalized: There are no pure supplements since supplements are mixed with the entities they supplement. Finally, in step five, (all?) entities are de-essentialized: They are not only mixed with their supplements but cannot be what they are unless they *need* their supplements.

Perhaps now, after demarcating these steps, we may back up to ask how Derrida was able to claim that culture exists within Nature or nature before culture even came into existence. Is Derrida talking about the potential for culture rather than culture itself? If so then we must ask whether potentials are existential, or whether they are back-projections from existence to a former absence. If potentials actually exist, then we must also ask whether absences exist. For example: Does land presently occupied by a house mean that the house's former absence on that land actually existed, that the house's potential actually existed, or instead that the words/concepts, *potential* and *absence* have become so vivid and alive as to become existential? Surely the house's potential, itself, did not exist on the land before the house appeared there.

What kind of model does Derrida use when he has Nature demoted to nature-calling-forth, as impossible without culture (which he compares to a natural occurrence)? Is it the model of an organism calling forth its as-of-yet absent death? Returning to the house analogy: While all organisms (need to) die, not all land is, or need eventually be, occupied by homes. Unlike the seeming impossibility of an eternal organism, land would be every bit land without a house (however, it would not be what it precisely is without the potential of being occupied by a house). Nature obviously has the potential for culture, but to say potentials exist seems as metaphysical as saying absences exist. It is unlikely that Nature (again, this is a dubious notion that, for the present, I need to retain) either contained culture within it before culture came about, or that Nature needed culture to be what it is or to assist its entropic or chaotic tendencies—what someone like myself would want to call destruction in the case of anthropogenic ecocide. Derrida's notion of Nature calling forth culture renders Nature dependent on culture because Nature could not have been Nature unless the potential for culture was intermixed with Nature.

Is Derrida still holding onto lingering anthropocentrisms, still breathing the heady and intoxicating air of humanity or culture's hubristic importance even as he questions geo-, evo- (humans as the telos of evolution), and logo-centrisms? Would Derrida also have said that without calling forth whales' culture, Nature could not be Nature? Perhaps. And perhaps he is also right that Nature would be something different if it could not call forth humans or whales.[14] But is nature a metaphysical entity (Nature), one calling forth this or that manifestation? Or does this sound too much like old, transcendental thought that projects humans as humanlike gods, this world as a Platonic Form, and nature as a Nature calling forth (which, by the way, lapses into the logocentrism Derrida so keenly noticed and critiqued). If Nature calls forth, we might just as well go back to God's Word calling forth the universe in Genesis.

Initially striking about Derrida's deconstructionist rescue of supplementarity or substitutionality when applied to Nature and culture is its practical uselessness. The results of merging nature and culture is likely to justify the way most people already think and act with regard to N/nature and culture. Culture, outside of a certain (Rousseauist) tradition of metaphysics, is ususally constructed as the highest manifestation of nature, if not intrinsic to nature then nature's telos and perfection. Doesn't culture already routinely substitute and supplement itself for a nature considered knowable and improvable? Derrida takes up the rescue of culture when people already prefer to mix culture with nature, prefer differing degrees of domesticated nature rendered culture-friendly. Although deconstruction is a crucial theoretical tool, Derrida overapplies its results in trying to rescue all underprivileged supplements, when at least one of them, culture, hardly needs rescuing. I am not sure that within contemporary world scenarios writing—the major defendant in *Of Grammatology*—needs defending from speech. Perhaps from video and film.

I offer an alternative to the metaphysical culture/Nature problem, though there is indeed value for the fifth world and its resources in Derrida's deconstruction of the culture/Nature split. Most other deconstructionist efforts furthering the aims of environmentalism or animal rights proceed like this: Humanity, in spite of all efforts, has not *risen* out of nature but is still firmly anchored to it. Humans are descended from animals, are the product of innate drives, and like plants and animals, subject to a deteriorating environment. Or conversely, just like humans, animals (some would even include plants) suffer, reason, emote, make and wield tools, and use language. Both these familiar deconstructionist claims yank the badly worn carpet from under human supremacy. But Derrida's contribution gives a rather strange twist to the above strategies of equality and parity, *strange* unless one realizes that Derrida is addressing a certain metaphysical tradition rather than real-world practice, a metaphysical tradition that had elevated nature above culture. Derrida counters that tradition by simultaneously *elevating* humanity and *lowering* Nature in a way that precludes any move toward hierarchy:

> Since evil always has the form of representative alienation, of representation in its dispossessing aspect, all Rousseau's thought is in one sense a critique of representation, as much in the linguistic as in the political sense. But at the same time—and here the entire history of metaphysics is reflected—this critique depends upon the naivete of representation. It supposes at once that representation follows a first presence and restores a final presence. One does not ask how much of presence and how much of representation are found within presence. In criticizing representation as the loss of presence, in expecting a reappropriation of presence from it, in making it an accident or a means, one situates oneself within the self-evidence of the distinction between presentation and representation, within the *effect* of this fission. (296)

With Rousseau making the distinction between presence (Nature) and absence/distance/alienation (culture/representation) he can denounce the sign, writing, and by implication, culture, as fallen from an original Nature. To counter Rousseau, Derrida's deconstruction produces a kind of parity where culture is not above Nature and Nature is not above culture. But instead of hierarchy perhaps it is traditional geography that is at issue. Rather than an above/below relationship, nature and culture should be mapped in the fashion that Derrida implied when he wrote about culture within nature, that is culture as part of and permeable by nature in a biological rather than a metaphysical tradition. The area occupied by culture in relation to the much larger (even after culture's colonialist ventures in nature) totality of other animals, plants, and elements might put the question of nature/culture parity, in better perspective. Culture equating itself to the totality (nature) of which it is part is not unlike maintaining that the screw is as important as the machine, that lions are equal to the whole of nature, or that the desires of a tiny percentage of humans are as important as those of the entire population.

There is a tendency, resulting from his simultaneous raising of representation and lowering of presence to achieve a nonhierarchy, that Derrida himself cautions against. Derrida mentions those critics who, having deconstructed presence, go on to make the mistake of reverse-privileging the signifier (the "representer") over the signified (the "represented," the closest representation can come to the presence of the referent):

> One criticizes the sign by placing oneself within the self-evidence and the effect of the difference between signified and signifier. That is to say, without thinking *(quite like those later critics who, from within the same effect, reverse the pattern, and oppose a logic of the representer to the logic of the represented)* of the productive movement of the effect of difference: the strange graphic of differance [sic]. (296, my emphasis, except *effect*)

For Derrida, neither term of the binary, signified/signifier, should be privileged. Thus culture cannot, as a gesture of revenge, be privileged over nature, nor writing over speech. Still Derrida privileges writing—most likely to be provocative—by coining *arche-writing,* a term that indicates the essence or point of both speech and writing. Although Derrida does not make the following claim, one might say, following his example, that as writing and speech are based upon arche-writing, so too are nature and culture preconditioned by an *arche-culture* since both nature and culture are united as articulative realizations of an arche-culture. Just as speech and writing are articulations of arche-writing, both nature and culture are articulations of arche-culture. Yet *arche-writing* is far more effective than *arche-culture* since the former is not so metaphysical after all: ground markings, tracks, and naturally-occurring patterns might serve as the origin of both speech and writing, in other words, language. One finds oneself, however, firmly planted in the transcendent metaphysical when postulating something beyond nature, an arche-culture which evolved into nature on the one hand and culture on the other, somewhat like the Christian creation myth in which God is the origin of nature and humanity. There, though nature was created before humanity, humanity did not issue from nature but was molded from wet ground by God the potter and given spirit by God the Life-giving in mouth-to-mouth suscitation. That Derrida did not offer up the word *arche-culture* might indicate his knowledge that not all binaries are as ingeniously solved as speech and writing by *arche-writing*. There are other uneasy solutions as well: What might the common source be for a continuum from male to female: *arche-female*? Or from light to dark: *arche-dark*?

Though he is accused of being apolitical, it is clear from his use of *arche-writing* that Derrida recognizes some of the political ripples of his thought. He provokes his readers, who probably believe that writing derives from speech, to imagine and counterintuit the beginning of speech and writing as a kind of writing more than as speech (even while he also speaks against origins[15]). On the other hand, Derrida acknowledges the problem of retaining the notion of writing and the word *writing* since both are weighed down with the connotation of metaphysical fallenness and marginalization outside speech's centrality and naturalness. Still, as he chose to use *arche-writing* for political purposes, he also retains the word *writing* for political reasons:

> I would wish rather to suggest that the alleged derivativeness of writing, however real and massive, was possible only on one condition: that the "original," "natural," etc. language had never existed, never been intact and untouched by writing, that it had itself always been a writing. An arche-writing whose necessity and new concept I wish to indicate and outline here; *and which I continue to call writing only because it essentially communicates with the vulgar concept of writing.* The latter could not have imposed itself historically except by the dissimulation of the arche-writing, by the desire for a speech displacing its other and its double and working to reduce its difference. *If I persist in calling that difference writing, it is because, within the work of historical repression, writing was, by its situation, destined to signify the most formidable difference.* It threatened the desire for the living speech from the closest proximity, it *breached* living speech from within and from the very beginning. (56, my emphasis, except *breached*)

Retaining a notion of writing, and the word *writing,* is subversive for Derrida because writing has historically threatened anointed speech, because writing, he emphasizes, involves play and the proliferation of textuality, both of which undermine the notion of truth and the univocal self—in a word, authority. The subaltern word *writing*, in that it poses a threat, is retained for political purposes. Derrida's move is similar to the choice of political groups who defiantly and strategically retain labels used to denigrate them.[16]

But the term *culture*, except perhaps metaphysically, is not, in common parlance, a label of condemnation, or a subversive term, as *nature* is when used to mean wild, uncivilized, chaotic, undeveloped, uninhabitable, savage, indifferent (notwithstanding *nature's* additional implications of Arcadia, a tamed nature). *Nature* in its condemning senses is by far more subversive than *culture* since it is frequently thought of as culture's other, designating those fifth worlders who, or which, exist without money and recognizable institutions. Perhaps this is partially why activists prefer to use the word *environment* to make nature seem more like culture, like something close or even intrinsic to culture instead of indifferent, wholly other, or threatening to it; or it could be that environment is used to combat *nature* in its connotations as romantic spectacle or poetic inspiration.[17] Using Derrida as my guide, I retain the word *nature* at least in part for its subversive tendencies and for the word's potential to serve as a critique of culture.[18]

Though Derrida is perspicuous, on epistemological grounds, to maintain Nature and culture as not mutually exclusive—culture as part of and within Nature and Nature involved in culture—nature and culture can, and at times, should be thought of as distinct primarily for this reason: *while culture is a subset of worldnature, worldnature is not a subset of culture.* Therefore I refuse, especially at this point in history, in this place (the United States, the West, the North), to coin any one term that risks conflating nature and culture; no *arche-culture*, *arche-nature*, or *natural culture*, perhaps not even *ecology*, which too often figures nature as a system based on an institutional model of human society. Humans and their culture(s), though certainly part of nature (humans as animals), are now better characterized as nature's internal enemy, the enemy of plants, animals, and elements, just as a tyrannical regime, though composed of the people is also its enemy. The politics of calling culture *natural,* even as it mows nature down (however unintentionally) has been made to seem rather harmless, or not worth addressing. Though nature and culture are intermixed, they are also increasingly distinct. Culture, while part of nature, mutilates it to such a degree that for the time being culture earns the non-metaphysical labels of *corrupt* and *outside*. After all, one should try to figure out who the enemy is, especially when that enemy is oneself.

To give Derrida his due, he does introduce the crucial, and in my experi-ence, rare, issue of degree. He writes: "It [Rousseau's 'naivete' that the thing represented is real] supposes at once that representation follows a first pres-ence and restores a final presence. One does not ask *how much* of presence and *how much* of representation are found within presence" (296, my emphasis). Derrida's "how much" draws attention to the idea of degree and implies the importance of asking how much of one thing is in another in order to name, categorize, distinguish, and if need be, separate them. For example, given the options of an organic banana, a chemically-treated banana, a plastic banana, or a photo of a banana, provided all are free, I would choose to eat the organic one, if it is not rotten, bruised, etc. I could eat the banana photo—it *is* of a real banana and is made of paper and inks from nature—but it retains too much culture for my taste. By virtue of com-parative degree, the photobanana can be deemed *culture*, and the organic banana, *nature*.[19] For purposes of eating, nature is privileged over culture, and the banana photo, in terms of eating, is a banana devoid of presence, a corruption within the category, food. As with food, there are times when cul-ture is best privileged. Not all binaries are best leveled. As it would be unwise to look to pictures of bananas as a source of food, it would be imprudent to feed plants into a film projector, even though celluloid is from plants.

Deconstruction, in *Of Grammatology*, participates in a conspicuously luxurious and overgeneralized metaphysics at a time when the majority of the fifth world is suffering under a leaden oppression and a constant threat from the four worlds of culture. If I am accused of misusing and trivializing Derrida's elegant and intoxicating deconstruction by yoking it with vulgar political agendas, I would suggest deconstructing the metaphysics/real world opposition. A metaphysical discourse is produced by and reverber-ates in (dangerous) real-world minds connected to (dangerous) real-world bodies. Even in the tradition of metaphysics Derrida critiques (the Rousseauist rhapsodization of nature), nature was, out of mere whim, or in the name of ideals, physically butchered. As valuable as is Derrida's method of deconstruction, a philosophical method is tainted by a lack (which is not a play) when it fails to examine its formation by, and its impact on, that other "text": fifth-world destruction.

8

BEYOND A CREEPING METONYMY

Simians, Cyborgs, and Women

Horrible beings advance, taking over the bodies of those they invade or incorporating them completely. The scenario illustrates a subgenre of horror, which I term *creeping metonymy.* In creeping metonymy, culture trespasses the already culturally-besieged boundary between itself and nature (including the very limits of the bodies of natural entities), and replaces nature by deeming itself nature, or by deeming nature culture. In other words, culture invades nature by calling itself *natural* or *part of nature,* or culture portrays nature with terms that are more applicable to culture. Yet culture's often laudable desire to question and transgress boundaries (which have rules) risks vilifying difference and leaving behind a dump where distinctions become a uniform and toxic sludge, where culture and nature collapse into one entity defined, not surprisingly, to human advantage. Herein lies what might be a serious caveat against poststructuralism (that Derridean approach wary of binaries and borderlines): When boundaries, distinctions, or differences are regarded as no longer useful, as the mark of an arrogant and fearful society keeping itself away from all that is believed threatening and abject in terms of class, gender, race, sexuality, and nature, then the other extreme, an expedient uniformity, is apt to take its place. Jürgen Habermas's strategy against these extremes—a polarized modern and structural society or a uniform poststructural one— takes the middle away, combines the need for boundaries with a frequent and open communication between them.[1] Jean-Francois Lyotard is even more fearful of poststructural uniformity than Habermas. Lyotard wants to combat homogeneity by welcoming a multiplication of distinctions, and, to an unspecified extent, applauding the non-communication between them. If individuals, disciplines, institutions, and societies should communicate as much as Habermas advocates, Lyotard fears a oneness, syncretism, and consensus attained by hucksterism, and coercion—Lyotard's rather broad notion of totalitarianism—will soon follow.[2] But then Lyotard's postmodernism also has its extreme: balkanization, segregation, separatism. On a continuum—and this issue of uniformity *can* be seen in terms of a line marked by degrees—one end is occupied by the totalized mass(es) of extreme poststructuralism, and the other by non-cooperating groups/individuals of extreme postmodernism (perhaps Enlightenment truth is dead center).

From Donna J. Haraway there is little need to fear the frigidity of polar postmodernism: Her warm advocacy of affinity groups or temporary coalitions tempers that position. Still, it is necessary to guard against the heat emanating from her employment of a poststructuralism whose danger is characterized by a creeping metonymy whereby culture threatens to erase any difference between itself and nature. Haraway colonizes the poststructural pole with cyborgs (she uses the term to define humans wielding high-technology),[3] who are an undelineated and quasi-heroic mixture of nature and culture. Against Haraway, I posit that we cyborgs are far more cultural (not to be confused with *cultured*) than natural—and therefore monstrous. My argument, however, is not a reassertion of the firm boundary between nature and culture—whose narrative tells of culture's heroic escape from nature's violent grip—nor is it a plea for nature's re-enchantment. It is not even a declaration of nature as a cultural paradigm. Instead, I argue for the (political) conditionalizing of the erasure of the nature/culture border. If I am convincing, Haraway's story just might earn a new classification: horror's frightening subgenre, creeping metonymy. Or a categorization even more terrifying . . . .

Nature as Subject:
The Animal

In addition to symbolizing the connection between human and machine, Haraway's cyborgs signify a joyful breach in the boundary between animal and human, a breach already in question:

> By the late twentieth century in the United States scientific culture, the boundary between human and animal is thoroughly breached. The last beachheads of uniqueness have been polluted if not turned into amusement parks—language, tool use, social behaviour, mental

events, nothing really convincingly settles the separation of human and animal. And many people no longer feel the need for such a separation; indeed, many branches of feminist culture affirm the pleasure of connection of human and other living creatures. Movements for animal rights are not irrational denials of human uniqueness; they are a clear-sighted recognition of connection across the discredited breach of nature and culture.[4]

Haraway's defense of animal rights is based on the human-animal connection, just as potential repeal of those rights might be founded on lack of connection, or of disconnection.[5] But is this the most viable way rights should be asserted (for animals)? Might not rights be granted to or demanded from those with whom humans feel no connection or even to those we see as radically different? Must connection to the human species be the grounds on which to bestow *consider*ation? While it becomes increasingly difficult to posit lack of connection between any two entities, disconnection need not preclude rights. With or without connection, rights can be argued on the basis of autovalence or multivalence (the latter a condition where all entities are complex and serve multi-purposive ends).

It is curious that Haraway represents the animal-human connection with the cyborg. But Haraway explains:

> Biological-determinist ideology is only one position opened up in scientific culture for arguing the meanings of human animality. There is much room for radical political people to contest the meanings of the breached boundary. The cyborg appears in myth precisely where the boundary between human and animal is transgressed. Far from signalling a walling off of people from other living beings, cyborgs signal disturbingly and pleasurably tight coupling. (152)

Yet Haraway, I presume, chooses the cyborg not so much because of its relationship to the human-animal connection, but more because of its link to breached boundaries in general. Perhaps a therianthrope like a sphinx would better have represented the breached animal-human boundary. But then the overall goal of Haraway's chapter, "A Cyborg Manifesto," which embraces technology, would be absent. Perhaps a better choice would be a superhero like Batman or Spiderman, who combines technology and the human form to produce an "animal." But these characters are too male in form and fantasy. Maybe Catwoman would have been the answer.

Ham, the chimp sent into space by the United States on a 1961 Mercury launch and discussed in Haraway's *Primate Visions*, might also have been a choice.[6] Ham would combine technology, animals, and people in the service of discovery—breaching the boundary between sky and space. But the image of a chimp strapped into a capsule is problematic. It isn't far removed from imagery animal rights activists use of lab animals implanted with and bound to devices that look more punitive than investigative.[7]

Lynn Randolph, whose illustration appears on the cover of *Simians, Cyborgs, and Women: The Reinvention of Nature*, tried her hand at Haraway's human-animal-machine cyborg. The picture shows a woman-cyborg facing the viewer, sitting at a "desk," a desert landscape: Atop the landscape sits a computer keyboard being used by a woman with an integrated circuit board chest and a living wild cat draped around her like a shawl, the feline's head rests on the woman's head and the cat's arms hang over the woman's shoulders. But even though the woman seems somewhat incorporated into landscape and machinery, the feline is not connected to the land and more resembles a fur cowl or an aura than a necessary addition to the woman's body. Further, the cat is made curiously insubstantial by the portrayal of its limbs as though x-rayed. This is not necessarily to blame Randolph since an unproblematic image of machinery fused with animals is difficult. Favorable imagery must show animals *wielding* technology, but this is unusual since animals have for so long been at the receiving end of contraptions and machines. Why *would* an animal want anything to do with machinery (though some might slightly appreciate cars and tractors which eliminate the need for the animal-drawn carriages and plows)? Besides, a cyborg showing a fusion of human and animal is peculiar since the more humans connect to machines the less they view themselves as animals.

The cyborg illustrates no breach between animal and human—only breach. If the cyborg resonates with anything, it is with humans finally becoming the machines they have long operated—highly trained, de- or unsensitized, instrumental creatures terminating, teasing, and torturing animals.[8] But this is not at all what Haraway promotes: "Perhaps, ironically, we can learn from our fusions with animals and machines how not to be Man, the embodiment of Western logos. From the point of view of pleasure in these potent and taboo fusions, made inevitable by the social relations of science and technology, there might indeed be a feminist science" (173).

The ways humans *have* concretely "fused" with animals are by bestiality, adornment with animal parts, and in-corporation of animal flesh and organs. This is an instance of humans forcing animals to fuse with humans: animals made to *in*fuse, disappear within our bodies and get lost in our appearances.[9] Our ability to make this happen and still maintain our human appearance reaffirms humanity more than animality. Perhaps because we are beginning to suspect that our status is no better than animals', humans seek desperately to separate from animals, or to fuse with them only after bringing them up to our level, or when we need their organs. Humans may configure animals as almost human, but less often are we willing to think of ourselves as animals (except perhaps in bed or biology).

Haraway wants it otherwise, wants us to be unafraid of our "joint kinship with animals and machines" (154). But how to grant animals subjectivity through kinship or fusion needs more discussion lest "joint kinship" and "potent fusions" (154) result in maintaining the devastating practice of viewing animals as pets or organ donors.[10] If animals would be made pets or organ donors because they are called our kin, they might do better as evil others. Animals should always break and run whenever hearing the words *fusion* and *kinship*.

Haraway's last and most provocative attempt at attributing subjectivity to nature through animals—besides "potent fusions" and "joint kinship"— is nature as "coding trickster," "Coyote," a "conversant nature" with "an independent sense of humor" (198–99). Andrew Ross thought these personifications might be perceived as "profane ecology," and "anthropocentric," perhaps meaning to say *anthropomorphic*.[11] But anthropomorphism does not seem to be the major problem here. The dilemma at this historical juncture is characterizing nature with a sense of humor and nature as civilly conversant. Although I find it plausible that many animals have a sense of humor, for politico-historical reasons I proffer an angry, exiled, enslaved, imprisoned, tortured, colonized, sacrificed, exterminated, and disenfranchised nature all less problematic attributions than that of nature with a sense of humor. My version is not of animals as passive victims but as fighters who do not muster humor in the grip of humanity.

Haraway's move to grant animals a sense of humor even as they are made into commodities and possessions exemplifies culture attributing to nature traits that lessen human guilt and complicity (animal products are advertised with laughing or content cows, grinning chickens, or Charlie the tuna eager to be caught). Haraway selectively stops short of a full-bodied anthropomorphism wherein animals might suffer as we would under similar persecution. Nature with a sense of humor might have subjectivity but Haraway's analysis risks removing nature too far from laboratory, farm, slaughterhouse, movie set, circus, rodeo, leash, enclosure.

"Conversant nature" is addressed from another important angle in "The Promises of Monsters." Haraway is irritated at the question: "Who speaks for the jaguar [the animal]?"[12] Why? Because it "was precisely like that [question] asked by some pro-life groups in the abortion debates: Who speaks for the fetus?"[13] Both questions bother Haraway because they complicate her pro-choice position. Though I do not doubt Haraway's "care about the survival of the jaguar,"[14] I believe she tries to dissect a simply stated, yet difficult, question by interpreting it literally, that is, "Who will speak the thoughts of the jaguar?" Interpreted this way, the original question *does* represent the jaguar as if a speechless dummy on a ventriloquist's knee. But the question, "Who speaks for the jaguar?" is not so easily dismissed if translated as "Who speaks *in the name of* the jaguar, for the survival, the continued well-being of the jaguar?" This interpretation is the more intellectually honest and also applicable to a fairer discussion of the abortion issue. Without this interpretation, representation is regarded too literally and animals suffer because they cannot speak for themselves like human plaintiffs, as in June 1994 when a federal appeals court ruled that people denouncing laboratory torture of birds and rodents failed to qualify these complainants as legal plaintiffs.[15]

However, human plaintiffs often do not speak for themselves. Lawyers do. Still, what is so interesting about this criticism of ventriloquism by those seeking a fusion with nature is its implied call for a *separation* of animal and human, and nature and culture. If, as Haraway asserts, there is no firm boundary between human and animals, why shouldn't animals be represented by people, just as people are represented by people. It could even be convincingly argued that animals, like people who cannot or do not represent themselves, need representation.

But Haraway, and most assuredly, Ross, would presumably dislike even the phrase *speaking in the name of* since it neglects to connect jaguars to a larger picture, namely, forests with fourth worlders or fetuses to mothers. Though connecting individuals to the environment is different in the cases of jaguars and fetuses, the complaint that the larger picture is overlooked is worth entertaining. It is part of that quotidian argument in which calling for preservation of nature usually is said to indicate a callousness toward people. This claim resembles the conservative response to identity politics or multiculturalism. Marginalized groups targeted for what is termed "special treatment" make the white-right fear marginalization by "reverse discrimination," by attention to the rights of women, people of color, and gays and lesbians. And regarding the rights of nature, even a portion of the left boards this special treatment bandwagon, claiming that focus on nature hurts jobs, ignores third- and fourth-world people, and is anti-human. Even within the ranks of environmentalists, some Earth-Firsters and ecologists maintain that animal rights activists call for the special treatment of animals. These are flawed arguments; special treatment is most often about getting decent, equal, or appropriate treatment, about avoiding the worst kinds of treatment.

And how are plants, animals, and elements, even marginalized people, to gain decent and equal treatment within and outside theory/cultural studies? The logic that individuals and environments are all connected only goes so far: mother and fetus can be disconnected, as can animals and plants deemed necessary for the survival of habitat and humanity. In cases like these a plea for people to only *connect* is ineffective. Regretfully, connection is ignored or scoffed at by people who are increasingly cut off from each other and from nature. Cannot care and rights be given to those deemed different or unconnected? Isn't it time to argue for life and liberty without tediously arguing about an entity's difference and similarity to humans, arguments not surprisingly rooted in those old bulwarks, intelligence or consciousness?

Nature Loses Subjectivity to Technology

The old saw, "we can't go back" gets salvaged and sharpened by Donna J. Haraway: "We cannot go back ideologically or materially," (162) and, "We have no choice but to move through a harrowed and harrowing artifactualism to elsewhere."[16] These assertions are probably accurate for the immediate future at least. But prescience is less problematic than a tendency toward optimistic fatalism: acceptance turning into comfort becoming desire for a pleasure-promising technofuture. Or perhaps the order is better reversed:

> I know that there's a lot going on in technoscience discourses and practices that's not about the devil, that's a source of remarkable

pleasure, that promises interesting kinds of human relationships, not just contestatory, not always oppositional, but something often more creative and playful and positive than that. And I want myself and others to learn how to describe those possibilities. And . . . even technoscience worlds are full of resources for contesting inequality and arbitrary authority.[17]

This picture is pretty because what goes unmentioned is that technoculture appropriates (destroys, kills, imprisons), transforms (mutilates), uses (deprives), and discards (trashes) worldnature so that humans *and only humans* may be creative and enjoy themselves. While it is obvious that scientists, engineers, and consumers benefit from technoscience's creative and playful human pleasures, it is less certain that technoscience can effectively contest the inequality between itself and worldnature while at the same time arbitrarily and routinely employing its authority about, and over it. And while some technoscientists may indeed be interested in "contesting inequality and arbitrary authority," I have never, before reading Haraway, heard or read this explanation for choosing a career in technology or science. The lure of science is more often than not about fascination for the subject and pursuit of money, knowledge, and authority rather than equality between genders, cultures, or nature and culture. Even when that large contingent of scientists and engineers in what used to be called the military-industrial complex stays up late into the night "contesting inequality and arbitrary authority," the results are often unsavory.

But the idealism embodied in Haraway's previous statement reaches its apogee with her declaration: "[In the technological polis] nature and culture are reworked; the one can no longer be the resource for appropriation or incorporation by the other"(151). Haraway's strategy is to mysteriously transform worldnature into non-resource and culture into non-appropriator in order to allow reinvented nature to escape technological sacrifice, and culture to acquire salvation through a reverse-Mass, by transubstantiating nature's flesh and blood into culture's bread and wine. While it may be obvious, it seems necessary to assert that outside the imagination no culture exists that doesn't appropriate and incorporate worldnature as resource—with even minimal or "low" technology. Muting the destruction inherent in technology, Haraway imagines an impossible state where worldnature is unappropriated and unincorporated by "creative" and "playful" technology.

But isn't my critique disingenuous? Haraway surely means to call for only a reduction of cultural consumption, a state in which appropriation is no longer the primary characteristic of the culture/nature relationship. The trouble, however, is not her attempt to replace an intrinsic and perhaps distasteful, aspect of the culture/nature relationship with New Age science fiction, but the ease with which the corporate/consumer culture can appropriate it. If corporations and consumers are comfortable calling tree-killing *harvesting*, and dumping and polluting *discharge* and *emissions*, why further enable cultural decimations of worldnature to be neutralized as *reworking* rather than the innocuous-sounding *appropriating*?

Haraway's faith in technology seems partially founded on an alignment with what she calls "Marxist humanism":

> The labour process constitutes the fundamental human condition. Through labour, we make ourselves individually and collectively in a constant interaction with all that has not yet been humanized. *Neither our personal bodies nor our social bodies may be seen as natural, in the sense of existing outside the self-creating process called human labour.* What we experience and theorize as nature and as culture are transformed by our work. *All we touch and therefore know, including our organic and our social bodies, is made possible for us through labour.* Therefore culture does not dominate nature, nor is nature an enemy. (10, my emphasis)

Marx construed labor as "an exclusively human characteristic"[18] because animals, he wrote, do not pre-envision what they construct.[19] How did Marx know this about animals[20] and, more importantly, why should foreknowledge and not, say, exertion be a condition of labor? While I hope asking the first question is enough, the second question requires an answer. If Marx were not to glorify labor with revered foreknowledge—a code word indicating Man and Reason—labor could not be used to elevate humans above animals and so inspire the animalized working class (especially with nineteenth-century working conditions) to the grand goal of owning, yet still laboring within, the modes of production, those very organs ravaging workers by turning them into machines alienated not just from the whole of production, but from their own tasks.

Haraway prepares the ground for a rather disappointing version of a workers' revolution through "The Cyborg Manifesto," which describes and calls for intelligent relationships between humans and high-technology, especially communications devices; in the name of this revolution (my term), human beings become essentialized as (communications) laborers in that their acts of perception count as labor. Humanity reduced to *Homo faber* is thus a natural for linkup with machines, not to mention the workplace. Rather than dispute Haraway's definition of labor, it might be more productive to substitute the italicized portions in Haraway's previous block quote with bracketed alternatives: "Neither our personal bodies nor our social bodies may be seen as [cultural] in the sense of existing outside the [un]self-creating process[es] called [nature]." And: "All we touch and therefore know, including our organic and our social bodies, is made possible for us through [nature]." My point here is that bodies cannot be cultural without also being first, and inescapably, natural (the definition of which is, of course, debatable).

Notice also that after Haraway walks readers through labor's fundamentality to the "human condition," she leaps to that penultimate pronouncement: "Therefore culture does not dominate nature."[21] The deconstruction is deft: The human processes Haraway construed as labor, as culture, now become so essential to humanity that they become natural. If labor is natural, Haraway asks, how then can labor dominate worldnature? Haraway's assaults on overconfident ideas of labor, nature, and culture, seem to force readers to come to terms with unquestioned definitions. It is also likely that certain readers will justify humanwide dominations of worldnature as natural, understandable, and acceptable, even if regrettable. The potential for outrage about global ecocide might become smothered by detached academic inquiry suitable for any agenda. Those in logging, chemicals, mining, oil, agribusiness, armaments, electronics, and utilities would be able to reasonably claim their labor as essential and therefore good because it does not dominate worldnature, but only processes it as does any other animal's labor. And why should understanding human labor as intrinsic, preclude domination? If this were true, would we say that tigers do not dominate their prey because hunting and killing are fundamental activities that can be construed as labor?

By construing all human function as fundamental cultural labor—and therefore non-dominational—Haraway naturalizes labor. Cultural activity becomes so intrinsic and unavoidable that it becomes part of nature. This position is, in a sense, so radically left that it can be confused with the radical right's position that human domination of worldnature through labor is natural and intrinsic labor. The only difference is that while the right construes labor as (rightful) domination of worldnature, Haraway does not. Even if the position of the radical right seems radically wrong, the right, at least, appears to better understand domination when it sees it. Through Haraway, the overall problem of human labor's relation to worldnature becomes primarily a matter of only egregious human labors and its products (for example, *toxic* waste). This leaves too much room to foist *our* (a *we* numbering in the hundreds of millions) ecocidal labor onto others who are available to blame for greater or more direct damage (even when it is our own acts we are more able to change). But there are two viable ways to alter or kill a corporation, government, or institution: by attacking it politically and by ceasing to feed it economically.

Rather than talk about what might happen if labor was non-dominational, it might be better to see what has already happened. Marx brought nature to the forefront of politico-economic dialogue—perhaps he even planted the seed of the Frankfurt School's notion of the domination of nature—yet also fostered the notion that nature is not dominated: "Living labor must seize on these things [worldnature], *awaken* them from the *dead*, change them into . . . *real* and *effective* use-values" (my emphasis).[22] Marx conceptualizes culture as creative labor and worldnature as dead, insensate modeling clay, or as a human "tool house" and "larder."[23] Marx's "awakening" of nature, like Haraway's "reworking" of nature is characterized by its naturalness to human development and its positive value. Without competing characterizations of worldnature as multi- or autovalent, Marx salves reservations about humans being laborers, seems to miss the human cost of construing human essence and activity as labor.[24] While the capitalist onslaught on worldnature is frequently admonished by the left, a critique of Marx's conception of nature and its connection to the monomaniacal drives of Lenin, Stalin, and Mao to industrialize, is ignored or shouted down as a betrayal to the left.[25]

But there is still one more process of labor on nature besides awakening and reworking. This is Haraway's "reinvention," which appears in the subtitle, *Simians, Cyborgs, and Women: The Reinvention of Nature.* What Haraway means by *reinvention* is a reimagination of nature—not the physical labor of reinventing its plants, animals, and elements—and is better referred to as reworking. Yet *the reinvention of nature* is unfortunate phrasing because it suggests worldnature as reinventable as culture, a nature like Marx's which benefits from (re)invention. Consider the problematic politics of hypothetical utterances like "the reinvention of the lower classes," "the reinvention of woman," and "the reinvention of homosexuals/bisexuals" issuing from a dominant class, from men, and from heterosexuals. How might othered groups receive such slogans from groups that appoint themselves as patriarchs and punishers? Dominant groups might do better to call for their own reinvention. And because culture does dominate by incarcerating, controlling, and killing individual animals, plants, and habitats, wouldn't *The Reinvention of Culture* have been a more apt subtitle than *The Reinvention of Nature?*

If labor "awakens," "reworks," or "reinvents" nature, science unlocks Nature's secrets. Technology is such an important key for scientifically unlocking nature-as-box that technology and science virtually collapse in Haraway's use of *technoscience*. Because technology enables science, Haraway accuses the "organicist" position of rejecting not just technology, but also science (knowledge, skill, playful experimentation):

> We can't afford the versions of the "one-dimensional man" critique of *technological* rationality, which is to say, we can't turn *scientific* discourses into the Other, and make them into the enemy, while still contesting what nature will be for us. We have to engage in those terms of practice, and resist the temptation to remain pure.[26] (my emphasis)

The difficult questions avoided by this shunting of a subtle Marcusian critique is: in *which* "terms of practice" must we engage? In other words, *to what extent* should we support the technological methods of science? And further, isn't our tendency to remain impure a far greater problem than any temptation to become "pure"? Vilifications of technology rarely include a call for the end of science and reason. Fewer and fewer doubt that scientific rationality is an invaluable, even if problematic, human tool; what forms science and reason should take is the more pertinent and vocalized problem.

Renouncing the technological part of science that kills or destroys what it "observes" and that invents products destroying what it has observed is a more effective way to challenge what nature can be for us than Haraway's rather insipid meliorism. Such a challenge might be accomplished by two strategies, which like Haraway's, are poststructuralist. First, conceiving of individual animals and plants as subjects first and objects (much) later—subjects who should no more directly or indirectly be destroyed for the sake of human knowledge than should human subjects. Second, thinking of plants, animals, and elements not as objects to exploit and obstacles to remove, but as friendly or unfriendly neighbors, to visit or tolerate. This is worldnature as another kind of culture with which to coexist and from which to learn, without colonial domination, or special (as in *species*) eviction. These two poststructural strategies might just be a more reasonable, less technological, and more accurate way to interrogate boundaries and deconstruct culture's hegemony in the nature/culture binary.[27]

To her credit, Haraway does acknowledge the problems of describing and prescribing our cyborgian identity. Yet despite what seem like overwhelming problems with technoscience she maintains optimism: "The main trouble with cyborgs, of course, is that they are the illegitimate offspring of militarism and patriarchal capitalism, not to mention state socialism. But illegitimate offspring are often exceedingly unfaithful to their origins. Their fathers, after all, are inessential" (151). While rightly stressing the legitimacy of bastardy and the inessentiality of fathers, Haraway's statement lacks application. High- and mass-technologies are impossible without State support and capital input. At most, "illegitimate offspring" can be only mildly unfaithful to the hands that feed them. And the more the Corporation and the State reform themselves, the more they look like indispensable institutions needing only improvement. Absent from this scenario is any significant dialogue about creating conditions whereby the State and Corporation could be dismantled or wither away, which would in turn diminish the need or desire for accumulation, militarism, and high-technology.

The Siamese twins of militarism and patriarchal capitalism are, indeed, intimidating problems for worldnature and culture, but preoccupation with these can preclude consideration of the pan-economic, pan-political phenomenon of production/consumption (destruction) by individuals and populations becoming entrenched consumers of artifacts, energy, and technology.[28] While the left nurtures its idealism of eventual State and corporate demise[29] and maintains its critique of individualism and liberalism whereby what it calls "isolated acts" cannot substitute for fundamental social change, its all or nothing attitude can have unfortunate results: unattainable goals about change can lead to devastating disappointments, or reduce individuals' acts to acts relevant only to those individuals. Instead, a politics of nature that includes worldnature *and* society would environmentalize and socialize all heretofore private decisions, exert influence, however limited, beyond the individual. Both fronts (the individual-in-terms-of-the-world and the world-in-terms-of-individuals) are necessary for any battle with the increasing cultural monstrosities of privacy and individualism.

If Haraway is right to claim that we cyborgs can rebel against patriarchal and militaristic origins by "both building and destroying machines, identities, categories, relationships, space stories," (181) other pronouncements seem more problematic: "Intense pleasure in skill, machine skill, ceases to be a sin, but an aspect of embodiment" (180), and "For [all of] us, in imagination and in other practice, machines can be prosthetic devices, intimate components, friendly selves" (178). If machines are prosthetic devices—and it is not hard to understand them as such—does *prosthetic* not also point to human disabledness as much as abledness? And what does intense pleasure (for example, sitting fixedly, sending and receiving disembodied words and images through cyberspace) have to do with anything but the most pathetic aspect of embodiment? Besides, who views machine skill as a sin? Even "organicist" countercultures, to greater and lesser degrees, have a love affair with technics (wind, solar, manual).

Love of technology is already so great that loss of technology is often compared to amputation, organ removal, regression, animalization, dehumanization. Haraway, surpassing even her cyborg metaphor, attempts to make it difficult to figure out where our bodies end and our machines begin: "The machine is not an *it* to be animated, worshipped, and dominated. The machine is us, our processes, an aspect of our embodiment. We can be responsible for machines; *they* do not dominate or threaten us. We are responsible for boundaries; we are they" (180). But if we can be responsible for machines, for boundaries, how can this next statement also be valid: "High-tech culture challenges . . . dualisms in intriguing ways. It is not clear who makes and who is made in the relation between human and machine" (177).

It is doubtful that we can be or will be responsible for machines since many of us cede responsibility for even our own and others' bodies partially because of the addiction to and the mediation of technology. But even if we responsibly use technics in such a way wherein overall benefits outweigh drawbacks, it is incontrovertible that even the smallest gestures of technical procurance, manufacture, distribution, use, maintenance, and disposal, destroys the plants, animals, and elements of worldnature; contextualized in terms of worldnature, virtually all tools, even those used by animals, are weapons.

Continually beating the drum (machine) for high-tech liberation further mires humans in modernism, no matter how poststructuralist (deconstructing fixed nature/culture, body/machine binaries), or postmodern (multiplying identities within the individual within and social formations). While technology obviously has useful aspects, in effect or intent technology increasingly means a weapon of mass destruction.

At the threshold of a new millennium, Haraway has effectively figured humanity as cyborgian. Yet she wields this sexy metaphor to sell the dated agenda of techno-optimism and liberation. Too bad. The cyborg could have been a somber metaphor for the cultural destruction and colonization of the last niches of worldnature.

A particular body part, organ, or mutualist parasite viciously attacks the body to which it is connected or which sustains it. This horror subgenre is deadly synecdoche. The configuration of (creeping) metonymy implies nature and culture as contiguous territories, a mapping similar to the visible distinctions between city/country, civilization/wilderness, and artifacts/organisms and elements. But a synecdochical picture views culture residing within nature, as a delineable and permeable part (picture a larger circle, nature, enclosing a much smaller circle, culture, whose border is a dotted line). Synecdoche is a more accurate cartography than metonymy for the nature-culture relationship because synecdoche not only shows culture within and as part of nature, but how culture moves into and incorporates nature, replacing or standing in for it. Haraway's cyborg is the agent of this sprawling culture (the enemy as ourselves), and a failed embodiment of nature and culture melded together. Instead, the cyborg should have been employed to show nature and culture *welded* together, a creature looking overwhelmingly cultural, far more human and technical than animal, vegetable, or elemental. Cyborgs or high-tech humans are part of nature only by being part of a culture, a monstrous culture trying to weld nature to itself through force and fantasy.

Epilogue

A Klee painting named "Angelus Novus" shows an angel looking as though he is about to move away from something he is fixedly contemplating. His eyes are staring, his mouth is open, his wings are spread. This is how one pictures the angel of history. His face is turned toward the past. Where we perceive a chain of events, he sees one single catastrophe which keeps piling wreckage upon wreckage and hurls it in front of his feet. The angel would like to stay, awaken the dead, and make whole what has been smashed. But a storm is blowing from Paradise; it has got caught in his wings with such violence that the angel can no longer close them. This storm irresistibly propels him into the future to which his back is turned, while the pile of debris before him grows skyward. This storm is what we call progress.

—Walter Benjamin, "Theses on the Philosophy of History," *Illiminations*, New York: Schocken Books, 1988, 257–58.

Vying for a potent image of millennial humanity is not only Haraway's sanguine cyborg but Benjamin's angel of history. Where the angel cannot help being blown backward, the cyborg, while also having its back to the future (not even a cyborg can see what lies ahead), confidently rides the tempest into the new day—confidently, despite the same mounting heap of debris produced by superannuated futures, hopes, optimisms. The storm from Paradise that produces the wreckage and the havoc in the angel's wings does not overwhelm the sleek, wingless cyborg moving as if under the thrust of its own will. Why such confidence? Is it because the cyborgian version of a bright future weds human technological progress to a "reinvention" of nature?

I ended the introduction to *Green Cultural Studies* with the image of a shotgun marriage between nature and culture (culture of course, also holding the shotgun). But isn't all *wedlock* between nature and culture under the gun, the product of cultural force or design? Perhaps what nature needs is not a bond with culture but a separation or divorce, some autonomy, at least some protection through "shelters" (preserves), offering sanctuary from culture's constant battering and stalking (I should interject that my metaphor falters to the extent that it genders nature). Wouldn't nature benefit from a respite from cultural attempts at marriage (couplings, fusions, connections, becomings one with), relief from culture's desire to own nature (possession, control, and oppression) or be owned by nature (affection, admiration, worship)?

Green cultural study just might be the cultural court in which nature is granted its much-needed restraining order.

Notes

Introduction

1. *Raw* connotes in need of cooking or processing.

2. The degree of misrepresentation and mistaking, though always hard to assess and therefore often ignored, remains extremely relevant. See Semansky and Hochman, "Ecotastrophes, Photography, and Millennial Doom," 1–15.

3. Ross, *Strange Weather*, 6.

4. "Elements" is a convenience under which are included minerals, the four elements (earth, air, fire, water), and "the elements" (meteorological phenomena).

5. See Raymond Williams, *Keywords*, for an introductory discussion of *nature* and *culture*.

6. See Glacken, *Traces on the Rhodian Shore*, Thomas, *Man and the Natural World*, Oelschlager, *The Idea of Wilderness*, and Wall, *Green History* for histories of cultural perceptions of nature.

7. Herein I include both wild and domesticated plants and animals. My project encompasses the rights of those unlucky enough to be under the (opposing) thumb of culture, and is coupled with the preservation and expansion of wild nature. While the worst in both camps privilege preservation and expansion, the best conceive of these interests, and those of human liberations as continuous.

8. The first four worlds are those human ones, from the industrialized to the indigenous.

9. Hall, "The Emergence of Cultural Studies," 16.

10. Horkheimer and Adorno, *Dialectic of Enlightenment*, 42.

11. Ibid., 40.

12. Slack and Whitt, "Ethics and Cultural Studies," 572.

13. See Ellul, *The Technological Society*. Instead of communism or capitalism Ellul blames "technique" for the destruction of nature. His catch-all term refers to the planning and administration of machines, institutions, and cultural phenomena such as the economy.

14. See Hoggart, *The Uses of Literacy*; E. P. Thompson, *The Making of the English Working Class*; and Williams, *Culture and Society 1780–1950*. For an overview see Turner, *British Cultural Studies*.

15. See Althusser, "Ideology and Ideological State Apparatuses," 127–86.

16. K. Marx, *Capital*, vol. 1, 285.

17. See also Engels, *Origin of Family, Private Property, and State* for a grounding of basic cultural institutions in nature or early culture.

18. Arendt, *Imperialism*, 72.

19. I have left out sexuality because gays, lesbians, and bisexuals are often castigated as unnatural even as they are reduced to objects in the same way as the *naturally* raced, classed, and gendered.

20. Jameson, *Postmodernism*, ix.

21. Sollors, "Ethnicity," 299.

22. Whatever the faults of environmentalism's whiteness, whites have more time for nature than blacks since blacks must use a great deal of energy resisting or coping with white hegemony. Whites, more than blacks, also have greater access to some semblance of nature because blacks have been forced into urban areas for jobs. Environmentalists have no corner on racism. Rather, racists more often betray a certain anti-environmentalism. Think of whites against environmental issues and you come up with the likes of anti-affirmative action Republicans, Patrick Buchanan, white supremacists, and militiamen (exceptions notwithstanding). Further, a focus on nature is not a devaluation of people. Such bad logic might be directed at feminists for not focusing enough time on gay rights, or gays for not addressing the rights of children.

23. Turner, *British Cultural Studies*, 6.

24. Zola, *The Experimental Novel*, 26.

25. However, in the film, *The Grapes of Wrath* (1940), John Ford blames nature. Peter Stowell, Ford's biographer, also falls prey to this notion: "From the beginning this story was conceived of as the quest of a human-sized deliverer, Tom Joad, who must fight the monster, which is, as Northrop Frye puts it, 'the sterility of the land itself'" (Peter Stowell, *John Ford* [Boston: Twayne, 1986], 58). The critic Joseph Warren Beach also privileges culture: "And we are left with the picture of the men on whom they [the women] all depend. It is reduced to the simplest terms—man pitted against the brute forces of nature—man with the enduring will that gives him power to use his brains for the conquering of nature" (Beach, *American Fiction, 1920–1940*, 334). At least Beach does not use naturalism to describe *The Grapes of Wrath*.

26. More precise readings are that the dust bowl provokes the Joads' odyssey while Death Valley reflects McTeague and Marcus's death battle.

27. Zola, "Preface to the Second Edition," 2.

28. Hobbes, *Leviathan,* vol. 1, 13.

29. A. Ross, "Green Ideas Sleep Furiously," 58.

30. Ferris, "On the Edge of Chaos," 43.

31. I have relied on Copleston's overview of Fichte (see Copleston, "Fichte (I)," vol. 7).

32. Haraway, "The Promises of Monsters," 297.

33. Spaying and neutering are mutilations, even if the greater good of pets is sought. In using this strong language, my hope is not that sterilization will be stopped immediately but eventually.

34. A. Wilson, *The Culture of Nature,* 124, my emphasis.

35. Ibid., 113.

36. Deleuze and Guattari, *A Thousand Plateaus,* 270.

37. Ibid., 276.

Chapter 1

1. Harris, *The Silence of the Lambs,* 326.

2. Herodotus, *The Histories,* 130.

3. Krupp, *Beyond the Blue Horizon,* 221.

4. Catherine also bears comparison to the tortured and intelligent Saint Catherine.

5. Krupp, *Beyond the Blue Horizon,* 221.

6. Compare to *Brewster McCloud* (Robert Altman, 1970) for a less reductive view.

7. Note Jame's androgynous name and voice.

8. See also Harris, *The Silence of the Lambs,* 302 for a discussion of Jame's hunting techniques.

9. Cf., *Cat People* (Jacques Tourneur, 1942).

10. Krupp, *Beyond the Blue Horizon,* 219.

11. Harris, *The Silence of the Lambs,* 337, my emphasis.

12. Ibid., 261.

13. Ibid., 261–62.

14. See *The Hellstrom Chronicle* (Walon Green, 1971), where insects are fascinating to Hellstrom because he believes they will inherit the earth.

15. Plato, *Collected Dialogues of Plato*, 12.965b, p. 1510, my emphasis.

16. Hopkins, *Poems of Gerard Manley Hopkins*, 69.

17. Plato, *Collected Dialogues of Plato*, 244b, p. 491.

18. Barber, *Vampires, Burial, and Death*, 89–94.

19. Lopez, *Of Wolves and Men*, 206.

20. Plato, *The Collected Dialogues of Plato*, 565d, p. 794.

21. Barber, *Vampires, Burial, and Death,* 74.

22. Ibid., 9.

23. Stoker, *Dracula*, 283.

24. Ibid., 23 and passim.

25. Ibid., 283.

26. Ibid., 333.

27. The slow evolution from human to insect in David Cronenberg's *The Fly* (1986) is relevant to a border dispute about when a human becomes a monster.

28. See Arens, *The Man-Eating Myth.*

29. See, for comparison, the visual work of Sue Coe, especially her series, *Porkopolis.*

30. Adams, *Sexual Politics of Meat*, 42.

31. See Descartes, *Discourse on Method.*

Chapter 2

1. One might rightly object that *human* and *culture* are not closed identities, univocal and unmixed with animal or nature. But any study must interrupt a process at some point, concentrate on one part and allude to the other. One reason to call human's representation cultural is to draw attention to people's ability to change it.

2. Auden, "Some Notes on D. H. Lawrence," 48.

3. Auden, "D. H. Lawrence," 289.

4. Unless otherwise stated, passages from my discussion about "Reflections on the Death of a Porcupine" are quoted from the 1988 Cambridge University Press edition of *Reflections on the Death of a Porcupine and Other Essays,* edited by Michael Herbert, 352.

5. My statement does not imply that the existence of knowledge is unmediated by cultural construction, but that cultural construction is also tempered or mediated by direct observation.

6. Lawrence, *Women in Love*, 518–19.

7. Burgess, *Flame into Being*, 130.

8. Lawrence, "Aristocracy," 376.

9. Collapsing two entities in metaphor eradicates the ability to effectively contrast at all. Since comparison by metaphor seems inevitable and beneficial, metaphor repeatedly demands exposure as comparison, not identity, lest unreasonable fear result whenever crossing the border of simile. Exposure is especially important when contemplating the often metaphorized representation of nature.

10. Unless otherwise stated, passages from *Women in Love* are quoted from the 1920 Modern Library edition.

11. Ideally, it would not be offensive to compare humans to animals. The offense comes from knowing that people think of animals as lowly, savage, filthy, and stupid—a regrettable state of affairs. We might also imagine a horse indignant at the woman equals horse metaphor, since horses are normally treated far worse than women.

12. Gerald is also a rapist because he rapes Gudrun in Zurich (Lawrence, *Women in Love*, 457–58).

13. Palmer, *History of the Modern World*, 768.

14. Ritvo, *The Animal Estate*, 130.

15. Ibid., 130.

16. Eliade, *The Encyclopedia of Religion*, vol. 15, 90.

17. Herodotus, *The Histories*, 1.216, cf., 4.71–72, 7.113.

18. Shortly after writing this passage I attended a concert of Tuvan singers at Washington Square Church in New York City. The January 16, 1993, concert program offered a brief history of the Tuvans, who are "a South Siberian Turkic people numbering 150,000." Tuvans seem to be as obsessed with horses as Americans with horsepower. Tuvan three-stringed instruments all have horse heads carved atop the instruments' necks. Three of the twelve songs were about horses: a lament for a dead horse, a ditty about harnessing a horse, and one especially relevant song addressing the relationship between horses and women, "Eki A'ttar"—"a song admiring women and great race horses. When a beautiful woman wears her braid decorations and walks, the sounds are like those of a great horse—in Tuva, the supreme compliment."

19. Lawrence, *Apocalypse*, 9–10.

20. Tompkins, *West of Everything*, 101.

21. Lawrence, "Study of Thomas Hardy," 419–20.

22. D. H. Lawrence, quoted in Inniss, *D. H. Lawrence's Bestiary*, 50.

23. Ritvo, *The Animal Estate*, 137–38.

24. It seems evident that empathy for animals has everything to do with reason as reason has everything to do with feeling. For a different discourse on trains and nature see L. Marx, *The Machine in the Garden*.

25. The Hyads later become enshrined as stars in the head of the constellation, Taurus, the Bull.

26. Jowitt, *Time and the Dancing Image*, 82.

27. Beacham, "Appia, Jacques-Dalcroze, and Hellerau," 160.

28. S. W. Smith, ed., *Everyman's Smaller Classical Dictionary*, 110.

29. The bacchante's duty was to liberate Dionysian spirit by tearing apart an animal (the Titan body) and eating the body to gain divine power. The rending and eating perhaps commemorated the Titans' killing and eating of Dionysus, who tried to escape them disguised as a bull. The Titans left behind Dionysus' heart and Zeus ate it and with Semele begat a new Dionysus. Zeus then killed Dionysus' Titanic murderers with a thunderbolt and, out of their ashes, made man. Consequently, humanity is made of the evil, bodily Titans and the good, spiritual Dionysus. Despite Christians' somewhat deserved reputation as hostile to nature, they have improved matters by substituting wafers and wine for live animals.

30. "For when the god enters the body of a man/he fills him with the breath of prophesy" (Euripides, *The Bacchae*, 173). "Man" probably includes women.

31. Lawrence, *Fantasia of the Unconscious*, 101.

32. Lawrence, "St Luke," 325.

33. Euripides, *The Bacchae,* 167.

34. De Vries, *Dictionary of Symbols and Imagery*, 69.

35. Euripides, *The Bacchae,* 173–74.

36. Ibid., 211.

37. See Tindall, *D. H. Lawrence and Susan His Cow* for meditations on the pet cow Lawrence kept in Taos.

38. See Adams, *Sexual Politics of Meat*.

39. Capital (wealth), like the horned heads of cattle, represents life for its possessors and danger or death to those from whom it is taken (the heads of animals as literalized capital on a hunter's wall, or the heads on coin and paper money). A capital crime, for example, theft,

also once meant a crime punishable by beheading. Capital would seem to go to, and for, the head.

40. Other contributions to the transition from matriarchy to patriarchy were agriculture, metal-working, and weaving.

41. Engels, *Origin of Family, Private Property, and State*, 50.

42. Gerald is vulnerable because he has the mark of Cain from accidentally killing his brother when both were children (Lawrence, *Women in Love*, 195).

43. Eliseo Vivas writes: "In the final analysis it [the rabbit scene] is ineffable in abstract terms, and nothing but the full synoptic grasp of the chapters in which it is dramatically defined will yield its complexity" (Vivas, "The Substance of *Women in Love*," 246). Though I agree with Vivas, a certain fear of explaining complexity, and a questionable adoration of the auratic (as in *aura*) artwork seem to underlie a reluctance shared by F. R. Leavis: "There is no need to analyze here how, in the violence of response engendered in Gerald and Gudrun by the struggle with the rabbit, there is engendered too an effect as of a dangerous field of force between the lovers—an intimation, not even now taken by their conscious minds, of latent tension and potential conflict. The nature of the significance is suggested well enough in such places as these" (Leavis, *D. H. Lawrence: Novelist*, 193). Leavis follows this with a lengthy quote describing the main action with the rabbit. Like Vivas, Leavis seems intimidated by Lawrence's constant reference to Bismarck as "mysterious," and perhaps, as well, by the artist's well-known accusation: that the critic is a talentless, meddling parasite.

44. For more on the rabbit-victim see Lawrence's poem, "Rabbit Snared in the Night," in *The Complete Poems of D. H. Lawrence*, eds. Vivian de Sola Pinto and Warren Roberts (New York: Viking, 1936), 240; D. H. Lawrence, *The White Peacock* (London: J. M. Dent, 1935); and D. H. Lawrence, *Phoenix: The Posthumous Papers of D. H. Lawrence*, ed. Edward McDonald (New York: Viking, 1936), 7–13. The latter contains an account of Adolph, his childhood pet rabbit. In the assessments of the way Lawrence uses animals as consistent symbols, I am indebted to the work of Inniss, *D. H. Lawrence's Bestiary*.

45. Lawrence, "Love on the Farm," 42.

46. "He [Halliday] gave Gerald the impression that he loved his terror. He seemed to relish his own horror and hatred of her, turn it over and extract every flavour from it, in real panic. Gerald thought of him as Gudrun is to think of Bismarck, a strange fool, yet piquant" (Inniss, *D. H. Lawrence's Bestiary*, 149). Loercke "ate biscuits rapidly, as a rabbit eats leaves" (Lawrence, *Women in Love*, 536) just before Gerald attacked him. Gerald will not eat this rabbit food perhaps because it is offered by Loercke.

47. "Typologically, the rabbit has a natural connection with the lamb-figure and the pacific principles of increase, but what Lawrence vividly and concretely presents in the poem ["Rabbit Snared in the Night] is an image of aggression inwardly directed against self, a strange lust for destruction by which the meek can implicate the strong in their taste for disaster" (Inniss, *D. H. Lawrence's Bestiary*, 63).

48. Lawrence asserts, "The *Lion* shall never lie down *with* the *Lamb*" (Lawrence, "The Lemon Gardens," 80–81, my emphasis).

49. This may be a fallacy. It might be that animals are sometimes better understood because they do not likely make a habit of cloaking behavior with manipulable language. But whatever the case, such generalizations about the huge class, animals, is a dubious enterprise.

50. Some birds fake a flight-preventing injury to draw predators away from their young. When the predator approaches the *injured* bird flies away.

51. Such a theory might be mustered to justify *sport* hunting, or even slaughter. The purveyors and consumers of meat maintain, "Animals wouldn't allow themselves to get shot unless they wanted to."

52. Lawrence, *Letters of D. H. Lawrence*, vol. 1, 503.

53. Lawrence, "Study of Thomas Hardy," 205.

54. One critic writes:

> Simplistic reading tends to attribute to Lawrence a one-sided, exclusively Dionysian sexual ecstasy, primitive religiosity, and intellectual irrationalism. In Lawrence's view, it is true, the times demanded a reassertion of these Dionysian elements to correct the imbalance on the side of Apollonian forces in decadent form—the imbalance on the side of spiritual will, rationalized faith, and sterile reason—which had resulted from the unholy wedlock of the industrial revolution and Christian idealism: the one divorced from natural cycles, the other divorced from religious cycles, and both united in the service of the utilitarian ethic that defined creativity as production, and progress as the proliferation of technology. But Lawrence no more advocated an imbalance on the opposite side than Nietzsche did. In every arc of his thought . . . Lawrence makes his plea for a balanced polarity between the Apollonian and the Dionysian (Cowan, *D. H. Lawrence and the Trembling of the Balance*, 34).

55. See Thomas Hardy's novels, especially *The Return of the Native*, for such efforts.

56. If anthropomorphism is unavoidable the only thing to do is use it more critically.

Chapter 3

1. Michael Ciment, referring to the forest in *Deliverance,* says, "The Garden of Eden is a poisonous jungle" (Ciment, *John Boorman,* 125).

2. Forest ghettos are reserved not only to maintain patches of forest for human use, but to ensure that development is perceived as greenly sustainable, human yet humane, productive yet preserving (even the National Forest Service *is* a part of the Department of Agriculture). Perhaps urban ghettos function as negative examples—peopled monuments showing society an image to avoid. Urban ghettos also seem to serve as inexpensive holding tanks or jails, especially for Latinos and African-American males, perhaps en-natured as *wild*. In the forest ghetto, wild plants and animals need not be imprisoned since they can be killed (often called "controlling" or "thinning") unless, that is, they are lucky enough to be labeled as endangered.

3. Parks, though marginalized, are not so much ghettos since they are visited for pleasure. But this is the case only if these areas have been remade from dangerous ghettos into attractive parks, gardens, arboretums, theme parks, zoos, etc.

4. Perhaps the forest might even spread, move into so-called civilization. For an advancing forest see Birnham Wood in *Macbeth* and Akira Kurosawa's remake of *Macbeth, Throne of Blood* (1957).

5. While the ghetto is neglected and undeveloped its cultural production is not.

6. Remember Bobby's remarks at the gas pump, that Oree might be the place everything ends up, even his '51 Dodge where "all [his] youth and passion were spent in the back seat." The soon-to-be engulfed forest gets its comeuppance for being the all-engulfing forest.

7. The forest as a place of the past can also be positive. If the forest is old enough to have seen it all, it must be wise or at least a place to attain wisdom.

8. This is not necessarily inappropriate except in its damaging effects on nature.

9. Jameson, "Great American Hunter" 185.

10. Ibid., 185.

11. Parks and forests gain speed because they are used as places to jog, speed walk, or let dogs run.

12. Some of nature's preexisting speed *is* utilized in activities such as rafting or canoeing.

13. Readers might wonder why I use *mountain* instead of *forest* people since I am writing about the forest. *Forest people*, unlike *mountain people*, is often associated with tales and legends.

14. For failed machines see other John Boorman films, *Point Blank* (1967), *Hell in the Pacific* (1968), and *Leo the Last* (1970).

15. Jameson, "Great American Hunter," 186.

16. Alighieri, *Inferno*, Canto I, lines 1–7.

17. Ibid., Canto IV, lines 64–66; Canto XIII, *passim*.

18. While the nature in *Deliverance* is not strictly hellish, Boorman did seek to create a menacing nature: "The film's downbeat mood is sustained in its cinematography as well as its dramaturgy. Seeking to lend what he called an 'ominous quality' to the 'pleasant and restful' greens and blues of sky, river and trees, Boorman (in conjunction with Technicolor) developed a new color desaturation technique for *Deliverance*. The result is a film shot in threatening grey-greens, not so much washed-out as evacuated of conventionally pretty nature imagery. . . . As befits a story of liberal complacency confronted by brutal antagonism, it is the struggle to survive that predominates, the big screen used more to document that in close-up than to celebrate the pictorial splendours of the setting" (Tudor, *International Dictionary of Films and Filmmakers*, 222–23). For more on color desaturation in *Deliverance* see Ciment, *John Boorman*, 130.

19. Alighieri, *Inferno*, Canto XIII, lines 2–6.

20. Ovid, *Metamorphosis*, Book IX, lines 115–16.

21. Ibid., Book IX, line 129. Ovid does not convey who removed the arrow.

22. Ibid., Book IX, line 169.

23. Recall that Lewis's exposed bones are in the same place as the scar of that other arch-archer, Odysseus.

24. Alighieri, *Inferno,* Canto XV, line 114; and see Mandelbaum's note for lines 112–14, 369, where he writes that the sinful strain was due to repeated acts of sodomy.

25. Ibid., Canto XVII, lines 62–63; and Mandelbaum's note to line 62, 368.

26. Ibid., Canto III, line 9.

27. Ovid, *Metamorphosis,* Book XI, line 166.

28. My description of Apollo courtesy of Bullfinch, *Bullfinch's Mythology*, Ovid, *Metamorphosis*, and Smith, *Everyman's Smaller Classical Dictionary*.

29. In the novel, the fall into the river cleans the arrow paint from Ed's wound, saving him from blood poisoning (Dickey, *Deliverance*, 179). For a film/novel comparison see Griffith, "Damned If You Do, and Damned If You Don't," 47–59.

30. Alighieri, *Inferno,* Canto XVI, lines 93–136.

31. Ibid., Canto XVII, lines 1–2.

32. Ibid., Canto XVI, lines 133–34. In *Inferno*'s "rope passage," Dante offers advice with strange resonance for *Deliverance*'s canoeists: "Faced with that truth which seems a lie, a man/should always close his lips as long as he can—/to tell it shames him, even though he's blameless" (Ibid., Canto XVI, lines 124–26). In *Deliverance*, the truth would refer to the mountain men's shameful violations, which the canoeists lie about.

33. The mountain men might be thought to belong to the forest, and not the forest to them because the forest is all around them even while they live in it. If the forest owns the men, they are, from the cultural view, morally depraved. If men own the forest, usually by so-called improvement or development, the forest's dark amorality is eradicated.

34. Eliade, *The Encyclopedia of Religion*, vol. 2, 260.

35. The problem with this reading is that the surviving canoe is metal. Still, shape and function are duplicated enough to retain a close relationship to wood canoes and the indirect connection to trees.

36. Eliade, *The Encyclopedia of Religion*, vol. 2, 259.

37. Ibid., vol. 15, 29. For people as trees, also see Mark 8:22.

38. The word *wretch*, as in *wretched*, comes from the Old English *wrecca,* or exile, wanderer, and is a cognate of the Greek *recke,* meaning warrior or hero. The wretched forest is a place only for exiles and heroes.

39. Toni Morrison, "The Site of Memory," 302.

40. The deer excuse was offered by an Oregon logger interviewed on an evening news program.

41. Recall that in *Women in Love* the horse Gerald rode was conceived of as a machine. With the opposite transformation, the machine is transformed into a fairly innocent creature, or to farmers, one that destroys crops.

42. Perhaps Lot had been a sodomite after all and, drunk, missed the familiar anus; or perhaps incest was his way to swear off the sodomy for which he felt guilty.

43. On what might be deemed classism in *Deliverance*, or explained as a prejudice against those considered more as products of nature than culture, I offer comments from two critics. The first: "The actual residents of north Georgia angrily believe that Boorman scoured the hills looking for the worst sort of people" (Armour, *"Deliverance:* Four Variations of the American Adam," 284). And the second: "Boorman's film is vastly strengthened by its ambiguities; the flooding of the Chatooga [sic] Valley can be interpreted as a cleansing operation as much as a pollutive one forcing the illiterate, physically

deteriorating backwoodsmen out into a healthier environment" (Strick, Review of *Deliverance*, 228).

44. The notion of hunting as cruel would clash with Dickey's views—he was an avid bow and arrow hunter—and with Lewis's practical expertise in this method of food gathering.

45. At Christmas, trees are killed to be used for decoration, much like the baubles that hang from them.

46. It is especially important to the culture of consumerism that nature be held up as the final enemy. If nature is our opponent, we care little that consumption destroys nature and we continue consuming nature to protect ourselves from it in its several forms: natural "ugliness" is combated with soaps, cosmetics, jewelry, and clothing; natural distance with animal or vehicular transportation; natural decay with refrigeration, chemicals, and drugs; natural discomfort with furniture, clothing, air conditioners, fans, and heaters. But most of what are commonly thought to be natural foes can also be construed as cultural, since culture sets the standards of beauty, distance, and comfort.

47. Eliade, *The Encyclopedia of Religion*, vol. 12, 406.

48. Ibid., vol. 15, 28.

49. Eliade, *The Encyclopedia of Religion*, vol. 12, 381.

50. Ibid., vol. 12, 417.

51. Robert F. Wilson, Jr., writes, "Ed passes the test of nature and his own conscience and he returns to civilization with a renewed sense of its worth . . . a victory of humane values over bestiality, of creativity over destruction" (R. Wilson Jr., *"Deliverance* from Novel to Film," 57).

Chapter 4

1. I do not claim that people today necessarily shudder when they hear the word *forest*. With the popularization of the term *rain forest*, fear is probably disappearing. But I show the history embedded in words such as *forest*, to illustrate how people continue to survive and forests don't. See Thomas, *Man and the Natural World* and Glacken, *Traces on the Rhodian Shore* for histories of European and American attitudes toward nature. Also relevant is L. Marx, *The Machine in the Garden*.

2. If people in a crowd leave, no crowd exists. But if the people and animals in a forest leave, a forest remains, which is only to say that people and animals are not the defining features of a forest. Trees are. While I hope this is obvious, there is that pesky philosophical question, "If a tree falls in an (unpeopled) forest, does it make a sound?" Or the more visual variation, "If a forest is seen by no one, does it exist?" The defining feature of a forest in these questions is a

corroborating human presence. Such questions tempt people toward self-apotheosis by basing existence-at-large upon Human Witnessing and Human Consciousness.

3. Subjectivity in terms of for-itself, and less for-another.

4. See Stampp, *The Peculiar Institution*. White southerners, who called slavery that "peculiar institution," seemed to have had a gift for understatement, but peculiar is from the Latin, *peculium*, meaning property, which derived from the Latin, *pecu*, referring to flock, farm animals, and/or cattle.

5. For the connection of the name, *Sethe*, to the Biblical Seth and the Egyptian god Seth, as well as to animals, see Samuels and Hudson-Weems, "Ripping the Veil," 94–138.

6. Unless otherwise stated, all passages from *Beloved* are quoted from the 1987 Plume edition.

7. Sethe's backtree has also been compared to "a tree of life—as a symbol of Sethe's history" and the "symbol of the cross or burden she bears." Samuels and Weems, "Ripping the Veil," 115.

8. Rebecca Rupp, *Red Oaks and Black Birches*, 133–34.

9. Ibid., 141.

10. Little, *Audubon Field Guide to North American Trees*, 509.

11. My question throughout this chapter is: Why were particular kinds of trees named? Merely because Morrison wanted readers to picture the tree? Research leads me to believe there is more. If I am reading into the text my suggestions still serve to illuminate, not Morrison's intention, but the potential *for reader or writer* of closely attending to representations of nature.

12. Contrary to the need to forget, it is also sometimes politically effective to memorialize humanity's unspeakable acts, but not by something beautiful. This is the reason trees are rarely, if ever, monuments to infamy.

13. Horror film, however, does have its subgenre of people-eating trees.

14. In over twenty critical articles and interviews no mention is made of Morrison's identification of trees let alone that these species seem well-chosen. The identification of trees is rendered as mere detail because trees themselves, despite their size, are considered details.

15. This taxonomy is, as most botanical and zoological taxonomy, based on structural similarities between trees rather than between trees and people. Neither is it based on what people use trees for, as implied in the hardwood/softwood distinction.

16. Linda Krumholz emphasizes, "the Clearing [as] a place that signifies the necessity for a *psychological* cleansing from the past" (397, my emphasis). My views do not contradict but complement Krumholz's.

17. Thomas, *Man and the Natural World*, 216.

18. If the Clearing can be compared to a cathedral or temple, Denver's post oak- and box-wood-protected emerald closet (a kind of play-fort), might be called a sanctuary, "a place where salvation was as easy as a wish" (Morrison, *Beloved*, 29). Post oaks, in addition to being sacred to Druids, are known for their Maltese-cross-shaped leaves and boxwood have been a part of sanctuary walls: "The glory of Lebanon shall come unto thee, the fir tree, the pine tree, and the box together, to beautify the place of my [God's] sanctuary" (Isaiah 60:13, *The Holy Bible: King James Version*, see also Isaiah 41:19). The absence of firs and scarcity of pines in *Beloved* is attributable to their abFsence and scarcity in the native forests of Ohio. Denver stops going to the emerald closet when Beloved, a Christlike revenant, is reborn, indicating that there is no need for sanctuaries when the real thing has come back.

19. Rupp, *Red Oaks and Black Birches*, 6. In Greek, *dry* means oak or tree. Dryads are tree- or wood nymphs. Although I find no verification of a relationship, *Druidae*, meaning Druids, is Latin and could be derived from or related to the Greek *dry*. Here might be an explanation for the phonetic similarity of *dryad* and *druid*.

20. Ibid., 1. With most trees, lightning travels to the ground through the uniformly wet, conductive outer leaves, limbs, and trunk of the tree. But in oaks, the bark is so rough that parts of it dry quickly, and lightning, seeking a path, enters the pores of the inner tree: "The heat of the travelling lightning—50,000 degrees Fahrenheit, five times hotter than the surface of the sun—promptly vaporizes the sap, which, trapped in its tiny tubes, expands violently. The resultant explosion blasts the luckless oak to oblivion" (4).

21. This more rich and complex view of the forest is absent when *Beloved* negatively metaphorizes noncommunication as a forest, "trackless and quiet" (165), as though forests without humans lacked paths and sounds. This is also the case when wildness is called a jungle of "swift unnavigable waters, swinging screaming baboons" and bloodthirsty snakes (198–99). Hannah Arendt believes that such views of nature, especially of the jungle, played (plays?) a crucial role in Western conceptions of Africans:

> What made them [Africans] different from other [whiter] human beings was not at all the color of their skin but the fact that they behaved like a part of nature, that they treated nature as their undisputed master, that they had not created a human world, a human reality, and that therefore nature had remained, in all its majesty, the only overwhelming reality—compared to which they appeared to be phantoms, unreal and ghostlike. They were, as it were, "natural" human beings who lacked the specifically human character, the specifically human reality, so that when European men massacred them they somehow were not aware that they had committed murder. (Arendt, *Imperialism*, 72)

This statement is intrinsic to the animalization of Africans by Westerners. The hostile, superior attitude to the jungle renders it the polar opposite of a place of beauty, nurture, knowledge, and home—words also fit for a jungle. These words are now employed to describe the rain forest, which is the positive pole to *jungle* (few talk about "saving the jungle"). I do not argue that the negative conceptions of the *jungle* are without basis; dangers should not be forgotten. Rather, I argue that instead of simply inculcating a proper caution toward the jungle, *Beloved*'s few configurations of massed nature (forest, jungle) subtly reinforce fear of, hostility and imperiousness toward nature, as well as apathy or satisfaction when forests and jungles are cut down, its animals killed, and its rivers dammed. Combine *Beloved*'s negativized jungle with its characterization as empty ("trackless and quiet") and clearings pose as civilizing cure (while the rain forest is potential pharmacological cure). Could it be—with such rough use of *forest* and *jungle*—that my reading of the Clearing was hasty? Perhaps it is the place where jungle and forest aren't present that people get in touch with their bodies and with other people, where people become human by becoming better than "unnavigable rivers," "screaming baboons," and bloodthirsty snakes. Morrison then might be accused of having more problems with forests or jungles than with individual trees.

22. Deborah Ayer Sitter asserts "That Paul D is meditating *not on trees* [my emphasis] but on manhood in Sethe's bedroom is revealed in the concluding words of his reverie: 'Now *there* was a man, and *that* was a tree.'" Sitter concludes: "Paul D's refusal to acknowledge that her [Sethe's] scars cohere into an awful but beautiful image reveals his inability to accept Sethe's integrity, her wholeness" (Sitter, "The Making of Man: Dialogic Meaning in *Beloved*," 23). The problem with Sitter's reading is that based on Brother's juxtaposition with the male Sixo, the tree's male name, and the repugnance of Sethe's allegedly female backtree, Sitter concludes that trees are symbols of manhood to Paul D. Sitter understands *Beloved*'s trees only as anthropomorphic symbols without noticing that the novel also attempts to value trees as trees, as "pretty," as "inviting; things you can trust and be near, talk to" (not exactly male traits), in short, worthy of a relationship and a name. Rather than being emblems of manhood, Paul D's (and Sixo's) beloved trees represent the positive pole opposite the negative pole of whites, with the noticeable reversal that whites are less "human," (have fewer good traits) than trees. A more plausible explanation for Paul D's repugnance to Sethe's backtree than its femaleness is that it is a network of scars caused by vicious white males, the latter of which Paul D would be loathe to associate with trees.

23. Rupp, *Red Oaks and Black Birches*, 90.

24. Perhaps Morrison's specification of tree species allows visualization for readers and future filmmakers. If this is true, why does she not specify what kind of tree Brother is? Morrison strives not just for visual clarity, but for conceptual clarity. Specifying Brother's

classification would interfere with its paradigmatic quality as everytree—every beautiful, beckoning tree.

25. See the notion of interpellation in Louis Althusser, "Ideology and Ideological State Apparatuses," 127–86, for implications of even pronominal naming.

26. Trees are most often hermaphrodites with flowers containing both male stamens and a female pistil ending in a basal ovary. Even many of the trees with separate-sexed flowers have both sexes on the same tree.

27. Sitter writes, "In the center of many West African villages stands a large tree (like the baobab in the epic *Sundiata*) around which *men* gather to make decisions about tribal governance" (Sitter, "The Making of Dialogic Meaning in *Beloved*," 23).

28. Rupp, *Red Oaks and Black Birches*, 194.

29. MacCulloch, *Mythology of All Races*, vol. 2, 331.

30. If newer generations proceed upward, then tree roots must be buried ancestors and the trunk must be the parents or *stock*, a word derived from the Old Norse *stokkr* meaning tree trunk, which might also be related to *stalk*.

31. The lullaby, "Rock-a-bye baby in the tree tops, when the wind blows the cradle will rock, when the bough breaks the cradle will fall and down will come baby, cradle and all," is the opposite pole of *Beloved*'s tree trust.

32. Both autovalence and extravalence stand as complements to anthropocentric environmentalism (safe water, air, soil, and food for people).

33. See Descartes, *Discourse on Method*.

34. Since he is not expressly described as white, I am hesitant about asserting that the sawyer is white. I base my assertion on three criteria, first, the carnival has almost all white performers and attendance, with only Thursdays for "coloreds." Therefore the carnival is probably in a white area. Second, the lumberyard has been the sawyer's for twelve years, while blacks seem to get jobs only at the slaughterhouse. Last, Morrison expressly uses "coloredpeople" to describe the carnivalgoers as if to contrast them with the white sawyer.

35. The death-to-life transformation is especially apt after a *carni*val, an occasion for reversal and rebirth, when winter's quiescent dead become spring's living flesh. See Bakhtin, *Rabelais and His World*.

36. *Child*, from the Gothic *kilthai*, womb, diminishes the child to a bodily organ of the mother, and to the father when he likens both wo-man/fe-male and child to a part or extension of himself.

Chapter 5

1. Shallow burial and unsuccessful psychological repression are linked by John Cooke in his Northwestern University dissertation "The Novels of Nadine Gordimer," 1976 (201), as cited in Clingman, "Prophecy and Subversion," 247 n. 43. For another of Gordimer's views on "living" corpses see "A Watcher of the Dead," 33–38, and "Six Feet of the Country," 7–20. See also "Speak Out," 92, where Gordimer speaks of protest as a corpse that students should "dig up, alive and kicking."

2. Governmental or public ownership is not always better since governments sell logging, drilling, mining, and grazing rights to business.

3. For Karl Marx, it was "exchange value," not exchange that gave an entity or product commodity status. K. Marx, *Capital*, vol. 1, 955. Thus, if something is produced with exchange in mind, and where labor can be objectified into the price of that exchangeable object, the thing is already a commodity, even if not exchanged. This seems extreme in that thought becomes *transubstantiating*. For example, if a farmer raises grain for the market and understands it as a commodity but never sells it then it is more accurate to say that the grain was raised as a commodity, yet never became one. This quibble aside, I still owe my conception of commodity to Marx.

4. Unless otherwise stated, all passages from *The Conservationist* are quoted from the 1978 Penguin edition.

5. See *The Machine in the Garden* for L. Marx's discussion of the rural, including the farm, as ideal mediation between technological culture and wilderness, which relates to Mehring's equation between productive and beautiful. Rural land or farmland is probably better characterized as comfortable more than beautiful because it signals few or no predators, hospitable weather, and food-bearing fields. Rarely does it signal toil. See Williams, *The Country and the City* for a discussion of the necessary absence of rural toil in the picturesque landscape.

6. Christo's gargantuan wrappings or packagings, and the "bisection," *Running Fence,* draw attention to the commodification of real estate. His most recent wrapping was of the Reichstag (1995), which perhaps drew attention to the cloaked buying and selling of government.

7. Other animals or plants can also be said to commodify and own. They parcelize by taking animals or plants out of context and exchange them by passing them as food to offspring or cohorts, probably receiving something in return (society, affection, protection, food). However, their dictatorship of property is minimal and temporary compared to human dictatorship by property.

8. Africans lived closer to nature than Europeans who had fixed domiciles. This means that Africans, as either hunter-gatherers or nomadic pastoralists, had fewer machines and possessions, and less development, which usually accompanies a fixed, agricultural way of life. Developed land appears to belong (or once belonged) to people more than vice versa. Close to nature might be more accurately described as further from Western ideas of culture.

9. Calling plants *weeds* has a similar effect to calling rodents *vermin* (from the Latin *vermis* meaning worm or maggot). What might be thought of as beautiful (plants) or cute (rodents) are, through lexical alchemy conceived as something ugly and killable.

10. Stephen Clingman discusses the farm as another kind of battlefield: "In a country where land dispossession had been crucial historically, farms—perhaps significantly for Gordimer's novel—were key sites for battle" (Clingman, "Prophecy and Subversion," 138–39). See the same essay for a discussion of the farm as an instance of a cultural relationship to the South African environment (147). The farm and apartheid are further linked through a policy of separating people in the same way that commodified crops are separated within fields. Where different cultures and colors formerly intermingled in South Africa, apartheid demarcated Africans into Bantustans or homelands by a brand of racist monocultural engineering.

11. For thoughts relative to the way Mehring, as everyfarmer, deals with land in agricultural and conservational practice see Joel Synder's essay, "Territorial Photography," in which Snyder remarks on "the critical literature of the period [1860s America], which continually commends photographers for having achieved pictures faithful to nature that *coincidentally* share specific compositional and pictorial features with landscapes wrought in other media" (Mitchell, ed., *Landscape and Power*, 185). If Mehring saw photographs of "naturally occurring" land framed by trees, he might think he was replicating nature. While canopy-like trees might be found in nature, their selection as picture-worthy is culturally-constructed.

12. Nicholas Green discusses metropolitan production of the private ego through spectacle—products and places are designed for individual consumers to view. Green writes that metropolitan private egoism is not confined to the city but escapes to the country where viewing nature also produces, or aggravates, the private ego (Green, *The Spectacle of Nature*, 138). On a quiet dark night in the pasture, Mehring exhibits such egoism: "He feels what can only be a sense of superiority. Not because he is not among them [friends] any more, not this year . . . but because no one is watching this night the way he is. No one is seeing it but him. That's the feeling" (205). Isolation reinforces Mehring's private ego, but so does pride about having exclusive access to nature. This is the egoism of privilege.

13. In addition to marginalization and forced absorption into hegemonic institutions, otherness can garner respect and a certain distance. The problem with othering people is that they

are so much like us that if they do not become like us they are marginalized or exterminated. Animals and plants, on the other hand, might benefit from being granted otherness, unassimilable difference and space to live out autonomous or semi-autonomous lives. Maybe.

14. See Glacken, *Traces on the Rhodian Shore* for mining's decimating impact on land, especially the forest.

15. Gordimer grew up in the strange landscape of the world's then richest gold-mining area, Witwatersrand, in the Transvaal of South Africa. See Gordimer, *Conversations with Nadine Gordimer*, 13.

16. Owning might indeed be called Mehring's special pleasure: "Shall I [Mehring] tell you something, Antonia [Mehring's lover]? You don't know it, but there's a special pleasure in having a woman you've paid. Now and then. I can't explain it. It's very clear cut. For that one night, or that one afternoon or day, whatever it is. You've bought and paid for everything" (77–78).

17. Mehring has gone beyond spectacle by imagining touching this slagheap with his lips.

18. People are also silenced by being considered property, but that does not occur in this novel.

19. There is an additional sense of conservation mentioned when Mehring thinks to himself: "On the farm it is the time for conservation—buildings to be repaired, fire-breaks cleared, he must go round all the fences with Jacobus. The sort of jobs they'll [the African laborers] never think to do unless you push them to it. A place must be kept up" (74). This might be called farm conservation rather than nature conservation.

20. There are cases where relocation might be the only solution, but it is still an incomplete solution because it fails to address the real problem: cultural encroachment. When destroying animals or plants is advocated to improve ecosystem health, suspicion is justified because genocide has also been perpetrated in the name of the health of a people, culture, or race.

21. See Robert, "Stella," "Stella Through the Looking Glass," 73–86, and Mistress Vena, "Confessions of a Psyco-Mistress," 65–72. Also see Engle, *"The Conservationist* and the Political Uncanny," 148–64 for the farm as an eruption of repression.

22. See Griffin, *The Roaring Inside Her* for a discussion of the common trope of woman-as-land, especially pages 52–54 on arable land.

23. One might argue that squeamishness about killing (animals) for food or clothing is the result of cultural warping, and that such killing is ethically acceptable and natural. Thus, who kills is too fine a point to belabor. But it could be that acceptance of removed or absentee killing (of animals) is also a cultural construction or warping stemming from a division of labor and mostly acceptable because people do not see, hear, or think about the killing, let

alone wield the knife or gun. Further, killing for one's own food and clothing is hardly better, because the ability to kill (animals) is primarily the result of cultural influence. In this matter of natural versus cultural construction, it might be better to move the discussion to other topoi, like cultural and natural effects.

24. Mehring is also able to disown labor in which he has invested no land. He, in part, disowns the corpse because he has never given, leased, or allowed the man to work on the land.

25. "Names," says Gordimer, "are very important. I can't really tell how they come. For the central characters the name comes very early on. It seems to be there and the person couldn't have had any other name. At other times, I will get the first name and the surname may not come. It is a question of milieu as well as the personality of the character.... Names are very important for the feeling of the person and for the physical look of the person" (Gordimer, *Conversations with Nadine Gordimer*, 79–80).

26. Thomas and Alina are exceptions. Thomas, the farm's gatekeeper, enters the novel when the corpse "rises." Unlike Jesus' apostle, Gordimer's Thomas doubts nothing. Still, he spurs readers to connect the resurrected corpse to Jesus. The reason for Gordimer's choice of a German name for Mehring's only house servant Alina (which comes from *Adele* and is Germanic for *noble*) eludes me. *Mehring* is also a German name, meaning more+ing, the reason for the suffix is unclear. However, the meaning of *mehr*, or *more,* is fitting for arch-capitalist Mehring whose essential role involves acquisition of African wealth. Mehring's German name also sets him apart from Boers, Africans, and Indians in the novel. It also functions as a sign of domination over the Africans with their Hebrew-sounding names and as a reminder of the Germans' atrocities against black Africans (see Arendt, *Imperialism*). Curiously, Mehring's first name is not mentioned; is he an everycapitalist?

27. All Biblical sources are derived from consultation with both *The Oxford Annotated Bible*, Revised Standard Version and *The Holy Bible,* King James Version.

28. This is not to say that wonder and excitement cannot also hang about these places.

29. There are more and less offensive agricultural and horticultural methods. But whatever the method—chemical or organic—and whatever the scale—agribusiness or backyard gardening—farming is control—an iron hand, not just a green thumb.

30. Near Christmas Mehring goes out to his land more often and even spends a night in the field, but this is an exception. Later, he is kept out by the flood, and finally, at the end of the novel, readers wonder if he ever returns. See Wade, *Nadine Gordimer*, 209, for more on Mehring's isolation.

31. See Clingman, "Prophecy and Subversion," 158, for a slightly different take on the novel's eggs.

32. This quotation is a King James translation. In the Revised Standard Edition of the *Oxford Annotated Bible* no chestnut trees appear in these passages and the rods are not for fertility but for getting the cattle to produce *a certain kind* of offspring. I am indebted to Rupp's *Red Oaks and Black Birches*, 32, for this lead on chestnut trees.

33. Mehring also falls asleep and gets earth in his mouth, he thinks he will be killed, and his friend, an analogue industrialist, commits suicide.

34. See Matthew 26:69–75 where Peter denies knowing Jesus three times.

35. Frazer, *The Golden Bough*, 427.

36. Bullfinch, *Bullfinch's Mythology*, 70–71.

37. See Newman, *Nadine Gordimer* for the relation of Zulu myth to reeds, as Zulu myth is important to this novel. For a greater exploration of Zulu myth's influence, specifically Reverend Henry Callaway's *The Religious System of the Amazulu,* see Thorpe, "Motif of the Ancestor," 116–23.

38. Blacks-equal-labor has long been a South African equation: "It was this absolute dependence on the work of others and complete contempt for labor and productivity in any form that transformed the Dutchman into the Boer and gave his concept of race a distinctly economic meaning" (Arendt, *Imperialism,* 73). When Africans became labor, Europeans became leisure.

39. Ibid., 72.

40. This is the "price of indifference" Gordimer discusses in "Speak Out," 102.

Chapter 6

1. Creel, *"A Peculiar People,"* 38.

2. Moore, *Travels into Inland Parts of Africa*, 42–43.

3. For a positive (because non-literal) postmodern notion of deterritorialization see Deleuze and Guattari, *A Thousand Plateaus.*

4. This view of Africans did not end in the United States. In an *Address to the Public by the Committee of Correspondence of the Educational Commission (1862),* northerners were petitioned to help freed slaves: "'We may hope . . . to do for these *stepchildren* of nature all their masters have failed to do, but we must certainly begin by doing what their masters did not and could not omit'" (Rose, *Rehearsal for Reconstruction,* 40, my emphasis). Is the writer implying that in Africa, Africans were the *children* of nature?

5. I have found no instance where slave status in Africa was inherited by children. This would make American slavery not just a peculiar institution as whites had euphemized it, but a peculiarly cruel institution.

6. Unless otherwise stated, and where possible, all film quotations will be cited from the 1992 book/script published by New Press.

7. Creel, *"A Peculiar People,"* 36.

8. Ibid., 43–44.

9. Rose, *Rehearsal for Reconstruction,* 14.

10. Ibid., 7. While talking with urbanite Julie Dash, she told me she discovered a feeling for nature while filming *Daughters of the Dust* on the Sea Islands. She said it was a place she wanted to die in (from an informal conversation in April 1996).

11. French is quoted in Rose, *Rehearsal for Reconstruction,* 57.

12. Movimento Popular de Libertaçao de Angola.

13. Neto, "The Grieved Lands," 30.

14. Rose, *Rehearsal for Reconstruction,* 82–83.

15. Lewis Mumford mentions an advantage of feudalism: "The meanest serf had a right to certain portions of the land, and if he could not leave it, neither could the land leave him" (Mumford, *The Culture of Cities,* 327). Lafargue writes about feudalism as a community (from *com-*, together and *munus*, duty): "Under the feudal system the landlord has obligations and is far from enjoying the liberty of the capitalist—the right to use and abuse. The land is not marketable; it is burdened with conditions, and is transmitted according to traditionary customs which the proprietor dares not infringe; he is bound to discharge certain defined duties towards his hierarchical superiors and inferiors" (Lafargue, *The Evolution of Property,* 47).

16. Kirkpatrick Sale, for example, explains a community land trust:

> In contemporary America the most fruitful example of communal owner-
> ship—though there are in truth many examples, from building co-ops in
> major cities to communes in the hinterlands—is the community land trust.
> The CLT is a nonprofit corporation, open to all members of a local commu-
> nity, that acquires a parcel of land to be held in trust in perpetuity and then
> rents it out on long-term, low-cost leases, renewable and inheritable,
> restricted by whatever original agreements the trust makes as to ecological
> practices, kinds of building, pooling of surpluses, and the like. (85)

For more, see Sale, *Dwellers in the Land,* 84–88. For a vision of universal land ownership after the anarchist revolution see Guillaume, "On Building the New Social Order," 356–61.

17. Locke, *Essay Concerning Human Understanding*, 254.

18. Rousseau, "Discourse on the Origin of Inequality," 60. Rousseau's version of history figures humans in nature as independent, self-sufficient individuals ("the first person who"). It is more likely that land was held in common by clans or communities.

19. Lafargue, *The Evolution of Property*, 41, n. 1.

20. Ibid., 59.

21. Ibid., 46.

22. The foregoing history courtesy of K. Marx, *Capital*, vol. 1, 878–79, and Polanyi, *The Great Transformation*, 34–39.

23. In order to prevent begging and thieving and to create a more just economy Thomas Paine argues in 1797 that landowners owe the community a ground rent, to be paid into "a national fund, out of which shall be paid to every person, when arrived at the age of twenty-one years, the sum of fifteen pounds sterling, as a compensation, in part, for the loss of his or her natural inheritance, by the introduction of landed property; and also the sum of ten pounds per annum, during life, to every person now living, of the age of fifty years, and to all others as they shall arrive at the age" (cited in Robertson, 14).

24. The first of many such laws was enacted in 1530. Marx enumerates some of them: "Beggars who are old and incapable of working receive a beggar's licence. On the other hand, whipping and imprisonment for sturdy vagabonds. They are to be tied to the cart-tail and whipped until the blood streams from their bodies, then they are to swear on oath *to go back* to their birthplace or where they have lived the last three years and to 'put themselves to labor' (K. Marx, *Capital*, 896, my emphasis). Marx remarks on the irony of the "beggars" being sent back to the land they were forced off. A 1547 law that Marx describes, like the events at Port Royal, indicates an unusual progression of property relationships: "A statute . . . ordains that if anyone refuses to work, he shall be condemned as a slave to the person who has denounced him as an idler" (K. Marx, *Capital*, 897).

25. At the time I was writing this chapter numerous corporations were downsizing. Downsizing redistributes wealth into the fewer but larger pockets of (trans)national corporate executives, their political yes-men, stockholders, and stockbrokers.

26. What follows is an extreme condensation of the events that led to black land ownership. For elaboration I recommend Willie Lee Rose's *Rehearsal for Reconstruction: The Port Royal Experiment*. Unless otherwise noted, the following passages come from the 1964 book published by Bobbs Merrill.

27. Here are some statistics on the decrease of privately-owned land: "From 1851 to 1879 the number of landed proprietors [in France] deserving the name had dwindled [from

7,846,000] to 1,420,000" (Lafargue, *The Evolution of Property,* 77–78). And in England, 3,511,770 acres of common land were confiscated by "parliamentary devices" between 1800–1831 (Lafargue, *The Evolution of Property,* 70). For more on enclosure see Williams, *The Country and the City* and Merchant, *The Death of Nature.*

28. Locke, "Of Property," 30. Both money and agricultural technology allow people to possess and work increasingly-larger areas of land. Technology, before the reign of money, consisted primarily of tools that could be wielded by humans and powered by animals, so excessive private appropriation was less a problem.

29. Lafargue, *The Evolution of Property,* 23.

30. In Genesis, the ground is cursed *before* agriculture not because of it. This is the myth's weakness. On the other hand, the ground *is* cursed on account of human action. This remains the story's strength.

31. Rousseau, "Discourse on the Origin of Inequality," 47.

32. See Shepard, *Man in the Landscape,* 230.

33. See my chapter on Donna Haraway who proposes a "reinvention of nature" by which she means a reinvention of human constructs of nature.

34. Trula may leave because of her lesbian or bisexual relationship with Yellow Mary, which might be difficult to maintain in a small, close-knit heterosexual society.

35. The script is unambiguous: Dash refers to Haagar—the family member most opposed to African ways and especially nature-worship—as "unenlightened" and "disenfranchised" (161).

36. While Snead has seen beautiful people and clothes before, he may not have seen them in such a beautiful setting. This beauty impacted not only Snead, but also the film's viewers, for *Daughters of the Dust* was criticized for being excessively beautiful. For a discussion of beauty in African American film and in *Daughters of the Dust,* see Rich, "In the Eyes of the Beholder," 60.

37. I refer to the video version whose framing is different from the film.

38. See Toni Cade Bambara's perspicacious assessment of Dash and Jafa's "democratic" and "Africentric" use of space in Dash, *Daughters of the Dust,* xiii.

39. Trachtenberg, ed., *Classic Essays on Photography,* 11.

40. This is, of course, simplistic: negative experiences are often turned into sources of pride as positive experiences can become shameful. The former slaves of *Beloved* might take exception with my simplification since they were not misled by the metonymy connecting slavery to land. Rather, they held on to the promise and memory of beautiful land (or was it just trees?) the more fiercely they were incarcerated and mutilated.

41. See Steinbeck's, *The Grapes of Wrath* for the indomitable turtle as an analogue of exiled farmers forced to make homes of their vehicles , 12–13.

42. Creel, *"A Peculiar People,"* 52–53.

43. Recall Haagars' critique: "Those old people, they pray to the sun, they pray to the moon, . . . sometimes just to a big star!" (131) These prayers are simultaneously to the ancestors and the unborn; or the spheres themselves may be prayed to as ancestors.

44. Ilogu, *Christianity and Ibo Culture*, 124.

45. Ibid., 176.

46. In the attempt to convert Ibos to Christianity it is unclear who converted who:

> The Faith and Order Commission of the World Council of Churches in their continued search for the Theology of nature remind us that "nature is both man's servant and his sister," and these two aspects have to be kept in balance. . . . The Ibo's reverential or "sacred" attitude to nature while accepting the Christian tradition of nature as the "creation of a transcendent God," is their attempt to treat nature as sister and this need not be destroyed. . . . We must avoid the one sided desire for handling, changing and transforming nature which puts western technology and secularization in danger of "forgetting what nature has to contribute in her sister-function," for if man "exercises a dominion which more and more makes the display of nature's sister-aspect impossible, man will pay the price for his fault." (Ibid., 179–80)

47. Wiredu, "Philosophy, Humankind and the Environment," 46. Plato has a similar ethic, even if his version of property lies somewhere between communal and private:

> First, then, let them [in the best society] make a division of lands and houses among themselves, and to till the soil in common, for that were a project beyond their birth, breeding, and education. But let the division be made with some such thought as this, that he to whom a lot falls is yet bound to count his portion the common property of the whole society, and, since the territory is his fatherland, to tend it with care passing that of son for mother, the more that the land is the divine mistress of her mortal children, and to think likewise of all the gods and spirits of the locality. (Plato, Collected Dialogues of Plato, 740a, p. 1325).

While people need to steward the lands they damage with agriculture and development, the rest of nature should most often be exempted from this well-meaning ethic. Fifth world inhabitants can take care of themselves.

48. Heidegger, "Building Dwelling Thinking," 361.

49. Ibid., 362.

50. Why is the noun, *resters*, used so little? Is someone who rests unworthy of anything but being arrested or called such maledictions as *loafer, bum, idler*? See Lafargue, *The Right to be Lazy*.

51. But contrary to my feeling about the film, the stills in the eponymous book, and in promotional stills, are preoccupied with faces and bodies.

52. Even bones probably have more to do with eternality than those highly dubious entities, souls and spirits.

53. Heidegger, "Building Dwelling Thinking," 351.

54. *Daughters of the Dust* does not include the activity of searching. Whether leisure or labor, searching can be a heightened way in which to allow the land to metaphorically guide us and make us a part of it. It is possible that food-gathering cannot properly be called labor. But if it is considered labor, it is because culture has catapulted food gathering into the world of commercialism and toil through agriculture, packaging, distribution, and even shopping. While looking for food outside culture might appear laborious, it is not usually characterized as labor when animals do it.

55. Another important reason the Islands are relatively undeveloped is that its sandy soils must be stabilized for development—a costly venture. For more information about the modern Sea Islands see Jones-Jackson, *When Roots Die*.

56. Ibid., 7.

57. Or almost. In 1950, the reality of development came to Hilton Head when timber magnate Joseph B. Fraser set off a chain reaction in other islands. Tight-knit, largely self-sufficient economies were replaced by mostly low-paying, low-skilled, service (servant) jobs with bosses, money, transportation, and all those conditions that Marx described as alienated labor. Not only were workers alienated from their products, but also from their labor, self, knowledge, community, and nature.

58. Wiredu, "Philosophy, Humankind and the Environment," 46.

59. Jones-Jackson, *When Roots Die*, 22.

60. Ibid., 23.

61. Ibid., 240. For communalism without cooperation see Godwin, *Political Justice* .

62. Even in the graveyard scene Nana tells Eli that he does not own his wife, Eula.

63. Wiredu, "Philosophy, Humankind and the Environment," 47.

64. By itself, communalism guarantees nothing. Even in furthering the aims of the community, a community can act against some of its own and nature's best interests. Superior political arrangements need developed ideologies. And vice versa.

65. Leopold, *A Sand County Almanac*, xix.

66. Before Leopold, Locke called nature a community:

> The state of nature has a law of nature to govern it, which obliges every one; and reason, which is that law, teaches all mankind who will but consult it that, being all equal and independent, no one ought to harm another in his life, health, liberty, or possessions; for men being all the workmanship of one omnipotent and infinitely wise Maker—all the servants of one sovereign Master, sent into the world by His order, and about His business— they are His property, whose workmanship they are, made to last during His, not one another's pleasure; and being furnished with like faculties, sharing all in one community of nature, there cannot be supposed any such subordination among us, that may authorize us to destroy one another, as if we were made for one another's uses, as the inferior ranks of creatures are for ours. (Locke, The Second Treatise of Government, Part 6, 5–6, my emphasis)

While primarily argued in the name of equality between persons, Locke's community of nature is pro-property and anti-animal. The latter is striking because animals are thought part of the "community of nature" more than people. Yet Locke's community of nature relates of course to harmony between people. Nature becomes a community of peaceful people taking advantage of a kind of Hobbesian nature, that since it is at war, is supposedly improved by being subdued by communal humans.

67. For another line of criticism on Leopold, see Fromm, "Aldo Leopold: Eccentric Anthropocentrist," 43–49. Fromm believes Leopold was willing to sacrifice individuals to (eco)systems or communities.

68. Sale, *Dwellers in the Land*, 53.

69. Polanyi, *The Great Transformation*, 178.

70. See LeFevre, *The Philosophy of Ownership* for an extended argument *for* private property as a crucial component of freedom. On the first page of LeFevre's treatise, a problem besets the greener reader: "Since the concern of this study relates entirely to man's well-being, and is not concerned with the well-being of other living things, the approach here will be to develop a philosophy of property ownership within a human context."

71. Daniel Coleman also calls opening public lands to resource extraction, "enclosure." See Coleman, *Ecopolitics*.

72. For practical methods toward these ends, see CLTs (Community Land Trusts) in Coleman, *Ecopolitics,* 133; Sale, *Dwellers in the Land,* 85–86; and Mumford, *The Culture of Cities,* 330, on governmental schemes of communal land distribution and management. See *Democracy and Nature 3*, no. 2, issue 8 (1996) for an extended discussion of the future of government and land distribution. Other promising possibilities include guerrilla and community gardens and community supported agriculture, all of which are attempts to take charge of one's food, if not one's land.

73. Perhaps the distance between an American CEO and the lowest-paid worker is similar to the distance between the lower classes and the fifth world.

Chapter 7

1. Substantive choice is already sabotaged by supplanting it with an appearance of choice, better deemed *option*. From the option to buy different brands of toilet paper, to the option of selecting candidates in political parties, we are told we have freedom because we can choose. Still, though different brands of toilet paper, or Democrats and Republicans are at this time highly similar (largely because the context in which they operate is virtually identical), products and parties are not identical. Through deconstructing polarized or similar terms, one risks losing sight of this. Notice, however, that the potential for harm is infinitely greater when deconstructing polarized terms, as in the case of deconstructing the nature/culture binary.

2. Unless otherwise stated, all passages from *Of Grammatology* are quoted from the 1974 Johns Hopkins edition.

3. I employ *decriminalize* to provoke, to indicate that cultural acts on nature are primarily criminal. I imply no attribution of human evil, but am attempting to find words suitable to describe the magnitude of avoidable human damage.

4. Supplementalization is the process whereby an entity (here, Nature) is demoted from its exalted status as irreplaceable to the rank of a replaceable substitute or supplement. The question crucial to this discussion will be: With what can Nature (or for that matter, nature) be replaced?

5. This is nature as Nature, as analogue to The Word or to Speech, One, self-identical, nondivisible, like God and at the other extreme from the fallenness of writing, humanity, culture.

6. *Supplement* and *substitute* are conflated in *Of Grammatology* but are somewhat different elsewhere. All definitions of *supplement* in the *Oxford English Dictionary* describe a deficiency completed by a supplement. Thus Nature or nature become deficiencies completed

by culture, that is nature as incomplete without culture. But *supplement* has the connotation of added on to as in the French *ajouter* meaning to add. While the denotation is highly problematic, the connotation is not. On the other hand, *substitute* does not have the connotation of added on to, but generally means something that can replace or stand for another. Speaking of nature and culture as totalities, culture cannot (ever) be said to be a substitute for nature, except as culture is substituted for nature in terms of affection or attention. So while I almost completely object to calling culture a substitute for nature, I only object to the denotation of *supplement*—filling a lack—not the connotation of something added to.

7. In Genesis, the human Fall, instead of Derrida's act of deconstruction, was a catalyst for the Fall of Nature. There, material nature became fallen successor to Edenic Nature. See Glacken, *Traces on the Rhodian Shore* for more on this idea of nature dragged down with human folly, most likely in order that toilsome agriculture could be explained.

8. The traditional answer would be God or Eden. This, however, would not be my answer.

9. Human culture is *always already* only in terms of humans.

10. To accriminalize means to erase the stigma of being a criminal. In this case, culture is the criminal who is acriminalized.

11. To de-supplementalize is to preclude understanding an entity as a mere supplement since, in order to be a supplement, it must share a great deal with that which it supplements. Thus *supplement* is a word that does not correspond to any state of affairs.

12. Beware possible justifications for planned obsolescence.

13. As de-supplementalization called into question supplementarity, de-essentialization does the same with essentiality; not only are things what they are not, but are not what they are.

14. But then why did Derrida not say "culture and every other entity"?

15. Here is that famous passage against origins: "In this play of representation, the point of origin becomes ungraspable. There are things like reflecting pools, and images, an infinite reference from one to the other, but no longer a source, a spring. There is no longer a simple origin. For what is reflected is split *in itself* and not only as an addition to itself of its image" (36).

16. As when gays and lesbians affectionately and politically retain the word, *queer*. But words relating to culture such as *refined, civil(ized), well-bred, genteel, cultivated, sophisticated*, and *cultured* are positive. About the only negative words attached to culture are synonyms of *decadent*, words relating to cultural excess, not the core idea of culture.

17. Although *environment* is a nonthreatening word, the term *environmentalist* assumes, on occasion, a subversive character when this type of person is cast as *wild, out of control,*

uncivil, terms that, unsurprisingly, are applied to nature. But like its paronym, *environment, environmentalist* stands to lose its subversive character when sportsmen, business people, and conservationists (those who want to conserve or reserve nature for future exploitation), begin to identify themselves as environmentalists.

18. I do not retain the word *nature* to serve factional agendas like Social Darwinism or the castigation of certain practices or people as unnatural. These uses of *nature* serve factions of culture similar to the way people use God to say He is on their side or that they are serving Him. Retaining use of *nature* means that culture must rest on a firm foundation of human parity in the name of no particular group. The use of *nature* is more often legitimate when employed to critique general cultural practice, such as production, consumption, and employment, not to serve cultural factionalism.

19. I have left out wild bananas because they are virtually unavailable to anyone reading this book. They are more nature than the agricultural, organic banana.

Chapter 8

1. Habermas, "Modernity—An Incomplete Project," 3-15.

2. Lyotard, *The Postmodern Condition*, 71-84.

3. Haraway said in an interview that her cyborg is female ("Interview with Donna Haraway," 20). But also that "The cyborg is a creature in a post-gender world" (*Simians, Cyborgs, and Women,* 150). Whatever she says or writes to her primary audience—women—there seems little problem with the cyborg as a model for both males and females since her overall agenda is to defend technoscience and assuage organicist fear or disgust with technology.

4. Haraway, *Simians, Cyborgs, and Women,* 151-52.

5. In a 1991 Stony Brook University lecture, Haraway was asked what she thought about the rights of lab animals. She said that if someone close to her were dying and an animal's sacrifice could keep the person alive, she would sanction the killing. Perhaps Haraway was being realistic, a view of herself as problematically self-centered. But this became dubious when she went on to maintain that people should be flexible, not dogmatic about animal rights. What can happen with flexible categories of nature and culture? Nature is more easily deemed expendable. Why not—if we are to blur the boundary between nature and culture—view humans as ethically fit laboratory subjects for the good of other humans, animals, or plants? Because only nature is allowed to suffer for culturally constructed boundaries, including the "flexible" ones.

6. Haraway, *Primate Visions*, 137-39.

7. Perhaps they are being punished for being animals, for not being human.

8. Some might say that an emotionless, nonorganic view of machines is narrow and out-dated. Perhaps someday it will be (compare Ridley Scott's *Blade Runner* [1982]). At the present time, and as far as I am aware, there is little confusion in deciding what is a machine and what is an organism, let alone a human organism. An appearance of emotion, move-ment, or reaction in a machine, at the present time, need not confuse one as to its machine status. Descartes, in *Discourse on Method,* used this same argument—not to be misled by appearances of emotions in animals—among others, to assert the mechanical nature of ani-mals. The fact that we manufacture machines and all their mechanisms, and do not do so with natural organisms, is crucial. We know less about animals and plants, which we do not manufacture than we do about machines, which we do manufacture. The possibility that animals (and humans for that matter) have emotions, thoughts, etc. is much greater than that machines do.

9. When furs, feathers, and skins are worn they are accouterments or adornments of our humanness. An obvious exception is a costume where the animal character dominates.

10. It might be argued there is little difference between killing a wild animal because no other food is available, and killing for an organ to be put in a desperately failing human body. But this fails to account for many factors. Organ killing could be avoided by research-ing the preservation of human organs for transplant rather than by treating animals as expendable subjects of human experiment. Second, transplants are only made possible by the killing and torture of multitudes of animals to improve the process of transplantation. Third, animals are imprisoned and commodified to make them available. Last, organ killing could easily become a quotidian activity of hospitals. One should be wary of institutional and mechanized slaughter—slaughter made easy and bloodless—especially where there's a profit motive. These considerations illustrate that killing for organs, even in desperation, is a more involved and severe transgression than killing animals when no other food is avail-able. My argument does not attempt to make clear lines between forms of killing, but to make distinctions that problematize tendencies toward excess, unproblematic killing. These are questions not just for medical ethicists but for any of us who might one day have the choice to be preserved by the organ of an animal.

11. A. Ross, "Wet, Dark, and Low," 230.

12. Haraway, "The Promises of Monsters," 311.

13. Ibid.

14. Ibid.

15. Burd, "Monitor Care of Lab Mice," A29.

16. Haraway, "The Actors are Cyborg," 25.

17. Haraway, "Interview with Donna Haraway," 8.

18. K. Marx, *Capital*, vol. 1, 284.

19. Ibid., 284.

20. Karl Marx's vision of animals is probably as machines. Thus no envisioning.

21. Which nature is it that Haraway claims we do not dominate? Nature as in Laws of Nature? These *patterns* indeed appear beyond domination. Or nature, as in plants, animals, and land (worldnature)? Perhaps the confusion is with the word *nature*, which tends to mold individual plants, animals, and elements into a huge mass that seems indomitable (the "inexhaustibility of nature"). Perhaps Enlightenment individualism, even if culturally problematic, might thus be of some service to worldnature?

22. K. Marx, *Capital*, vol. 1, 289.

23. Ibid., 285.

24. See Lafargue, *The Right to be Lazy* for a more balanced view of labor. Lafargue, Marx's Marxist son-in-law, construes labor—as even Victor Frankenstein came to regard his creative, humanitarian labors—as toil. See Mary Shelley, *Frankenstein* (London: Penguin, 1985), 102.

25. For an exception see Murray Bookchin, *Remaking Society: Pathways to a Green Future*, (Boston: South End), 1990.

26. Haraway, "Interview with Donna Haraway," 5.

27. See my previous chapter on Jacques Derrida's *Of Grammatology* for a deconstruction of *nature* as the privileged term (Haraway deconstructs *culture* as a privileged term) in the nature/culture binary. More than Derrida, Haraway works to blur any clear conception of both nature and culture, not just to—as Derrida does—deprivilege nature (as presence, voice, authenticity) over culture (absence, writing, artificiality).

28. This does not imply a call for top-down regulations or laws to restrict "private" consumption, but for uncoerced, voluntary renunciations or substitutions brought about through massive re-education by instructors attempting to be as unfaithful as possible to *their* fathers, who previously had regimented and inculcated students with a culture of consumption (with insufficient chewing).

29. See especially Murray Bookchin's "libertarian municipalism" and Takis Fotopoulos's "direct democracy" in *Democracy and Nature* 8 3:2 (1996).

Bibliography/Filmography (I)

Adams, Carol J.
  The Sexual Politics of Meat: A Feminist-Vegetarian Critical Theory. New York:
    Continuum, 1991.

Alighieri, Dante
  Inferno. Translated by Allen Mandelbaum. New York: Bantam, 1982.

Althusser, Louis
  "Ideology and Ideological State Apparatuses." In *Lenin and Philosophy.* New York &
    London: Monthly Review Press, 1971. 127–86.

Arendt, Hannah
  Imperialism: Part Two of the Origins of Totalitarianism. New York: Harvest/Harcourt
    Brace Jovanovich, 1968.

Arens, O. W.
  The Man Eating Myth: Anthropology and Anthropophagy. New York: Oxford
    University Press, 1979.

Armour, Robert
  "*Deliverance:* Four Variations of the American Adam." *Literature/Film Quarterly*
    (Summer 1973): 280–85.

Auden, W. H.
  "D. H. Lawrence." In *The Dyer's Hand and Other Essays.* New York: Random House,
    1962. 277–95.
  "Some Notes on D. H. Lawrence." In *Critics on D. H. Lawrence.* Edited by W. T.
    Andrews. Miami: University of Miami Press, 1979. 47–51.

Bakhtin, M. M.
  Rabelais and His World. Translated by Helene Iswolsky. Cambridge: MIT, 1968.

Barber, Paul
  Vampires, Burial, and Death: Folklore and Reality. New Haven: Yale University Press,
    1988.

Beach, Joseph Warren
  American Fiction, 1920–1940. New York: Macmillan, 1942.

Beacham, Richard C.
  "Appia, Jacques-Dalcroze, and Hellerau, Part One: 'Music Made Visible.'" *New
    Theatre Quarterly* 2 (May 1985): 155–64.

Bullfinch, Thomas
   Bullfinch's Mythology. Garden City, New York: Doubleday, 1968.

Burd, Stephen
   "U.S. Told It Needn't Monitor Care of Lab Mice, Rats, Birds." *Chronicle of Higher Education* 1 June 1994, A29.

Burgess, Anthony
   Flame Into Being. New York: Arbor House, 1985.

Ciment, Michael
   John Boorman. Translated by Gilbert Adair. London: Faber and Faber, 1986.

Clingman, Stephen
   "Prophecy and Subversion: *The Conservationist*." In *The Novels of Nadine Gordimer: History from the Inside*. 2nd ed. Amherst: University of Massachusetts Press, 1986. 135–69.

Coleman, Daniel
   Ecopolitics: Building a Green Society. New Brunswick: Rutgers University Press, 1994.

Copleston, Frederick
   "Fichte (I)." In *A History of Philosophy*. Vol. 7, *Fichte to Nietzsche*. New York: Image/Doubleday, 1985. 32–58.

Cowan, James C.
   D. H. Lawrence and the Trembling of the Balance. University Park: Pennsylvania State University Press, 1990.

Creel, Margaret Washington
   "A Peculiar People": Slave Religion and Community Culture Among the Gullahs. New York & London: New York University Press, 1988.

Dash, Julie
   Daughters of the Dust: The Making of an African American Woman's Film. New York: New Press, 1992.
   Daughters of the Dust. Screenplay by Julie Dash. Dir. Julie Dash. Perf. Adisa Anderson, Barbara O, Cheryll Lynn Bruce, Cora Lee Day. Kino International, 1991.

Descartes, René
   Discourse on Method. Indianapolis: Hackett, 1980.

Deleuze, Gilles and Félix Guattari
   A Thousand Plateaus: Capitalism and Schizophrenia. Translated by Brian Massumi. Minneapolis & London: University of Minnesota Press, 1987.

Deliverance
   Screenplay by James Dickey. Dir. John Boorman. Perf. Jon Voight, Burt Reynolds, Ned Beatty, Ronnie Cox. Warner Bros., 1972.

Derrida, Jacques
   Of Grammatology. Baltimore: Johns Hopkins, 1974.

De Vries, Ad.
Dictionary of Symbols and Imagery. Amsterdam: North Holland, 1974.

Dickey, James
Deliverance. New York: Laurel, 1970.

Eliade, Mircea
The Encyclopedia of Religion. New York: Macmillan, 1987.

Ellul, Jacques
The Technological Society. New York: Vintage, 1964.

Engels, Frederick
The Origin of the Family, Private Property, and the State. New York: New World, 1963.

Engle, Lars
"*The Conservationist* and the Political Uncanny." In *The Later Fiction of Nadine Gordimer.* Edited by Bruce King. New York: St. Martin's, 1993. 148–64.

Euripides
The Bacchae. In *Euripides V.* Edited by David Grene and Richard Lattimore. New York: Washington Square Press, 1969.

Ferris, Timothy
"On the Edge of Chaos." Review of *The Quark and the Jaguar: Adventures in the Simple and Complex,* by Murray Gell-Mann. *The New York Review of Books* Vol. XLII, Sept. 1995 40–43.

Frazer, Sir James George
The Golden Bough. New York: Macmillan, 1958.

French, Mrs. A. M.
Slavery in South Carolina and the Ex-Slaves; or The Port Royal Mission. New York: Negro Universities Press, 1969.

Fromm, Harold
"Aldo Leopold: Eccentric Anthropocentrist" *ISLE* 1.1 (Spring 1993): 43–49.

Glacken. Clarence
Traces on the Rhodian Shore: Nature and Culture in Western Thought from Ancient Times to the End of the Eighteenth Century. Berkeley & Los Angeles: University of California Press, 1967.

Godwin, William
Political Justice. London: Geo. Allen & Unwin, 1929.

Gordimer, Nadine
Conversations With Nadine Gordimer. Edited by Nancy Topping Bazin and Marilyn Seymour. Jackson: University Press of Mississippi, 1990.
The Conservationist. London: Penguin Books, 1978.
"Six Feet of the Country." In *Six Feet of the Country.* London: Penguin, 1982. 7–20.
"Speak Out: The Necessity for Protest." In *The Essential Gesture: Writing, Politics and Places.* New York: Knopf, 1988. 87–103.

"A Watcher of the Dead." In *Why Haven't You Written: Selected Stories 1950–1972*. New York: Penguin, 1992. 33–38.

Griffith, James J.
"Damned If You Do, and Damned If You Don't: James Dickey's *Deliverance*." *Post Script* (Spring–Summer 1986): 47–59.

Guillaume, James
"On Building the New Social Order." In *Bakunin on Anarchy*. New York: Vintage, 1971. 356–61.

Habermas, Jürgen
"Modernity—An Incomplete Project." In *The Anti Aesthetic: Essays on Postmodern Culture*. Edited by Hal Foster. Seattle: Bay Press, 1983. 3–15.

Hall, Stuart
"The Emergence of Cultural Studies and the Crisis of the Humanities." *October* 53 (Summer 1990): 11–23.

Haraway, Donna J.
"The Actors are Cyborg, Nature is Coyote, and the Geography is Elsewhere: Postscript to 'Cyborgs at Large.'" In *Technoculture*. Edited by Constance Penley and Andrew Ross. Minneapolis: University of Minnesota Press, 1991. 21–26.
"Cyborgs at Large: Interview with Donna Haraway." In *Technoculture*. Edited by Constance Penley and Andrew Ross. Minneapolis: University of Minnesota Press, 1991. 1–20.
Primate Visions. New York & London: Routledge, 1989.
"The Promises of Monsters: A Regenerative Politics for Inappropriate/d Others." In *Cultural Studies*. Edited by Lawrence Grossberg, Cary Nelson, and Paula Treichler. New York & London: Routledge, 1992. 295–337.
Simians, Cyborgs, and Women: The Reinvention of Nature. New York & London: Routledge, 1991.

Harris, Thomas.
The Silence of the Lambs. New York: St. Martin's, 1988.

Hecht, Susanna, and Alexander Cockburn
The Fate of the Forest: Developers, Destroyers, and Defenders of the Amazon. New York: Verso, 1989.

Heidegger, Martin
"Building Dwelling Thinking." In *Basic Writings*. Edited by David F. Krell. San Francisco: Harper, 1993. 347–63.

Heistand, Emily
"Economic Theory is Changing." *Orion* 12, no. 3 (Summer 1993): 52.

Herodotus
The Histories. London: Penguin, 1968.

Hesiod
Theogony. Ann Arbor: University of Michigan Press, 1959.

Hoggart, Richard
The Uses of Literacy. London: Penguin, 1958.

The Holy Bible
King James Version. New York: Meridian, 1974.

Hobbes, Thomas
Leviathan. Edited by M. Oakeshott. Oxford: Oxford University Press, 1946.

Homer
The Odyssey. Translated by Albert Cook. New York: W. W. Norton, 1967.

Hopkins, Gerard Manley
The Poems of Gerard Manley Hopkins. London: Oxford, 1967.

Horkheimer, Max and Theodor W. Adorno
Dialectic of Enlightenment. Translated by John Cumming. New York: Continuum, 1989.

Ilogu, Edmund
Christianity and Ibo Culture. Leiden, Netherlands: E. J. Brill, 1974.

Inniss, Kenneth
D. H. Lawrence's Bestiary. The Hague: Mouton, 1971.

Jameson, Frederic
"The Great American Hunter, or, Ideological Content in the Novel." *College English* 34 (Nov. 1972): 180–97.
Postmodernism or The Cultural Logic of Late Capitalism. Durham: Duke University Press, 1991.

Jones-Jackson, Patricia
When Roots Die: Endangered Traditions on the Sea Islands. Athens & London: University of Georgia Press, 1987.

Jowitt, Deborah
Time and the Dancing Image. New York: Morrow, 1988.

Kane, Joe
Review of *Fate of the Forest*, by Susanna B. Hecht. *Voice Literary Supplement* (Feb. 1990): 26.

Krumholz, Linda
"The Ghosts of Slavery: Historical Recovery in Toni Morrison's *Beloved*. *African American Review* 26, no. 3 (Fall 1992): 395–408.

Krupp, E. C.
Beyond the Blue Horizon. New York: HarperCollins, 1991.

Lafargue, Paul
The Evolution of Property. London: New Park, 1975.
The Right to be Lazy. Chicago: Charles H. Kerr, 1989.

Lawrence, D. H.
> *Apocalypse.* New York: Viking, 1932.
> "Aristocracy." In *Reflections on the Death of a Porcupine and Other Essays.* Edited by
> > Michael Herbert. Cambridge: Cambridge University Press, 1988. 365–76.
> *Fantasia of the Unconscious.* New York: Viking, 1922.
> "The Lemon Gardens." In *Twilight in Italy.* London: Wm. Heineman, 1950. 54–96.
> *The Letters of D. H. Lawrence.* Edited by Aldous Huxley. New York: Viking Press, 1936.
> "Love on the Farm." In *The Complete Poems of D. H. Lawrence.* Edited by Vivian de
> > Sola Pinto and Warren Roberts. New York: Viking, 1936. 42.
> *Phoenix: The Posthumous Papers of D. H. Lawrence.* Edited by Edward McDonald.
> > New York: Viking, 1936.
> "Reflections on the Death of a Porcupine." In *Reflections on the Death of a Porcupine
> > and Other Essays.* Edited by Michael Herbert. Cambridge: Cambridge
> > University Press, 1988. 347–64.
> "St Luke." In *The Complete Poems of D. H. Lawrence.* Edited by Vivian de Sola Pinto
> > and Warren Roberts. New York: Viking, 1936. 325.
> "Study of Thomas Hardy." In *Phoenix: The Posthumous Papers of D. H. Lawrence.*
> > Edited by Edward McDonald. New York: Viking, 1936. 398–516.
> *Women in Love.* New York: Modern Library, 1920.

Leavis, F. R.
> *D. H. Lawrence: Novelist.* New York: Simon and Schuster, 1955.

LeFevre, Robert
> *The Philosophy of Ownership.* Larkspur, Colorado: Pine Tree, 1966.

Leopold, Aldo
> *A Sand County Almanac.* New York: Ballantine, 1966.

Little, Elbert L.
> *The Audubon Field Guide to North American Trees: Eastern Region.* New York: Knopf,
> > 1980.

Locke, John
> *Essay Concerning Human Understanding.* Chicago: Gateway, 1956.
> "Of Property." In *The Second Treatise of Government.* New York: Liberal Arts, 1952.
> > 16–29.

Lopez, Barry
> *Of Wolves and Men.* New York: Scribner's, 1978.

Lyotard, Jean-Francois
> *The Postmodern Condition: A Report on Knowledge.* Translated by Geoff Bennington
> > and Brian Massumi. Minneapolis: University of Minnesota Press, 1989.

MacCulloch, John Arnott
> *The Mythology of All Races: Eddic.* Vol. 2. New York: Cooper Square Publishers, 1964.

Marx, Karl
> *Capital.* Vol. 1. Translated by Ben Fowkes. New York: Vintage, 1977.

Marx, Leo

> *The Machine in the Garden: Technology and the Pastoral Ideal in America.* London & Oxford: Oxford University Press, 1964.

Moore, Francis

> *Travels into Inland Parts of Africa.* London: J. Stagg, 1739.

Morrison, Toni

> *Beloved.* New York: Plume, 1987.
>
> "The Site of Memory." In *Out There.* Edited by Russell Ferguson, Martha Gever, Trinh T. Minh-ha, and Cornel West. Cambridge: MIT Press, 1990. 299–326.

Mumford, Lewis

> *The Culture of Cities.* Westport, Conn.: Greenwood, 1970.

Neto, Agostinho

> "The Grieved Lands." In *The Penguin Book of Modern African Poetry.* Edited by Gerald Moore and Ulli Beier. London: Penguin, 1984. 29–30.

Newman, Judie

> *Nadine Gordimer.* London: Routledge, 1988.

Norris, Frank

> *McTeague.* New York: Signet/Penguin, 1964.

Ovid

> *Metamorphosis.* Translated by Mary M. Innes. London: Penguin, 1955.

The Oxford Annotated Bible

> Revised Standard Version. New York: Oxford University Press, 1962.

Palmer, R. R.

> *A History of the Modern World.* New York: Knopf, 1965.

Plato

> *The Collected Dialogues of Plato: Including the Letters.* Edited by Edith Hamilton and Huntington Cairns. Princeton: Princeton University Press, 1973.

Polanyi, Karl

> *The Great Transformation: The Political and Economic Origins of Our Time.* Boston: Beacon, 1964.

Rich, B. Ruby

> "In the Eyes of the Beholder." *The Village Voice* (January 28, 1992): 60.

Ritvo, Harriet

> *The Animal Estate: The English and Other Creatures in the Victorian Age.* Cambridge: Harvard University Press, 1987.

Robert/"Stella."

> "Stella Through the Looking Glass." *Social Text* 37 (Winter 1993): 73–86.

Robertson, James

> "Institutional Restructuring and the Liberatory Transition." *Democracy and Nature* 9, 3:3, 1–20.

Rose, Willie Lee
Rehearsal for Reconstruction: The Port Royal Experiment. Indianapolis: Bobbs Merrill, 1964.

Ross, Andrew
"Green Ideas Sleep Furiously." Interview by Mike McGurl. *Lingua Franca* vol. 15 no. 1 (Nov./Dec. 1994): 57–65.
Strange Weather. London & New York: Verso, 1991.
"Wet, Dark, and Low, Eco Man Evolves from Eco Woman." *Boundary 2*, vol. 19, no. 2, (1992): 205–32.

Ross, Charles R.
Women in Love: A Novel of Mythic Realism. Boston: Twayne, 1991.

Rousseau, Jean-Jacques
"Discourse on the Origin of Inequality." In *The Basic Political Writings.* Edited and translated by Donald A. Cress. Indianapolis & Cambridge: Hackett, 1987. 25–110.

Rupp, Rebecca
Red Oaks and Black Birches: The Science and Lore of Trees. Pownal, Vt.: Storey, 1990.

Sale, Kirkpatrick
Dwellers in the Land: The Bioregional Vision. San Francisco: Sierra Club, 1985.

Samuels, Wilfred D. and Clenora Hudson Weems
"Ripping the Veil: Meaning Through Rememory in *Beloved.*" In *Toni Morrison.* Boston: Twayne Publishing, 1990. 94–138.

Semansky, Chris and Jhan Hochman
"Ecotastrophes, Photography, and Millennial Doom: Snapshots of the End." *Genre* 28 (Spring/Summer 1996): 1–15.

Shepard, Paul.
Man in the Landscape: A Historic View of the Esthetics of Nature. College Station: Texas A&M University Press, 1991.

The Silence of the Lambs
Screenplay by Ted Tally. Dir. Jonathan Demme. Perf. Jodie Foster, Anthony Hopkins. Orion, 1991.

Sitter, Deborah Ayer
"The Making of Man: Dialogic Meaning in *Beloved.*" *African-American Review* 26, no. 1 (Spring 1992): 17–30.

Slack, Jennifer Daryl and Laurie Anne Whitt
"Ethics and Cultural Studies." In *Cultural Studies.* Edited by Lawrence Grossberg, Cary Nelson, and Paula Treichler. New York & London: Routledge, 1992. 571–92.

Smith, Sir William, ed.
Everyman's Smaller Classical Dictionary. New York: E. P. Dutton, 1952.

Sollors, Werner
"Ethnicity." In *Critical Terms for Literary Study*. Edited by Frank Lentricchia and Thomas McLaughlin. Chicago & London: University of Chicago Press, 1990. 288–305.

Stampp, Kenneth M.
The Peculiar Institution: Slavery in the Ante-Bellum South. New York: Vintage, 1964.

Steinbeck, John
The Grapes of Wrath. Toronto: Bantam, 1954.

Stoker, Bram
Dracula. London: Penguin, 1979.

Strick, Philip
Review of *Deliverance*, directed by John Boorman. *Sight and Sound* (Autumn 1972): 228–29.

Thomas, Keith
Man and the Natural World: A History of the Modern Sensibility. New York: Pantheon, 1983.

Thompson, E. P.
The Making of the English Working Class. London: Penguin, 1978.

Thorpe, Michael
"The Motif of the Ancestor in *The Conservationist*." In *Critical Essays on Nadine Gordimer*. Edited by Rowland Smith. Boston: G. K. Hall, 1990. 116–23.

Tindall, William York
D. H. Lawrence and Susan His Cow. New York: Columbia University Press, 1939.

Tompkins, Jane
West of Everything. New York: Oxford University Press, 1991.

Trachtenberg, Alan, ed.
Classic Essays on Photography. New Haven, Connecticut: Leete's Island Books, 1980.

Tudor, Andrew
International Dictionary of Films and Filmmakers. Edited by Nicholas Thomas. Chicago: St. James Press, 1990. 222–23.

Turner, Graeme
British Cultural Studies: An Introduction. New York & London: Routledge, 1990.

Vena, Mistress
"Confessions of a Psyco Mistress." *Social Text* 37 (Winter 1993): 65–72.

Vivas, Eliseo
"The Substance of *Women in Love*." In *D. H. Lawrence: The Failure and Triumph of Art*. Evanston, Ill.: Northwestern University Press, 1960. 237–72.

Wade, Michael
Nadine Gordimer. London: Evans Brothers, 1978.

Williams, Raymond
The Country and the City. New York: Oxford University Press, 1973.
Culture and Society 1780–1950. London: Penguin, 1966.
Keywords: A Vocabulary of Culture and Society. New York: Oxford University Press, 1983.

Wilson, Alexander
The Culture of Nature: North American Landscape from Disney to the Exxon Valdez. Cambridge, Mass.: Blackwell, 1992.

Wilson Robert F. Jr.
"Deliverance from Novel to Film: Where is our Hero?" *Literature/Film Quarterly* (Winter 1974): 57.

Wiredu, Kwasi
"Philosophy, Humankind and the Environment." In *Philosophy, Humanity and Ecology.* Vol. 1. Edited by H. Odera Oruka. Nairobi: African Center for Technology Studies and The African Academy of Sciences, 1994. 30–47.

Zola, Emile
The Experimental Novel and Other Essays. Translated by Belle M. Sherman. New York: Haskell House, 1964.
"Preface to the Second Edition." In *Thérèse Raquin.* Translated by Andrew Rothwell. Oxford & New York: Oxford University Press, 1992. 1–6.

Green Cultural Studies Bibliography (II)

Adams, Carol J.
  The Sexual Politics of Meat: A Feminist-Vegetarian Critical Theory. New York:
    Continuum, 1991.

Altman, Nathaniel
  Sacred Trees. San Francisco: Sierra Club Books, 1994.

Anderson, William
  The Green Man: The Archetype of Our Oneness with Earth. London & San Francisco:
    HarperCollins, 1991.

Baker, Steve
  Picturing the Beast: Animals, Identity and Representation. Manchester & New York:
    Manchester University Press, 1990.

Berger, John
  "Why Look at Animals." In *About Looking.* New York: Vintage, 1980. 3–28.
  "Seker Ahmet and the Forest." In *About Looking.* New York: Vintage, 1980. 86–93.

Bermingham, Ann
  Landscape and Ideology: The English Rustic Tradition 1740–1860. Berkeley:
    University of California Press, 1986.

Collingwood, R. G.
  The Idea of Nature. New York: Oxford University Press, 1960.

Dekkers, Midas
  Dearest Pet: On Bestiality. Translated by Paul Vincent. London & New York: Verso, 1994.

Deleuze, Gilles and Félix Guattari
  A Thousand Plateaus: Capitalism and Schizophrenia. Minneapolis & London:
    University of Minnesota Press, 1987.

Fiddes, Nick
  Meat: A Natural Symbol. London & New York: Routledge, 1991.

Fjellman, Stephen M.
  Vinyl Leaves: Walt Disney World and America. Boulder, Colo.: Westview Press, 1992.

Gelbspan, Ross
  "The Heat is On: The Warming of the World's Climate Sparks a Blaze of Denial."
    Harper's (Dec. 1995): 31–39.

Glacken, Clarence J.
  *Traces on the Rhodian Shore: Nature and Culture in Western Thought from Ancient
      Times to the End of the Eighteenth Century.* Berkeley & Los Angeles: University
      of California Press, 1967.

Grant, Barry Keith
  Voyages of Discovery: The Cinema of Frederick Wiseman. Urbana & Chicago: University
      of Illinois Press, 1992.

Green, Nicholas
  *The Spectacle of Nature: Landscape and Bourgeois Culture in Nineteenth Century
      France.* Manchester & New York: Manchester University Press, 1990.

Griffin, Susan
  Woman and Nature: The Roaring Inside Her. New York: Harper & Row, 1978.

Haraway, Donna
  "The Actors are Cyborg, Nature is Coyote, and the Geography is Elsewhere: Postscript
      to 'Cyborgs at Large.'" In *Technoculture.* Edited by Constance Penley and
      Andrew Ross. Minneapolis: University of Minnesota Press, 1991. 21–26.
  "Cyborgs at Large: Interview with Donna Haraway." In *Technoculture.* Edited by
      Constance Penley and Andrew Ross. Minneapolis: University of Minnesota
      Press, 1991. 1–20.
  Primate Visions. London & New York: Routledge, 1989.
  "The Promises of Monsters: A Regenerative Politics for Inappropriate/d Others." In
      Cultural Studies. Edited by Lawrence Grossberg, Cary Nelson and Paula
      Treichler. London & New York: Routledge, 1992. 295–337.
  Simians, Cyborgs, and Women: The Reinvention of Nature. New York & London:
      Routledge, 1991.

Harrison, Robert Pogue
  Forests: The Shadow of Civilization. Chicago & London: University of Chicago Press,
      1992.

Hayles, N. Katherine
  "Simulated Nature and Natural Simulations: Rethinking the Relation Between the
      Beholder and the World." In *Uncommon Ground: Toward Reinventing Nature.*
      Edited by William Cronon. New York & London: W. W. Norton, 1995. 409–25.

Horkheimer, Max
  The Eclipse of Reason. New York: Oxford University Press, 1947.

Horkheimer, Max and Theodor W. Adorno
  Dialectic of Enlightenment. New York: Continuum, 1989.

Irwin, Mark
  "Toward a Wilderness of the Artificial." *The Ohio Review* 49. 105–19.

Merchant, Carolyn
  The Death of Nature: Women, Ecology and the Scientific Revolution. San Francisco:
      Harper & Row, 1989.

Mitchell, W. J. T., ed.
   Landscape and Power. Chicago & London: University of Chicago Press, 1994.

Oelschlager, Max
   The Idea of Wilderness. New Haven: Yale University Press, 1991.

Perlman, Michael
   The Power of Trees: Reforesting the Soil. Dallas: Spring Press, 1994.

Peterson, Dale and Jane Goodall
   Visions of Caliban: On Chimpanzees and People. Boston: Houghton Mifflin, 1993.

Price, Jennifer
   "Looking for Nature at the Mall: A Field Guide to the Nature Company." In
      Uncommon Ground: Toward Reinventing Nature. Edited by William Cronon.
      New York & London: W. W. Norton, 1995. 186–203.

Regan, Tom and Peter Singer, eds.
   Animal Rights and Human Obligations. Englewood Cliffs, N.J.: Prentice Hall, 1976.

Ritvo, Harriet
   The Animal Estate: The English and Other Creatures in the Victorian Age. Cambridge:
      Harvard University Press, 1987.

Ross, Andrew
   The Chicago Gangster Theory of Life. London & New York: Verso, 1994.
   "Green Ideas Sleep Furiously." Interview by Mike McGurl. *Lingua Franca* vol. 15 no.
      1. (Nov./Dec. 1994): 57–65.
   Strange Weather. London & New York: Verso, 1991.

Schiebinger, Londa
   Nature's Body: Gender in the Making of Modern Science. Boston: Beacon, 1993.

Semansky, Chris and Jhan Hochman
   "Ecotastrophes, Photography, and Millennial Doom: Snapshots of the End." *Genre* 28
      (Spring/Summer 1996): 1–15.

Serres, Michel
   The Natural Contract. Translated by Elizabeth MacArthur and William Paulson. Ann
      Arbor: University of Michigan Press, 1995.

Shepard, Paul
   Man in the Landscape: A Historic View of the Esthetics of Nature. College Station: Texas
      A&M University Press, 1991.

Siebert, Charles
   "The Artifice of the Natural: How TV's Nature Shows Make All the Earth a Stage."
      Harper's (February 1993): 43–51.

Simmons, I. G.
   Interpreting Nature: Cultural Constructions of the Environment. London & New York:
      Routledge, 1993.

Slack, Jennifer Daryl and Laurie Anne Whitt
  "Ethics and Cultural Studies." In *Cultural Studies*. Edited by Lawrence Grossberg,
    Cary Nelson, and Paula Treichler. New York & London: Routledge, 1992.
    571–92.

Smith, Jonathan
  "The Lie That Blinds: Destabilizing the Text of Landscape." In
    Place/Culture/Representation. Edited by James Duncan and David Ley. London
    & New York: Routledge, 1993. 78–92.

Thomas, Keith
  Man and the Natural World: A History of the Modern Sensibility. New York: Pantheon,
    1983.

Tobias, Michael
  A Vision of Nature: Traces of the Original World. Kent: Kent State University Press,
    1995.

Tompkins, Jane
  West of Everything. New York: Oxford University Press, 1991.

Thompson, George F., ed.
  Landscape in America. Austin: University of Texas Press, 1995.

Tuan, Yi-Fu
  Passing Strange and Wonderful: Aesthetics, Nature, and Culture. Washington, D.C.:
    Island Press/Shearwater Books, 1993.

Virilio, Paul
  Popular Defense and Ecological Struggles. New York: Semiotext(e), 1990.

Wall, Derek, ed.
  Green History: A Reader in Environmental Literature, Philosophy, and Politics.
    London & New York: Routledge, 1994.

Wilson, Alexander
  The Culture of Nature: North American Landscape from Disney to the Exxon Valdez.
    Cambridge, Massachusetts: Blackwell, 1992.

Williams, Raymond
  The Country and the City. New York: Oxford University Press, 1973.

Wright, Will
  Wild Knowledge: Science, Language and Social Life in a Fragile Environment.
    Minneapolis: University of Minnesota Press, 1992.

Zukin, Sharon
  Landscapes of Power: From Detroit to Disney World? Berkeley: University of California
    Press, 1991.